A HANDBOOK OF CRITICAL APPROACHES
TO LITERATURE

A HANDBOOK OF CRITICAL APPROACHES TO LITERATURE

SECOND EDITION

WILFRED L. GUERIN

Louisiana State University in Shreveport

EARLE LABOR
LEE MORGAN

Centenary College of Louisiana

JOHN R. WILLINGHAM

The University of Kansas

HARPER & ROW, Publishers

New York, Hagerstown, Philadelphia, San Francisco, London

Sponsoring Editor: Phillip W. Leininger
Project Editor: Renée E. Beach
Designer: T. R. Funderburk
Production Manager: Marion A. Palen
Compositor: TriStar Graphics
Printer and Binder: The Murray Printing Company
Art Studio: Vantage Art, Inc.

A HANDBOOK OF CRITICAL APPROACHES TO LITERATURE, Second Edition
Copyright © 1979 by Harper & Row, Publishers, Inc.

Library of Congress Cataloging in Publication Data

Guerin, Wilfred L.
  A handbook of critical approaches to literature.

  Bibliography: p.
  Includes index.
  1. Criticism.   I. Title.
PN81.G8   1979   801.95   78-12477
ISBN 0-06-042554-7

To our first critics

Carmel Cali Guerin
Rachel Higgs Morgan
Sylvia Kirkpatrick Steger
Grace Hurst Willingham

CONTENTS

Contents

PREFACE

The first edition of this book had its genesis during the early 1960s. At that time the collaborators had become conscious of the problems of teaching literary analysis to young college students in the absence of a comprehensive yet elementary guide to some of the major critical approaches to works of literature. No work of that sort existed at the time, yet students clearly could have profited from a more formalized and contemporary introduction to the serious study of literature than they generally had received in lower levels of education. We found that most freshmen and many upperclassmen were entering and emerging from courses in literature still unenlightened about the most rewarding critical techniques that a keen reader could apply to good imaginative writing. Even students whose exposure to literature had been extensive often possessed only a narrow and fragmented concept of such interpretive approaches. Consequently, one of our first aims, then and now, has been to help establish a healthy balance in the student's critical outlook. We believed then, and are even more convinced now, that any college or university student—or, for that matter, any advanced high school student—should have at hand the main lines of the most useful approaches to literary criticism.

With these assumptions in mind, we marked off our areas of concern and laid claim to fill the need we sensed. We were gratified with the success of that claim, indicated by the acceptance of the book by our professional colleagues and by thousands of students throughout the land and abroad. (The book was translated into both Spanish and Portuguese.) However, there was also an acceptance we had not anticipated. Our original concern was to offer critical approaches to students in the early years of college work, but we found that in instance after instance the book was being used at upper division levels and even in graduate classes. Even so, this extent of use did not preclude the book's acceptance by some high school teachers as well.

We hope that in this second edition we have preserved that versatility, and we have even tried to improve upon it. Partly because of developing emphases in some recent criticism and partly to assist the least sophisticated of our readers, we have added to this edition a prologue on the precritical response to literature—the response of the "common reader." The first five chapters, though all have undergone some revision and updating, are essentially as they were in the successful first edition. The sixth chapter, however, has undergone thorough expansion and revision. In it we have tried to survey eleven approaches to literature in such a way that the least sophisticated can become aware of approaches other than the five that form the core of the book, but conversely the more accomplished student of literature can find both orientation and guides to seeking out much more information about these several approaches. Often these "other" approaches reflect recent and European developments, and as such would be especially helpful to those advanced students who responded so well to the first edition.

Even with these two expansions—the precritical response and the enlarged chapter of "other" approaches—

our aim in this second edition is still much the same as in the first: to provide a basic introduction to the major critical-interpretive perspectives that a reader beginning a serious study may bring to bear on literature. The book describes and demonstrates the critical tools that have come to be regarded as indispensable for the sensitive reader; these tools are what we call approaches. Furthermore, because this is a *handbook* of critical approaches, we have tried to make it suggestive rather than exhaustive. We make no claims to being definitive; on the contrary, the book's value lies in part in opening the student's eyes to the *possibilities* in literature and criticism. Today we read much about heuristics—the process of discovery. This sense of discovery was important in the first edition of this book, and it continues important here.

But heuristics can be guided, and for that reason we chose as guides five main approaches to literary criticism for that first edition. These five we have continued in this edition. Similarly we have preserved the nature and structure of these five main chapters. Each of them begins with an introduction to and definition of a particular interpretive approach, followed usually by a detailed practical application of that approach to the same four major works: one each from the genres of the novel, the short story, poetry, and drama; two British, two American. Each chapter also cites many other literary works for occasional illustrations, and in so doing extends the book beyond the four works treated more extensively while at the same time it leads the student to try his hand on the works thus briefly mentioned. There is no rigid sequence from chapter to chapter, and the four major works are not all treated in the same degree of detail in each chapter. This is so because not all works lend themselves equally well to a given approach. Consequently, one important aspect of our treatment of critical reading should be the student's recognition of the need to select the most suitable approach for a given literary work.

Following the discussion of the "common reader's" precritical response, Chapter 1 considers the cluster of perspectives generally accepted as "traditional"—the biographical, the historical, the moralistic and the philosophical, with some attention to textual matters, to genre, and to the time-honored technique of interpretive summary. Chapter 1 points out both the advantages and the limitations of such approaches. Chapter 2 deals with the formalistic approach, which has come to be especially associated with the "New Criticism." Chapter 3 is a treatment of psychology in literature, concentrating on Freudian criticism. Chapter 4 moves into the realm of Jungian archetypal patterns and cultural myths as they are manifested in literature. Chapter 5 demonstrates a sophisticated application of several of the preceding approaches as they may be fused and expanded into another perspective—the exponential—a perspective that gives further insight into patterns of image-metaphor-symbol. As indicated earlier, Chapter 6, because it is a survey of eleven different approaches, does not attempt to treat the four works chosen for detailed analyses in the five main chapters.

Those four works were chosen because of their rich potential for interpretation, because they will help make the beginning student aware of the joys of reading at increasingly higher levels of ability, and because they are generally important in introductory courses in literature. Two of them—*Adventures of Huckleberry Finn* and *Hamlet*—are easily available in paperback editions, if not in the student's anthology. The other two—"To His Coy Mistress" and "Young Goodman Brown"—are included in this book. But regardless of the availability of these four works, we hope that this book will be primarily a model or guidebook for the interpretation of *other* literary works. In short, this handbook may serve as a complementary text, best used with an anthology or a set of paperbacks.

The glossary at the end of the book is not intended as a substitute for the longer dictionaries of critical terms, but it does define the technical terms that have special relevance for the present discussions. The bibliography lists some of the most helpful books related to the respective interpretive approaches, books that are generally available in any academic library.

This handbook may be read as a continuous unit, of course, but it has both flexibility and adaptability. For example, although it is primarily organized by "approaches" rather than by genres, the instructor may assign at the beginning of the course the introductory section of each chapter and later the section of each of the five main chapters that deals with a certain genre. Thus the instructor who decides to begin with the short story may assign the introductory section of each of the chapters and then the five discussions of "Young Goodman Brown." In another possible use of this book, students might read several literary works early in the term and discuss them in class without immediate recourse to this handbook. Then they might read it, or pertinent sections of it and bring their resulting new insights to bear on the literature read earlier, as well as on subsequent reading. This double exposure would have the advantage of creating the sense of discovery that awaits the perceptive reader.

Finally, our debt to the canon of literary criticism and scholarship is obvious, and we acknowledge it with gratitude. Our bibliography suggests the breadth and depth of critical scholarship and teaching from which this volume derives. We once again acknowledge the many helpful suggestions that were made for the first edition. For these we thank Laurence Perrine, William B. Allmon, James A. Gowen, Donald F. Warders, Arthur Schwartz, Richard Coanda, and James Wilcox. Assistance in the preparation of the first edition was given by the late Kathleen Owens, and by Czarena Stuart, Irene Winterrowd, Yvonne B. Willingham, Mildred B. Smith, Melinda M. Carpenter, Alyce Palpant, and Jeanette DeLine. To these we wish to add the following, who have furthered the work on the second edition: Dean Mary McBride and Robert Leitz of Louisiana State University in Shreveport, Stephen J. Mayer, our colleague, and Jeff Hendricks, our former student at Centenary College, along with the students in Earle Labor's literary criticism seminar at the University of Aarhus in Denmark. We are grateful to Ruby George and Betty Labor and to the staffs of the libraries of Louisiana State University in Shreveport and Centenary College of Louisiana. For any errors in our book we, of course, take full responsibility.

Our wives, who we said a decade ago stoically endured the project, are our wives and stoics still.

W. L. G.
E. L.
L. M.
J. R. W.

PROLOGUE
THE PRECRITICAL RESPONSE

No less a professional critic than Dr. Samuel Johnson in the *Life of Gray* made the precritical response the ultimate criterion in determining literary merit:

> I rejoice to concur with the common reader; for by the common sense of readers, uncorrupted by literary prejudices, after all the refinements of subtility and the dogmatism of learning, must be finally decided all claim to poetical honours.

Now, Dr. Johnson's common reader in eighteenth-century England probably bears little resemblance to what would have to be defined as a common reader in twentieth-century, industrial, urban, mass-educated America. But if we make some allowance for changes in taste and the literary curriculum from the eighteenth to the twentieth century, we can perhaps agree that for the most part we are talking about relatively similar types of readers.

It was inevitable that literature should one day become a part of the academic curriculum. Anything that could so move and interest large numbers of people, including the most cultivated and enlightened, and that had such obvious and pronounced didactic uses was in the judgment of academicians bound to be worthy of intellectual analysis. Such a view may well have motivated educators to make literature an academic subject: It "taught" men something; it was a source of "knowledge." The study of modern literature as a subject in school, however, is relatively recent. For centuries in Western Europe, only the literature of classical antiquity was thought to have sufficient merit for systematic study. In any event, once literature was established in the curriculum, it was subjected to the formal discipline of criticism, which ultimately consisted of taking it apart (and putting it back together again) to see how and why as well as what it was and meant.

A popular opinion has it that because literary "technicians" have so rigorously pursued their studies, many "common readers" shy away from the rich and pleasurable insights that balanced, intelligent literary criticism can lead to. Whatever the reason, many students not innately hostile to literature may well have come almost to despise it, certainly to dread it in school, and to think of it in the same category as quantum physics, Erse philology, macro economic theory, or—worse yet—English grammar.

Some professional critics have apparently sympathized with this negative view of the effects of criticism and have espoused neosubjective and appreciative critical criteria that bear scrutiny in such a discussion as this. Susan Sontag, for example, in a 1964 article for the *Evergreen Review* entitled "Against Interpretation," mounted a frontal attack on most kinds of current criticism, which, she maintained, would actually usurp the place of a work of art. In her free-swinging assault Sontag is at once defending a precritical response somewhat similar to the one elaborated in this prologue and asserting that critical analysis is the desecration of an art form. She sees art as the uninhibited creative spirit in action, energetic and sensual. She sees criticism—at least, most of it—as a dry-as-dust intellectual operation, the intent of which is to control and manage art and the method of which is to reduce the work of art to *content* and then to interpret that. Her approach is highly provocative and stimulating. Yet despite some last-minute disclaimers that she is not condemning all critical commentary and some advice to critics to pay more attention to *form*, it is difficult to escape the conclusion that in her opinion interpretation impoverishes art and that its practice for the last half-century by most academic and professional critics has been unquestionably harmful. She concludes with the audacious pronouncement that "In place of a hermeneutics we need an erotics of art."

Such a view would seem to place her in general agreement with Leslie Fiedler, who, addressing the 1974 National Convention of the College English Association in Philadelphia, advocated "ecstatics" as a response to literature. The flamboyant Professor Fiedler would make the "gut reaction" the be-all and end-all of art. The traditionally accepted standards and classics are in his view elitist, academic opinions and productions that have been forced on the reading public, who demonstrably prefer sentimental literature, horror stories, and pornography—all of the Pop variety. Such popular writings produce almost exclusively emotional effects—particularly feelings of pathos, terror, and sexual titillation. They cause readers, says Fiedler, "to go out of control, out of [their] heads." He continues by pointing out that

> ... we do have a traditional name for the effect sought, and at its most successful achieved, by Pop: the temporary release from the limits of rationality, the boundaries of the ego, the burden of consciousness; the moment of privileged insanity[;] that traditional name is, of course, "Ekstasis," which Longinus spoke of in the last centuries of the Classic Era, not in terms of Popular Art or High Art, which in fact cannot be distinguished in terms of this concept; but of *all* art at its irrational best—or, to use his other favorite word, most "sublime."

That political principles underlie Fiedler's position is clear in the closing remarks of his article:

3

Once we have made *ekstasis* rather than instruction or delight the center of critical evaluation, we will be freed from the necessity of ranking mass-produced and mass-distributed books in a hierarchal order viable only in a class-structured society, delivered from the indignity of having to condescend publicly to works we privately relish and relieved of the task of trying to define categories like "high" and "low," "majority" and "minority" which were from the beginning delusive and unreal. ("Is There a Majority Literature?" *The CEA Critic,* 36 [May 1974], 3-8)

Both Sontag's and Fiedler's points of view are instructive for readers interested in familiarizing themselves with the variety of critical responses to a literary work. Whether one subscribes to them in their entirety or in part or disagrees with them categorically, they are invigorating polemics that can spark further intellectual exchange on the issue in the classroom, in the learned journals, and in magazines and newspapers.

Evidence that this more individualistic, less technical approach to literary analysis may now be seriously considered in the classroom is David Bleich's *Readings and Feelings: An Introduction to Subjective Criticism,* a textbook published in 1975 by the National Council of Teachers of English. Bleich stresses the effect that a given piece of literature has on an individual reader and the response the reader makes to the work. To identify, understand, and finally describe this response is one of the main purposes of "subjective criticism." After all, Bleich maintains, a work of literature does not have an independent existence but functions only as it affects those who write and read it. Thus the effects that it produces are highly important and worthy of study. Other academicians who have endorsed the more subjective techniques of criticism are Barrett Mandel in his *Literature and the English Department* (Champaign, Ill.: NCTE, 1970) and Norman Holland in "'English' and Identities" (*The CEA Critic,* 35 [May 1973], 10). Mandel's book is a provocative discussion of subjective and egalitarian approaches to literary study and pedagogy that he thinks have been rewarding to his students and to him and that he strongly urges other teachers to try. Holland's article (the keynote address at the 1973 CEA convention in Detroit) argues that a reader's interpretation of a work always derives from his own "identity theme" (the way that he perceives the world, based on his unique reaction to his experiences) and hence is invariably subjective. Holland acknowledges his "profound indebtedness" to Bleich, whose earlier book *The Subjective Reader*, he says, particularly influenced his thinking about the "whole relation of subjectivity and objectivity in literary response." Bleich has reaffirmed and elaborated his position more recently in "The Subjective Character of Critical Interpretation" (*College English*, 36 [March 1975], 739-755), where he writes:

> Interpretive knowledge is neither deduced nor inferred from a controlled experience. Rather, it is constructed from the uncontrolled experience of the interpreter, and the rules of construction are only vaguely known by anyone observing the interpreter. The consequences of interpretation are not made up of a finite set of possible events which logically follow from the interpretation. Rather, as is easily seen from the critical response to, say, Bradley's interpretations of Shakespeare, the events consequent to interpretive knowledge are in principle infinite and are determined only by the number and kind of people responding to Bradley.

Holland and Murray Schwartz coauthored an article in the same issue of *College English* entitled "The Delphi Seminar" (pp. 789–800). In it they describe a course in which they developed a "widely applicable teaching strategy for using and understanding, rather than avoiding, the subjective responses of both students and faculty. We ended, in fact, with a seminar built upon the Delphic principle, Know Thyself." The following admonitions appeared in the course memorandum:

5

> Whatever you write about, try to avoid the intellectual, analytical response of the ordinary English class. Try instead for three things: feelings, associations, persons.
>
> Feelings should form the foundation of your written response. Describe them as best you can . . . as precisely and as fully. Analogies will help you and lead you toward associations, that is, ideas, memories, or thoughts that come to mind as you let the literary work "float" in your consciousness. Some people who work with this kind of response . . . think that the richest, most feelingful associations are those to significant persons in the responder's life: parents, sibs, spouses, lovers, and friends.

This kind of precritical response suggests considerable concern with the reader's psychology; indeed, the literary work of art seems less an object worthy of contemplation in its own right, though with obvious extensional dimensions, than a means of reader self-analysis. This view is being articulated by literary scholars with pronounced psychological interests. Norman Holland has been not only a professor of English, but also Director of the Center for the Psychological Study of the Arts at the State University of New York at Buffalo; and Schwartz has been director of the Center's graduate program in literature and psychology. Subjective approaches are being given a forum among English professionals by the National Council of Teachers of English, which, as we have noted, published Bleich's *Readings and Feelings: An Introduction to Subjective Criticism* and Mandel's *Literature and the English Department* as well as the articles in *College English* by Bleich and Holland and Schwartz, referred to previously. (For additional comments that bear upon these points, see "The Phenomenological Approach" in Chapter 6 of this book.)

These advocates of more subjective, less "rational" responses to literature in the classroom have not gone unchallenged. Spirited rebuttals have been written by J. Mitchell Morse ("Are English Teachers Obsolete?" *The*

CEA Critic, 36 [May 1974], 9–18); Ann Berthoff ("Recalling Another Freudian Model—A Consumer Caveat," *CEA Critic,* 35 [May 1953], 12–14); and Eva Touster ("Tradition and the Academic Talent," *The CEA Critic,* 33 [May 1971], 14–17). And John Ciardi in the second edition of *How Does a Poem Mean?* (Boston: Houghton Mifflin, 1975) emphatically condemns "appreciation" and "free association" in discussing poetry in the classroom, calling the one "not useful," the other "permissive and pointless," and both together "dull" (pp. xix-xxi).

Perhaps as a result of this controversy, a dilemma has arisen in the classroom for some teachers of literature: namely, whether to discuss their subject merely in the enthusiastic, impressionistic manner of precriticism—the extreme of which could be as subjective and nonrational as a sensitivity session—or whether to employ the tools of formal analysis in studying literary art. We believe that these options do not necessarily constitute a dilemma.

There is unquestionably a kind of literary analysis that is like using an elephant gun to shoot a gnat. It is practiced by riders of all kinds of scholarly hobbyhorses and may manifest itself in such ways as ascertaining the number of feminine rhymes in *The Rape of the Lock* or instances of trochees in Book IV of *Paradise Lost* or the truth about Hamlet's weight problem. The early pages of Dickens's *Hard Times* illustrate the imagination-stifling effect of one such technique. Thomas Gradgrind, patron of a grammar school in an English industrial town, is listening to a class recite. He calls on one of the pupils, "girl number twenty," for the definition of a horse. "Girl number twenty" (in Gradgrind's world there is no personal identity) cannot produce the expected rote answer. A better-conditioned classmate can: "Quadruped. Graminivorous. Forty teeth, namely twenty-four grinders, four eye-teeth and twelve incisive. Sheds coat in the spring; in marshy countries sheds hoofs, too. Hoofs hard, but requiring to be shod with iron. Age known by marks in mouth.' 'Now girl number twenty,' said Mr. Gradgrind. 'You know what a horse is.' "

It hardly needs pointing out that such a "definition" would not do justice to the likes of Bucephalus, Pegasus, Black Beauty, or Flicka. But absorption with extraneous, irrelevant, or even too practical considerations that detract from aesthetic perception seems to be an occupational disease of many literary critics. This appears to be a problem, however, rather than a dilemma, and its solution is among the several aims of this book.

Our purpose in this chapter is to show that the precritical response is not only desirable but indeed essential in the fullest appreciation of literature. In doing so, we do not mean to suggest that analysis or expertise detracts from aesthetic sensitivity any more than we mean to suggest that a precritical response is an unworthy one. It is a truism to say that our senses can sometimes mislead us, hence the need to analyze literature that is being studied as well as read for pure pleasure.

We maintain that knowledge, even of a specialized kind, is not in and of itself a deterrent to the enjoyment of literature. On the contrary, this book is predicated on the assumption that such knowledge and the intelligent application of several interpretive techniques can enhance the pleasure that the "common reader" can derive from a piece of literature.

Let us illustrate with an analogy. The typical student in the crowded football stadium on a crisp November afternoon watching the exciting game between his school and its arch-rival knows an ecstasy denied to many, although his technical knowledge of football may be modest. The thrill he experiences as his team moves for a touchdown is matched only by the heightened sense of danger he feels when the other team threatens to score. Time-outs allow him to join in the cheers and clapping, to sing the fight songs blared out by the band, to drink in the colors and cuts of garbs modish and outlandish. Everything combines to please—the weather, the spectacle, the sounds.

One row behind, another spectator is equally interested in, even excited by the game. He is the student who played football in high school, regularly watches televised games on weekends, follows the nation's leading teams in the newspapers and *Sports Illustrated*, and has even become skilled in the intricacies of APBA. On the level of sense experience, he receives the same impressions as the first student. But because of his special knowledge, he *understands* what is happening. He sees line play, downfield blocking, fakes, options, shifting defenses. He often knows in advance what will come next in this titanic ritual. Yet his knowledge does not dim his pleasure; it does not nullify his "precritical," amateur response. It may intensify it; it certainly complements it. For there is no real opposition of responses here. This more knowledgeable fan does not say to himself at one point, "Now I'm *feeling*," and at another, "Now I'm *knowing*." By this stage the knowing is almost as instinctive as the feeling.

What the academic needs to keep always in mind is that the precritical response should not necessarily be an inferior response to literature. (After all, we may be sure that Shakespeare did not write *Hamlet* so that critical approaches to it could be formulated.) Rather, the precritical response employing primarily the senses and the emotions is an indispensable one if pleasure or delight is the aim of art. Without it the critic might as well be merely proofreading for factual accuracy or correct mechanical form.

Setting

The student's precritical response to the athletic spectacle parallels the "common reader's" precritical response to the literary spectacle. The colorful, crowd-filled stadium, the weather (sunny but cool), and the condition of the field (greener-than-life astroturf) correspond to the **Setting** of the work of literature (the antebellum South; Puritan Massachusetts; Cavalier England; eleventh-century Denmark).

Precritical responses to setting in the works to be dealt with in this handbook are likely to be numerous and freewheeling. One reader of *Huckleberry Finn* will respond to the nostalgia of an earlier, rural America, to the lazy tempo and idyllic mood of Huck and Jim's raft trip down the Mississippi. Still another will delight in the description of the aristocratic Grangerfords' bourgeois parlor furnishings or the frontier primitivism of Arkansas river villages and the "one-horse" plantation of the Phelpses. The Gothic texture of the New England forest in "Young Goodman Brown" will sober some readers, as will the dark and brooding castle of Hamlet. The actual setting of "Coy Mistress" must be inferred (a formal garden? the spacious grounds of a nobleman's estate? some Petit Trianon type of apartment?), but romantically connotative settings such as the "Indian Ganges" and the "tide of Humber" are alluded to, as are macabre or mind-boggling places like "marble vaults" and "deserts of vast eternity."

Plot

The student's partisan, uncomplicated view of the game itself (his team, the "good guys" [or heroes]; their opponents, the "bad guys" [or villains]) equals the reader's precritical response to the **conflict (plot)** involving **protagonist** and **antagonist** (Hamlet versus his uncle; Clint Eastwood and Charles Bronson versus hoods, freaks, and muggers). Readers who delight in action will thrill to the steps in Hamlet's revenge, even when it lights on the innocent, and will feel the keen irony that prevents Hamlet from knowing his Ophelia to be true and guiltless and from enjoying the fruit of his righteous judgment. Such time-honored plot ingredients as the escape, the chase, the capture, the release—liberally spiced with lynching, tar-and-feathering, swindling, feuding, murder, and treachery—will form the staple of interest for precritical readers of *Huckleberry Finn*. Such readers will also be rooting for the white boy and his black slave friend to elude their pursuers and attain their respective freedoms. Enigma and bewilderment may well be the principal precritical response elicited by the plot of "Young Goodman Brown": Is Brown's conflict an imaginary one, or is he really battling the Devil in this theological *Turn of the Screw?* Will the young Cavalier prevail with his Coy Mistress to make love before they are crushed in the maw of Time?

Character

The student at the ballgame assesses, after a fashion, the merits of the players (his, the outweighed underdogs composed of English and business majors, premeds and ministerial students fighting fairly and voluntarily for Alma Mater; the opponents, a horde of superjocks recruited for the sole purpose of playing dirty for ill-disguised payola at Preprofessional U.). Although these are cultural stereotypes, they bear some analogy to the "common reader's" commonsense **character** analysis of literary figures (perceiving the self-effacing, sacrificial nature of Sidney Carton in *A Tale of Two Cities,* the matter-of-fact courage and resourcefulness of Robinson Crusoe, the noble but frustrated humanity of John Savage in *Brave New World*). Precritical reactions to the **characters** in "Coy Mistress" will no doubt vary with the degree to which the reader subscribes to situation ethics or adheres to a clearly articulated moral code. "Strict constructionists" will judge the male aggressor a "wolf" and the girl a tease at best. Libertines will envy the speaker his "line." Women's libbers will deplore the "male-chauvinist-pig" exploitation that is being attempted. Although characters more complex than our stereotyped football players appear in *Huckleberry Finn,* a precritical perusal of the book will probably divide them into good (those basically sympathetic to Huck and Jim) and bad (those not). Similarly, the dramatis personae of *Hamlet* will be judged according to whether they line up on the side of the pathetic and tormented Hamlet or on that of his diabolically determined uncle. In more complex character analysis, the simplistic grouping into "good" and "bad" will not be adequate; it may in fact necessitate an appreciation of ambiguity. From this viewpoint, Gertrude and Polonius and Rosencrantz and Guildenstern appear more weak and stupid than vicious. Just as ambiguity was prominent in the plot of "Young Good-man Brown," so does it figure largely in a reader's precritical evaluation of character. Brown may appear a victim of trauma, an essentially shallow man suddenly made to seem profoundly disturbed.

Structure

The student's awareness of the four quarters of the game and the importance of each to the outcome is akin to the reader's or viewer's unconscious sense of **plot structure,** the "relatedness" of actions, the gradual buildup in suspense from a situation full of potential to a climax and a resolution (as in Macbeth's rise to be king of Scotland through foul and bloody means and the poetic justice of his defeat and death by one he had wronged). A precritical response to the **structure** of "Coy Mistress" could certainly involve the recognition of the heightening in intensity, stanza by stanza, of the lover's suit—from the proper and conventional complimentary "forms" of verbal courting to more serious "arguments" about the brevity of life and finally, to the bold and undisguised affirmation that sexual joy is "what it's all about." The "common reader" can discern the plot development in *Hamlet* step by step, from mystery, indecision, and torment to knowledge, resolute action, and catharsis. He may be fascinated by the stratagems that Hamlet and Claudius employ against each other and amused by the CIA-like techniques of Polonius to ferret out Hamlet's secret. Spellbinding horror and, later, cathartic pathos are possible emotions engendered by the climax and dénouement of this revenge tragedy. *Huckleberry Finn's* episodic plot is somehow coherent even though precritical readers must confront in rapid order thrill, suspense, danger, brutality, outrage, absurdity, laughter, tears, anger, and poetic justice as they respond to Huck and Jim's attempt to elude capture; the side-splitting charlatanism as well as the sinister and criminal behavior of the King and the Duke; wrecked steamboats; tent revivals; feuding, shooting in the street, and thwarted lynching; and finally the triumph of the heroes. The structural stages in "Young Goodman Brown" may result in ambivalent reader reactions: on the one hand, plain recognition of the destructive effects of the events of the plot on Brown; on the other, bewilderment as to whether the events really took place or were all fantasy.

Style

The style of play in the football game (straight power, razzle-dazzle, tight defense) has its counterpart in the verbal **style** of a literary work (the spare, understated prose of Hemingway; the sophisticated wit of *The Importance of Being Earnest*; the compressed, highly allusive idiom of modern poets like Eliot and Yeats; the crude, earthy plain talk of Mailer's *The Naked and the Dead*, Updike's *Couples*, and Vonnegut's *Slaughterhouse-5*). The precritical reader feels it in the Pike County dialect of *Huckleberry Finn*, its vocabulary and rhythms ringing true in every line; in the urbane diction, learned allusion, and polished couplets of "Coy Mistress"; in the magnificent blank verse of *Hamlet*, alternately formal and plain, yet somehow organic and right for both dramatic action and philosophical soliloquy; in the solemn, cadenced phraseology of "Young Goodman Brown," echoing in some unexplainable fashion what one imagines Puritan discourse to have been like, both in and out of the pulpit, its lightest touches still somehow ponderous.

[handwritten margin note: Twain as satirist]

Atmosphere

Atmosphere, the mood or feeling that permeates an environment, is a further common ingredient in the two parts of our analogy. Several factors combine to create it: at the football game, the weather, the excitement, the tension, the behavior of the fans; in a literary work, such similar factors as the eerie locales and stormy weather in Mary Shelley's *Frankenstein* and Emily Brontë's *Wuthering Heights*, the panic of the green troops in Crane's *The Red Badge of Courage*, the suspense and terror in Poe's "The Tell-Tale Heart," the indifference and listlessness of the characters in Faulkner's "That Evening Sun."

The four works that we are emphasizing for precritical responses afford interesting possibilities. "Coy Mistress," which on the surface seems to have fewer overt atmosphere-producing elements, in fact has a fairly pronounced atmosphere (or atmospheres, since there are shifts). The atmosphere results from the diction and the tone the speaker employs. The formal honorific "Lady" and its implied politeness create, if not a drawing-room atmosphere, a stylized one where there is romantic badinage, where gallants wax hyperbolic in a formulary way, and where fair maidens drop their eyes demurely or, if hyperbole becomes too warm, tap male wrists with a delicate fan. It is a mannered, controlled, ritualistic atmosphere. But in the second stanza, compliments give way to professorial lectures as the aggressive and more intellectual male grows impatient with coyness carried too far, hence a dispiriting philosophical discussion about the brevity of life and the nothingness of afterlife. Finally, in the third stanza, the atmosphere becomes electric and potentially physical as the diction becomes explicitly erotic.

In *Huckleberry Finn,* on a very obvious plane, setting contributes to atmosphere. The Mississippi River, sleepy villages, small towns, one-horse plantations, Victorian parlors: all combine to present an essentially "normal" nineteenth-century-Americana kind of security along with zest for life. Diction, character, and costume, however, also function to add subtle features to the atmosphere. The casual use of expressions like "nigger" and "harelip" (our nineteenth-century ancestors did not share our aversion to using racial epithets or to making fun of physical deformity); the toleration and acceptance of violence, cruelty, and inhumanity observable in conversation and exposition; the radical inconsistency of basically decent, religious people breaking up slave families while evincing genuine affection for them and concern for their welfare. The amalgam of their shocking and sometimes contradictory attitudes and actions results in an utterly convincing atmosphere.

Both setting and plot make for a gloomy, foreboding

atmosphere in *Hamlet* and "Young Goodman Brown." The Shakespearean drama opens with sentries walking guard duty at midnight on the battlements of a medieval castle where a ghost has recently appeared. It is bitter cold and almost unnaturally quiet. Though later the scene changes many times, this atmosphere persists, augmented by the machinations of the principals, by dramatic confrontations, by reveries on death, by insane ravings, and finally by wholesale slaughter. In only slightly less melodramatic form, Hawthorne's story takes the reader to a witches' sabbath deep in the forests of seventeenth-century Massachusetts, where a cacophony of horrid sounds forms the auditory background for a scene of devilish human countenances and eerie natural images of trees, stones, clouds. The protagonist's ambiguous role in the evil ceremony, which ruins his life, adds to the dark atmosphere pervading the story.

Theme

Our analogy, like any other analogy, begins to break down when we come to **theme,** the often rich and varied underlying idea of action. In the football game, theme may be no more than "Win at all costs," "We're Number One," or "These gladiators are better than those." In a literary work, theme may be as obvious as the message in *Uncle Tom's Cabin* that "Slavery is cruel and morally degrading and must go" or the implicit point of *Robin Hood* that "Some rich folks deserve to be taken from, and some poor folks need to be given to." These scarcely compare with such profound thematic implications as those in *Adam Bede, The Scarlet Letter,* or "The Love-Song of J. Alfred Prufrock." As theme is a complex aspect of literature, one that requires very intentional thinking to discern, it is not likely to elicit the precritical response that the more concrete features do. This is not to say that it will not be felt. Twain's criticisms of slavery, hypocrisy, chicanery, violence, tastelessness, and other assorted evils will move both the casual reader and the scholar. So does Marvell's speaker's spunky defiance of all-conquering Time. The poignancy of young Hamlet's having to deal with so many of life's insolubles at once and alone is certainly one of the play's major themes, and is one available at the precritical level of response. There are others. Despite complexity and ambiguity, the precritical reader will sense the meaning of faith and the effects of evil in "Young Goodman Brown" as two of the more urgent themes in the story.

None of these feelings, whether at the football game or in one's private reading, is contingent upon a technical knowledge of football or a graduate degree in the humanities. Without either, one may appreciate and respond "precritically" to both NFL play-offs and the cold setting of Jack London's "To Build a Fire," to the sequence of events that causes Oedipus to blind himself, or to the phantasmagoric atmosphere of horror pervading Poe's "The Masque of the Red Death."

In short, regardless of the extent to which close scrutiny and technical knowledge aid in literary analysis, there is no substitute for an initial personal, appreciative response to the basic ingredients of literature: setting, plot, character, structure, style, atmosphere, and theme. The reader who manages to proceed without that response sacrifices the spontaneous joy of seeing any art object whole, the wondrous sum of myriad parts.

CHAPTER 1

TRADITIONAL APPROACHES

I. NATURE AND SCOPE OF TRADITIONAL APPROACHES

At the opposite extreme of such precritical or appreciative responses as those discussed in our prologue is the type parodied some years ago, when a story was making the rounds in academic circles and was received in good humor by all the enlightened teachers of literature. A professor of English in one of our great Eastern universities, so the story goes, entered the classroom one day and announced that the poem under consideration for that hour was to be Andrew Marvell's "To His Coy Mistress." He then proceeded to discuss Marvell's politics, religion, and career. He described Marvell's character, mentioned that he was respected by friend and foe alike, and speculated on whether he was married. At this point the bell rang, signaling the end of the class. The professor closed his sheaf of notes, looked up, smiling, and concluded, "Damn' fine poem, men. Damn' fine."

The story was told to ridicule the type of analysis that dominated the study of literature until the 1930s and that is still widely employed today. In this approach the work of

19

art frequently appeared to be of secondary importance, something that merely illustrated "background." Such an approach often (many would say inevitably) led to the study of literature as essentially biography or history, rather than as art.

Well on in the twentieth century, however, a new type of literary analysis emerged in which the literary work per se (that is, as a separate entity divorced from "extrinsic" considerations) became the dominant concern of scholars. The "New Critics," as the proponents of this position were called, insisted that scholars concentrate on the work itself, on the text, examining it as art. This method revolutionized the study of literature. It frequently divided critics and teachers into opposing factions: those of the older school, for whom literature provides primarily an opportunity for exercising the "really relevant" scholarly and cultural disciplines (for example, history, linguistics, and biography) and the New Critics, who maintain that literature has an intrinsic worth, that it is not just one of the media of transmitting biography and history. Now that the controversy has lessened, the rationale of the New Criticism seems to have put into clearer focus what a poem or play or piece of fiction is trying to do; it has unquestionably corrected many wrongheaded interpretations resulting from an unwise use of the older method. To this extent it has expanded our perception and appreciation of literary art.

Nevertheless, in their zeal to avoid the danger of interpreting a literary work solely as biography and history— the end result of the traditional method, they thought— many twentieth-century followers of New Criticism have been guilty of what may well be a more serious mistake, that of ignoring any information not in the work itself, however helpful or necessary it may be. Fortunately, the most astute critics have espoused a more eclectic approach and have fused a variety of techniques. They have certainly insisted on treating literature as literature, but they have not ruled out the possibility of further aesthetic illumination from traditional quarters. Oscar Cargill, in the introduction to his *Toward a Pluralistic Criticism* (Carbondale: Southern Illinois University Press, 1965), endorses the eclectic approach unequivocally:

> I have always held that any method which could produce the meaning of a work of literature was a legitimate method. . . . I came to the conclusion that . . . the critic's task was . . . to procure a viable meaning appropriate to the critic's time and place. Practically, this meant employing not any one method in interpreting a work of art but every method which might prove efficient. [pp. xiii–xiv]

In any event, while we may grant the basic position that literature is primarily art, it must be affirmed also that art does not exist in a vacuum. It is a creation by someone at some time in history, and it is intended to speak to other human beings about some idea or issue that has human relevance. Any work of art for that matter will always be more meaningful to knowledgeable people than to uninformed ones. Its greatness comes from the fact that when the wisest, most cultivated, most sensitive minds bring all of their information, experience, and feeling to contemplate it, they are moved and impressed by its beauty, by its unique kind of knowledge, and even by its nonaesthetic values. It is surely dangerous to assume that a work of art must always be judged or looked at or taught as if it were disembodied from all experience except the strictly aesthetic. Many literary classics are admittedly autobiographical, propagandistic, or topical (that is, related to contemporary events).

Thus, although we have not yet elaborated these critical methods, let us be aware from the outset that in succeeding chapters we will be dealing with some widely divergent interpretive approaches to literature and that, regardless of what newer modes of analysis may be in the ascendant, the traditional methods retain their validity.

A. Textual Scholarship: A Prerequisite to Criticism

Before we embark upon any interpretive ventures, we should look to that branch of literary studies known as textual criticism. In the words of James Thorpe, author of one of the best modern books on the subject, *Principles of Textual Criticism* (San Marino, Calif.: Huntington Library, 1972), textual criticism has as its ideal the establishment of an *authentic* text, or the "text which the author intended" (p. 50). This aim is not so easy to achieve as one might think, however, and it is a problem not only with older works, where it might be more expected, but also in contemporary literature. There are countless ways in which a literary text may be corrupted from what the author intended. The author's own manuscript may contain omissions and errors in spelling and mechanics; these mistakes may be preserved by the next copyist, be he scribe or printer, who may add a few of his own. Or, as has often happened, a copyist or editor may take it upon himself to improve, censor, or correct what the author wrote. If the author or someone who knows what the author intended does not catch these errors during proofreading, they can be published, disseminated, and perpetuated. (Nor does it help matters when the author himself cannot decide what the final form of his work is to be but actually releases for publication several different versions or, as is frequently the case, delegates broad editorial powers to others along the line.) So many additional mishaps can befall a manuscript in the course of producing multiple copies for the public that, to quote Thorpe again, the "ordinary history of the transmission of a text, without the intervention of author or editor, is one of progressive degeneration" (p. 51). Shocking as such an assertion may sound, it is nevertheless true and can be documented.

We frequently assume that the text before us has come down unchanged from its original form. More often than not, the reverse is the case; what we see is the result of painstaking collation of textual variants, interpretation, and emendation or conjecture. Because it is pointless to study inaccurate versions of anything, from economic theories to works of literature, except with a view to ascertaining the true (that is, the authorial) version, our debt to textual criticism is well-nigh incalculable. For example, the student who uses the eight-volume Chicago edition of *The Canterbury Tales,* a collation of scores of medieval manuscripts, should certainly appreciate the efforts of precomputer scholars. Similarly, the studies of W. W. Greg, A. W. Pollard, and a host of others have gone far toward the establishment of a satisfactory Shakespearean text. This type of scholarship should create in the student a healthy respect for textual criticism and expert editing, and well it might, for as Thorpe has aptly phrased it, "where there is no editing the texts perish" (p. 54).

Textual criticism plays an especially important role in studying the genesis and development of a piece of literature. Thus it has enabled us to see how Ezra Pound's editorial surgery transformed T. S. Eliot's *The Waste Land* from a clumsy and diffuse poem to a modern classic. (The poem still presents textual problems, however, because Eliot himself authorized versions containing substantive differences.) Other famous textual "cases" include Dickens's two endings for *Great Expectations:* After seeing the first "unhappy" ending in proof, Dickens wrote another and authorized only it. Later editors have published the first version as having more aesthetic integrity, but Dickens never authorized it. Thomas Hardy made so many substantive character and plot alterations in the four versions of *The Return of the Native,* all of which he authorized for publication between 1878 and 1912, that James Thorpe understandably asks, "Which is the real *Return of the Native?*" (p. 34). Moreover, textual criticism is, contrary to what ill-informed people may think, anything but an essentially mechanical operation. Although its practitioners are very much concerned with such matters as spelling, punctuation, capitalization, italicization, and paragraphing ("accidentals" as they are called in textual criticism) in the establishment of an authentic text, they deal with much more than close proofreading. They must be highly skilled in linguistics, literary history, literary criticism, and bibliography, to mention only the most obvious areas.

However, though textual critics must and do make aesthetic judgments, not only in accidentals but also in "substantives" (actual verbal readings), they do so in order to establish by means as scientific as possible an authentic text for the literary critic, who may then proceed to interpret and evaluate. Textual criticism is therefore treated in this book not as a traditional interpretive approach to literature but as an indispensable tool for further meaningful analysis. This relationship between textual and strictly interpretive criticism may be expressed in a surgical metaphor: The textual critic is the first in a team of critics who prepare the literary corpus for further dissection. Nevertheless, we should not push any analogy between textual criticism and science too far. The textual critic is not and should not be considered a scientist. He has no predetermined or inviolable laws that he can use to come out with an "authentic text." Perhaps it would be more accurate to concede that a textual critic is a scientist of sorts; he simply isn't an exact scientist (that is, one dealing in an exact science). He is more of a combination of a scientist and an artist. As A. E. Housman says, textual criticism is the "science of discovering error in texts and the art of removing it" ("The Application of Thought to Textual Criticism," in Ronald Gottesman and Scott Bennett, eds., *Art and Error: Modern Textual Editing* [Bloomington: Indiana University Press, 1970], p. 2).

Thorpe, however, is highly critical of any scientific claims for textual criticism. Indeed, one of the main points of his book is the failure of textual studies to measure up to their alleged scientific status. Somewhat resignedly he concludes:

> It would be cheerful to be able to report that a mastery of sound principles, an application of effective methods, and an exercise of conscientious care will enable the textual critic to reach the ideal which is incorporated in the first principle of his craft. But it would not be true. In textual criticism, the best that one can do is to cut the losses, to reduce the amount

of error, to improve or clarify the state of textual affairs, to approach the ideal. After all has been done that can be done, however, the results of textual criticism still are necessarily imperfect. [p. 55]

Whether one agrees with Thorpe or with those who view textual criticism as less tentative and more scientific, all critics can agree on one thing: It is far more preferable to have a version of a literary work that textual criticism can make available to us than to have one that has not been subjected to the rigorous methodology of that discipline.

B. Types of Traditional Approaches

We are presenting traditional critical approaches to literature under two headings, "Historical-Biographical" and "Moral-Philosophical," which will be defined, discussed, and subsequently applied to each of the four works selected for emphasis. Early in the discussions of each work we will also treat textual matters, summarizing the narrative line of the literary work and making some nontechnical observations about genre. (The generic approach will receive additional attention in Chapter 6.) These steps may be thought of as preliminaries to traditional literary analysis and can certainly be useful in other interpretive approaches as well.

1. Historical-Biographical

Although the historical-biographical approach has been evolving over many years, its basic tenets are perhaps most clearly articulated in the writings of the nineteenth-century French critic H. A. Taine, whose phrase *race, milieu, et moment*, elaborated in his *History of English Literature*, bespeaks a hereditary and environmental determinism. Put simply, this approach sees a literary work chiefly, if not exclusively, as a reflection of its author's life and times or the life and times of the characters in the work.

At the risk of laboring the obvious, we will mention the historical implications of William Langland's *Piers Plowman*, which is, in addition to being a magnificent allegory,

25

a scorching attack on the corruption in every aspect of fourteenth-century English life—social, political, and religious. So timely, in fact, were the poet's phrases that they became rallying cries in the Peasants' Revolt. John Milton's sonnet "On the Late Massacre in Piedmont" illustrates the topical quality that great literature may and often does possess. This poem commemorates the slaughter in 1655 of the Waldenses, members of a Protestant sect living in the valleys of northern Italy. A knowledge of this background clarifies at least one rather factual reference and two allusions in the poem. Several of Milton's other sonnets also reflect events in his life or times. Two such are "On His Blindness," best understood when one realizes that the poet became totally blind when he was forty-four, and "On His Deceased Wife," a tribute to his second wife, Katherine Woodcock. Milton was already blind when he married her, a fact that explains the line, "Her face was veiled." In fact, Milton affords us an excellent example of an author whose works reflect particular episodes in his life. *Samson Agonistes* and *The Doctrine and Discipline of Divorce* may be cited as two of the more obvious.

A historical novel is likely to be more meaningful when either its milieu or that of its author is understood. James Fenimore Cooper's *The Last of the Mohicans*, Sir Walter Scott's *Ivanhoe*, Charles Dickens's *A Tale of Two Cities*, and John Steinbeck's *The Grapes of Wrath* are certainly better understood by readers familiar, respectively, with the French and Indian War (and the American frontier experience generally), Anglo-Norman Britain, the French Revolution, and the American Depression. And, of course, there is a very real sense in which these books are *about* these great historical matters, so that the author is interested in the characters only to the extent that they are molded by these events.

What has just been said applies even more to ideological or propagandist novels. Harriet Beecher Stowe's *Uncle Tom's Cabin*, Frank Norris's *The Octopus*, and Upton

Sinclair's *The Jungle* ring truer (or falser as the case may be) to those who know about the antebellum South, railroad expansion in the late nineteenth century, and scandals in the American meatpacking industry in the early twentieth century. Sinclair Lewis's satires take on added bite and fun for those who have lived in or observed the cultural aridity of *Main Street*, who have been treated by shallow and materialistic physicians like some of those in *Arrowsmith*, who have sat through the sermons and watched the shenanigans of religious charlatans like Elmer Gantry, or who have dealt with and been in service clubs with all too typical American businessmen like Babbitt. Novels may lend themselves somewhat more readily than lyric poems to this particular interpretive approach; they usually treat a broader range of experience than poems do and thus are affected more by extrinsic factors.

It is a mistake, however, to think that poets do not concern themselves with social themes or that good poetry cannot be written about such themes. Actually, poets have from earliest times been the historians, the interpreters of contemporary culture, and the prophets of their people. Take, for example, a poet as mystical and esoteric as William Blake. Many of his best poems can be read meaningfully only in terms of Blake's England. His "London" is an outcry against the oppression of man by society: He lashes out against child labor in his day and the church's indifference to it, against the government's indifference to the indigent soldier who has served his country faithfully, and against the horrible and unnatural consequences of a social code that represses sexuality. His "Preface" to *Milton* is at once a denunciation of the "dark Satanic Mills" of the Industrial Revolution and a joyous battle cry of determination to build "Jerusalem/In England's green and pleasant Land." It has been arranged as an anthem for church choirs, is widely used in a hymn setting, and was sung in London in the 1945 election by the victorious Labor party. The impact of the Sacco-Vanzetti case upon young poets of the 1920s or of the opposition to the war in Vietnam upon almost every important American poet in the 1960s resulted in numerous literary works on these subjects. Obviously, then, even some lyric poems are susceptible to historical-biographical analysis.

Political and religious verse satires like Dryden's in the seventeenth century and personal satires like Pope's in the eighteenth century have as one of their primary purposes the ridiculing of contemporary situations and persons. Dryden propounds his own Anglican faith and debunks that of Dissenters and Papists in *Religio Laici*. Later, when he had renounced Anglicanism and embraced Roman Catholicism, he again defended his position, and in *The Hind and the Panther* he attacked those who differed. His *Absalom and Achitophel* is a verse allegory using the Biblical story of Absalom's rebellion against his father, King David, to satirize the Whig attempt to replace Charles II with his illegitimate son, the Duke of Monmouth. Pope's *Dunciad* is certainly a satire against all sorts of literary stupidity and inferiority, but it is also directed against particular literary people who had the bad fortune to offend Pope. All these works may be understood and appreciated without extensive historical or biographical background. Most readers, however, would probably agree with T. S. Eliot that "No poet, no artist of any art, has his complete meaning alone" (from "Tradition and the Individual Talent") and with Richard D. Altick that "almost every literary work is attended by a host of outside circumstances which, once we expose and explore them, suffuse it with additional meaning" (*The Art of Literary Research*, rev. ed. [New York: Norton, 1975], p. 5).

The triumph of such verse satires as those of Dryden and Pope is that they possess considerable merit as poems, merit that is only enhanced by their topicality. That it should ever have been necessary to defend them because they were topical or "unpoetic" is attributable to what Professor Ronald S. Crane calls in *A Collection of English Poems, 1660–1800* (New York: Harper & Row, 1932) the tyranny of certain Romantic and Victorian "presuppositions about the nature of poetry" and the "inhibitions of taste which they have tended to encourage." He mentions among such presuppositions the notions that

> true poetry is always a direct outpouring of personal feeling; that its values are determined by the nature of the emotion which it expresses, the standards being naturally set by the preferences of the most admired poets in the nineteenth-century tradition; that its distinctive effort is "to bring unthinkable thoughts and unsayable sayings within the range of human minds and ears"; that the essence of its art is not statement but suggestion. [p. v]

In short, even topical poetry can be worthwhile when not limited by presuppositions that make poetry a precious, exclusively personal, even esoteric thing.

2. MORAL-PHILOSOPHICAL

The moral-philosophical approach is as old as classical Greek and Roman critics. Plato, for example, emphasized moralism and utilitarianism; Horace stressed *dulce et utile*, (delight and instruction). Among its most famous exemplars are the commentators of the age of neoclassicism in English literature (1660–1800), particularly Dr. Samuel Johnson. The basic position of such critics is that the larger function of literature is to teach morality and to probe philosophical issues. They would interpret literature within a context of the philosophical thought of a period or group. From their point of view Sartre and Camus can be read profitably only if one understands existentialism. Similarly, Pope's *Essay on Man* may be grasped only if one understands the meaning and the role of reason in eighteenth-century thought. Such teaching may also be religiously oriented. Fielding's *Tom Jones*, for example, illustrates the moral superiority of a hot-blooded young man like Tom, whose sexual indulgences are decidedly atoned for by his humanitarianism, tenderheartedness, and instinctive honor (innate as opposed to acquired through training). Serving as foils to Tom are the real sinners in the novel—the vicious and the hypocritical. Hawthorne's *The Scarlet Letter* is likewise seen essentially as a study of the effects of secret sin on a human soul, that is, sin unconfessed before both God and man, as the sin of Arthur Dimmesdale with Hester Prynne, or, even more, the sin of Chillingworth. Robert Frost's "Stopping by Woods on a Snowy Evening" teaches that duty and responsibility take precedence over beauty and pleasure.

A related attitude is that of Matthew Arnold, the Victorian critic, who insisted that a great literary work must possess "high seriousness." (Because he felt that Chaucer lacked it, Arnold refused to rank him among the very greatest English poets.) In each instance the critic working from a moral bent is not unaware of form, figurative language, and other purely aesthetic considerations, but they are for him secondary. The important thing is the moral or philosophical teaching. On its highest plane this is not superficially didactic, though it may at first seem so. In the larger sense, all great literature teaches. The critic who employs the moral-philosophical approach insists on ascertaining and stating *what* is taught. If the work is in any degree significant or intelligible, this meaning will be there.

It seems reasonable, then, to employ historical-biographical or moral-philosophical analyses among other methods (such as textual study and recognition of genre) in getting at the total meaning of a literary work when the work seems to call for them. Such approaches are less likely to err on the side of overinterpretation than are more esoteric methods. And overinterpretation is a particularly grievous critical error. A reader who stays pretty much on the surface of a piece of literature has at least understood part of what it is about, whereas a reader who extracts interpretations that are neither supportable nor reasonable may miss a very basic or even key meaning. Obviously, a dull, pedestrian, uniformly literal approach to literary analysis is the antithesis of the informed, imaginative, and creative approach that this book advocates. But it must be remembered that, brilliant and ingenious criticism notwithstanding, words in context, though they may mean many things, cannot mean just anything at all. Daring, inventive readings of metaphorical language must have defensible rationales if they are to be truly insightful and convincing.

If, as has been contended by its enemies, the traditional approach to literary analysis has tended to be somewhat deficient in imagination and has neglected the newer sciences, such as psychology and anthropology, and if it has been too content with a "commonsense" interpretation of material, it has nevertheless performed one valuable service: In avoiding cultism and faddism, it has preserved scholarly discipline and balance in literary criticism. We do not mean that we favor the traditional criticism over predominantly aesthetic interpretive approaches. We do suggest, however, that any knowledge or insight (with special reference to scholarly disciplines like history, philosophy, theology, sociology, art, and music) that can help to explain or clarify a literary work ought to be given the fullest possible chance to do so.

The reader who intends to employ the traditional approaches to a literary work will almost certainly employ them simultaneously. That is, he will bring to bear on the poem, for instance, all the information and insights these respective disciplines can give him in seeing just what the poem means and does.

II. THE TRADITIONAL APPROACHES IN PRACTICE

A. Traditional Approaches to Marvell's "To His Coy Mistress"

1. THE TEXT OF THE POEM
Some words on textual problems in Andrew Marvell's "To His Coy Mistress" will set the stage for our consider-

ation of the poem. One of these problems is the last word in this couplet:

> Now therefore, while the youthful hue
> Sits on thy skin like morning dew.

Instead of "dew," the first edition of the poem had "glew," which we now know is a dialectal variant of "glow," although it was earlier thought to be another spelling of "glue," a senseless reading in the context. "Lew" (dialectal "warmth") was also suggested as a possibility. But when someone conjectured "dew," probably in the eighteenth century, it was apparently so happy an emendation that virtually all textbooks have long printed it without any explanation. The first edition of this handbook followed those textbooks. But two recent texts restore the earliest reading. Both *The Anchor Anthology of Seventeenth-Century Verse* (ed. Louis L. Martz [Garden City, N.Y.: Doubleday, 1969], vol. I) and *Andrew Marvell, Complete Poetry* (ed. George de F. Lord [New York: Random House (Modern Library), 1968] print "glew" (meaning "glow") as making more sense in the context and being quite sound linguistically. Two other words in the poem that must be explained are "transpires" and "instant" in this couplet:

> And while thy willing soul transpires
> At every pore with instant fires.

In each case, the word is much nearer to its Latin original than to its twentieth-century meaning. "Transpires" thus means literally "breathes forth," and "instant" means "now present" and "urgent." Admittedly, this sort of linguistic information borders on the technical, but an appreciation of the meaning of the words is imperative for a full understanding of the poem.

2. THE GENRE OF THE POEM

Most critics are careful to ascertain what literary type or genre they are dealing with, whether a poem (and if so, what particular kind), a drama, a novel, or a short story. This first step—the question "What are we dealing with?"—is highly necessary, because different literary genres are judged according to different standards. We do not expect, for example, the sweep and grandeur of an epic in a love lyric, nor do we expect the degree of detail in a short story that we find in a novel. From a technical and formal standpoint, we do expect certain features in particular genres, features so integral as to define and characterize the type (for example, rhythm, rhyme, narrative devices such as a point-of-view character, and dramatic devices such as the soliloquy). The lyric, the genre to which "Coy Mistress" belongs, is a fairly brief poem characterized primarily by emotion, imagination, and subjectivity. Having ascertained the genre and established the text, the employer of traditional methods of interpretation next determines what the poem says on the level of statement or, as John Crowe Ransom has expressed it, its "paraphrasable content." The reader discovers that this poem is a "proposition," that is, an offer of sexual intercourse. At first it contains, however, nothing of the coarseness or crudity usually implied in the word "proposition." On the contrary, though impassioned, it is graceful, sophisticated, even philosophical. The speaker, a man, has evidently urged an unsuccessful suit on a lady. Finding her reluctant, he is, as the poem opens, making use of his most eloquent "line." But it is a "line" that reveals him no common lover. It is couched in the form of an argument in three distinct parts, going something like this: (1) If we had all the time in the world, I could have no objection to even an indefinite postponement of your acceptance of my suit. (2) But the fact is we do not have much time at all; and once this phase of existence (that is, life) is gone, all our chances for love are gone. (3) Therefore the only conclusion that can logically follow is that we should love one another now, while we are young and passionate, and thus seize what pleasures we can in a world where time is all too short. After all, we know nothing about any future life and have only the grimmest observations of the effects of death.

3. HISTORICAL-BIOGRAPHICAL CONSIDERATIONS

We know several facts about Marvell and his times that may help to explain this framework of logical argument as well as the tone and learned allusions that pervade the poem. First, Marvell was an educated man (Cambridge B.A., 1639), the son of an Anglican priest with Puritan leanings. Because both he and his father had received a classical education, the poet was undoubtedly steeped in classical modes of thought and literature. Moreover, the emphasis on classical logic and polemics in his education was probably kept strong in his mind by his political actions. (He was a Puritan, a Parliamentarian, an admirer of Cromwell, a writer of political satires, and an assistant to Milton in the Latin secretaryship of the government.) That it should occur, therefore, to Marvell to have the speaker plead his suit logically should surprise no one.

There is, however, nothing pedantic or heavy-handed in this disputatious technique. Rather, it is playful and urbane, as are the allusions to Greek mythology, courtly love, and the Bible. When the speaker begins his argument, he establishes himself in a particular tradition of love poetry, that of courtly love. No one would mistake this poem for love in the manner of "Frankie and Johnny," "O my luve's like a red, red rose," or "Sonnets from the Portuguese." It is based on the elevation of the beloved to the status of a virtually unattainable object, one to be idolized, almost like a goddess. This status notwithstanding, she is capable of cruelty, and in the first couplet the speaker accuses her of a "crime," the crime of withholding her love from him. Moreover, because she is like a goddess, she is also capricious and whimsical, and the worshipper must humor her by following the conventions of courtly love: He will "complain" (of her cruelty and his subsequent pain and misery) by the Humber. He will "serve" her through praise, adoration, and faithful devotion from the fourth millennium B.C. (the time of Noah's Flood) to the conversion of the Jews to Christianity, an event prophesied to take place just before the end of the world. Doubtless, this bit of humor is calculated to make the lady smile and to put her off her guard against the ulterior motive of the speaker. However pronounced courtly love may be in the opening portion of the poem (the first part of the argument), by the time the speaker has arrived at his conclusion, he has stripped the woman of all pretense of modesty or divinity by his accusation that her "willing soul" literally exudes or breathes forth ("transpires") urgent ("instant") passion and by his direct allusion to kinesthetic ecstasy: "sport us," "roll all our strength," "tear our pleasures with rough strife/Thorough the iron gates of life" (the virginal body). All of this is consistent with a speaker who might have been schooled as Marvell himself was.

Many allusions in the poem that have to do with the passage of time show Marvell's religious and classical background. Two have been mentioned: the Flood and the conversion of the Jews. But there are others that continue to impress the reader with the urgency of the speaker's plea. "Time's wingèd chariot" is the traditional metaphor for the vehicle in which the sun, moon, night, and time are represented as pursuing their course. At this point, the speaker is still in the humorous vein, and the image is, despite its serious import, a pleasing one. The humor grows increasingly sardonic, however, and the images become in the second stanza downright repulsive. The allusions in the last stanza (the conclusion to the argument or case) do not suggest playfulness or a Cavalier attitude at all. Time's "slow-chapped [slow-jawed] power" alludes to the cannibalism of Chronos (Time), chief of the gods, who, to prevent ever being overthrown by his own children, devoured all of them as they were born except Zeus. Zeus was hidden, later grew up, and ultimately became chief of the gods himself. The last couplet,

> Thus, though we cannot make our sun
> Stand still, yet we will make him run,

suggests several possible sources, both Biblical and classical. Joshua commanded the sun to stand still so that he could win a battle against the Amorites (Joshua 10:13). Phaeton took the place of his father, the sun, in a winged chariot and had a wild ride across the sky, culminating in his death (Ovid, *The Metamorphoses*). Zeus bade the sun to stand still in order to lengthen his night of love with Alcmene, the last mortal woman he embraced. In this example it is, of course, easy to see the appropriateness of the figures to the theme of the poem. Marvell's speaker is saying to his mistress that they are human, hence mortal. They do not have the ear of God as Joshua had, so God will not intervene miraculously and stop time. Nor do they possess the power of the pagan deities of old. They must instead cause time to pass quickly by doing what is pleasurable.

In addition to Marvell's classical and Biblical background, further influences on the poem are erotic literature and metaphysical poetry. Erotic poetry is, broadly speaking, simply love poetry, but it must emphasize the sensual. In "Coy Mistress" this emphasis is evident in the speaker's suit through the references to his mistress's breasts and "the rest" of her charms and in the image of the lovers rolled up into "one ball." The poem is metaphysical in its similarities to other seventeenth-century poems that deal with the psychology of love and religion and—to enforce their meaning—employ bizarre, grotesque, shocking, and often obscure figures (the metaphysical conceit). Such lines as "My vegetable love should grow" (the warning that worms may violate the mistress's virginity and that corpses do not make love), the likening of the lovers to "amorous birds of prey," and the allusion to Time's devouring his offspring ("slow-chapped") all help identify the poem as a product of the seventeenth-century revolt against the saccharine conventions of Elizabethan love poetry. As for its relation to *vers de société*, "To His Coy Mistress" partakes more of the tone than the subject matter of such poetry, manifesting for the most part wit, gaiety, charm, polish, sophistication, and ease of expression—all of these despite some rough metaphysical imagery.

4. MORAL-PHILOSOPHICAL CONSIDERATIONS

An examination of what "Coy Mistress" propounds morally and philosophically reveals the common theme of *carpe diem*, "seize the day," an attitude of "eat and drink, for tomorrow we shall die." Many of Marvell's contemporaries treated this idea (for example, Robert Herrick in "To the Virgins, To Make Much of Time" and Edmund Waller in "Go, Lovely Rose"). This type of poetry naturally exhibits certain fundamental moral attitudes toward the main issue this poem treats—sex. These attitudes reflect an essentially pagan view. They depict sexual intercourse as strictly dalliance ("Now let us sport us while we may"), as solely a means of deriving physical sensations. Although not a Cavalier poet, Marvell is here letting his speaker express a typically Cavalier (as opposed to Puritan) idea.

One more aspect of the historical background of the composition of the poem may be helpful in understanding its paradoxically hedonistic and pessimistic stance. The seventeenth century, it should be remembered, was not only a period of intense religious and political struggle, but a period of revolutionary scientific and philosophical thought. It was the century when Sir Francis Bacon's inductive method was establishing itself as the most reliable way of arriving at scientific truth; it was the century when the Copernican theory tended to minimize the uniqueness and importance of the earth, hence of man, in the universe; it was the century when Thomas Hobbes's materialism and degrading view of human nature tended to outrage the orthodox or reflective Christian. Given this kind of intellectual milieu, readers may easily see how the poem might be interpreted as the impassioned utterance of a man who has lost anything resembling a religious or philosophical view of life (excluding, of course, pessimism). The paradox of the poem consists in the question of whether the speaker is honestly reflecting his view of life—pessimism—and advocating sensuality as the only way to make the best of a bad situation or whether he is simply something of a cad—typically male, conceited, and superior, employing eloquence, argument, and soaringly passionate poetry merely as a "line," a devious means to a sensual end. If the former is the case, there is something poignant in the way the man must choose the most exquisite pleasure he knows, sensuality, as a way of spitting in the face of his grand tormentor and victorious foe, Time.

B. Traditional Approaches to *Hamlet*

1. THE TEXT OF THE PLAY

Few literary works have received the amount and degree of textual study that Shakespeare's *Hamlet* has. There are some obvious reasons for this. To begin with, even the earliest crude printings, shot through with the grossest errors, revealed a story and a mind that excited and challenged viewers, producers, readers, critics, and scholars—so much so that the scholars decided not to let the matter drop but to do everything possible to ascertain what Shakespeare actually wrote. The other reasons are all related to this one. Shakespearean editors ever since have realized the importance of establishing an accurate text if students and audiences are to discover the meaning of *Hamlet*.

It is difficult at this remove in time for the college student embarking on a serious reading of *Hamlet* to realize that the beautiful anthology or the handy paperback before him, each edited by an eminent authority, contains the product of over 300 years of scholarly study of four different versions of *Hamlet* and that it still includes some moot and debatable readings. Besides questionable readings, there are a number of words whose meanings have changed over the years but that must be understood in their Elizabethan senses if the play is to be properly interpreted. To be sure, modern editors explain the most difficult words, but occasionally they let some slip by or fail to note that reputable scholars differ. Obviously, it is not possible here to point out all the variants of a given passage or to give the seventeenth-century meaning of every puzzling construction, but the student can catch at least a glimpse of the multiplicity and the richness of interpretations by examining some of the more famous ones.

One of the best-known examples of such textual problems occurs in Act I, scene ii, "O that this too too solid flesh would melt." This is perhaps the most common rendering of this line. The word "solid" appears in the first folio edition (1623) of Shakespeare's complete works. Yet the second quarto edition (1604-1605), probably printed from Shakespeare's own manuscript, has "sallied," a legitimate sixteenth-century form of "sully" (to dirty, or make foul). These words pose two rather different interpretations of the line: If one reads "solid," the line seems to mean that Hamlet regrets the corporeality of the flesh and longs for bodily dissolution in order to escape the pain and confusion of fleshly existence. If, on the other hand, one reads "sullied," the line apparently reveals Hamlet's horror and revulsion upon contemplating the impurity of life and, by extension, his own involvement in it through the incest of his mother. J. Dover Wilson, in *What Happens in "Hamlet"* (London: Cambridge University Press, 1935), sees "sullied flesh" as the clue to many significant passages in the play (for example, to Hamlet's imaginations "foul as Vulcan's stithy"); to his preoccupation with sexuality, particularly with the sexual nature of his mother's crime; and to his strange conduct toward Ophelia and Polonius. This view becomes even more credible when one considers Hamlet's seemingly incomprehensible remark to Polonius in II, ii, where he calls the old man a "fishmonger" (Elizabethan slang for "pimp"); implies that Ophelia is a prostitute by referring in the same speech to "carrion" (Elizabethan "flesh" in the carnal sense); and warns Polonius not to let her "walk i' the sun" (that is, get too close to the "son" of Denmark, the heir apparent, him of the "sullied flesh" and "foul" imaginations). Wilson explains Hamlet's ambiguous remark as obscene because Hamlet is angry that Polonius would stoop to "loose" his daughter to him (as stockmen "loose" cows and mares to bulls and stallions to be bred) in order to wheedle from him the secret of his behavior, and he is angry and disgusted that his beloved would consent to be used in this way. Hence his later obscenities to her, as in III, i, when he tells her repeatedly to go to a "nunnery" (Elizabethan slang for "brothel").

One final example must suffice to illustrate the importance of textual accuracy in interpreting this piece of literature. In Quarto Two the speeches of the officiant at Ophelia's funeral are headed "Doct." This is probably "Doctor of Divinity," the term that one editor of *Hamlet*, Cyrus Hoy, inserts in the stage directions (Norton Critical Edition; New York: Norton, 1963). The "Doctor of Divinity" reading was one reason for J. Dover Wilson's asserting positively that Ophelia's funeral was a Protestant service, contrary to the way directors often stage it. Indeed, the point seems to be relevant, because it affects one's interpretation of the play. Although Shakespeare used anachronisms whenever they suited his purpose, a careless disregard of facts and logic was not typical of him. For example, both Hamlet and Horatio are students at Wittenberg. That this university was founded several hundred years after the death of the historical Hamlet is beside the point. What does seem important is that Wittenberg was the university of Martin Luther and a strong center of Protestantism. It is not unreasonable to assume, then, that Shakespeare wanted his audience to think of Denmark as a Protestant country (it was so in his day)—indeed that he wanted the entire drama to be viewed in contemporary perspective, a point that will be elaborated later in this chapter.

2. A SUMMARY OF THE PLAY

The main lines of the plot of *Hamlet* are clear. Hamlet, Prince of Denmark and heir presumptive to the Danish throne, is grief-stricken and plunged into melancholy by the recent death of his father and the "o'erhasty" remarriage of his mother to her late husband's brother, who has succeeded to the throne. The ghost of the prince's father appears to him and reveals that he was murdered by his brother, who now occupies the throne and whom he describes as "incestuous" and "adulterate." Enjoining young Hamlet not to harm his mother, the ghost exhorts him to take revenge on the murderer. In order to ascertain beyond question the guilt of his uncle and subsequently to plot his revenge, Hamlet feigns madness. His sweetheart Ophelia and his former schoolfellows Rosencrantz and Guildenstern attempt to discover from him the secret of his "antic behavior" (Ophelia because her father, Polonius, has ordered her to do so, Rosencrantz and Guildenstern because the king has ordered them to do so). All are unsuccessful. Before actually initiating his revenge, Hamlet wants to be sure it will hit the guilty person. To this end, he arranges for a company of traveling players to present a drama in the castle that will depict the murder of his father as the ghost has described it. When the king sees the crime reenacted, he cries out and rushes from the assembly. This action Hamlet takes to be positive proof of his uncle's guilt, and from this moment he awaits only the right opportunity to kill him. After the play, Hamlet visits his mother's apartment, where he mistakes Polonius for the king and kills him. The killing of Polonius drives Ophelia mad and also convinces the king that Hamlet is dangerous and should be gotten out of the way. He therefore sends Hamlet to England, accompanied by Rosencrantz and Guildenstern, ostensibly to collect tribute, but in reality to be murdered. However, Hamlet eludes this trap by substituting the names of his erstwhile schoolfellows on his own death warrant and escaping through the help of pirates. He reaches Denmark in time for the funeral of Ophelia, who has apparently drowned herself. Laertes, her brother, has returned from Paris vowing vengeance on Hamlet for the death of his father. The king helps Laertes by arranging a fencing match between the two young men and seeing to it that Laertes's weapon is naked and poisoned. To make doubly sure that Hamlet will not escape, the king also poisons a bowl of wine from which Hamlet will be sure to drink. During the match, Laertes wounds Hamlet, the rapiers change hands, and Hamlet wounds Laertes; the queen unwittingly drinks the poisoned wine; and Laertes confesses his part in the treachery to Hamlet, who then stabs the king to death. All the principals are thus dead, and young Fortinbras of Norway becomes king of Denmark.

3. HISTORICAL-BIOGRAPHICAL CONSIDERATIONS

It will doubtless surprise many students to know that *Hamlet* is considered by some authorities, (for example, the Oxford historian A. L. Rowse, in his *William Shakespeare, A Biography* (New York: Harper & Row, 1963) to be highly topical and highly autobiographical. In view of the recent death of Elizabeth I and the precarious state of the succession to the British crown, Shakespeare's decision to mount a production of *Hamlet,* with its usurped throne and internally disordered state, comes as no surprise. Indeed, the timeliness of such a play must have struck Shakespeare even earlier (*Hamlet* was probably written between 1598 and 1602), as Queen Elizabeth's advanced age and poor health called increasing attention to the problem of the succession. There is some ground for thinking that Ophelia's famous characterization of Hamlet may be intended to suggest the Earl of Essex, formerly Elizabeth's favorite, who had incurred her severe displeasure and been tried for treason and executed:

> The courtier's, soldier's, scholar's, eye, tongue, sword
> The expectancy and rose of the fair state,
> The glass of fashion and the mould of form,
> The observed of all observers. . . . [III, i]

Also, something of Essex may be seen in Claudius's observation on Hamlet's madness and his popularity with the masses:

How dangerous it is that this man goes loose!
Yet must we not put the strong law on him:
He's loved of the distracted multitude,
Who like not in their judgment but their eyes;
And where 'tis so, the offender's scourge is weighed,
But never the offence. [IV, viii]

Yet another contemporary historical figure, the Lord Treasurer Burghley, may well be seen in the character of Polonius. Rowse points out that Shakespeare had probably often heard his patron, the young Henry Wriothesley, Earl of Southampton, express contempt for Elizabeth's old Lord Treasurer; indeed, this was the way many of the gallants of Southampton's generation felt. Burghley possessed most of the shortcomings Shakespeare gave to Polonius; he was boring, meddling, and given to wise old adages and truisms. (He left a famous set of pious yet shrewd precepts for his son, Robert Cecil.) Moreover, he had an elaborate spy system that kept him informed about both friend and foe. One is reminded of Polonius's assigning Reynaldo to spy on Laertes in Paris (II, i). This side of Burghley's character was so well known that it might have been dangerous for Shakespeare to portray it on stage while the old man was alive (because Burghley had died in 1598, Shakespeare could with safety do so in this general way).

Other topical references include Shakespeare's opinion (II, ii) about the revival of the private theater, which would employ children and which would constitute a rival for the adult companies of the public theater, for which Shakespeare wrote. It is also reasonable to assume that Hamlet's instructions to the players (III, ii) contain Shakespeare's criticisms of contemporary acting, just as Polonius's description of the players' repertoire and abilities (II, ii) is Shakespeare's satire on dull people who profess preferences for rigidly classified genres. Scholars have also pointed out Shakespeare's treatment of other stock characters of the day: Osric, the Elizabethan dandy; Rosencrantz and Guildenstern, the boot-licking courtiers; Laertes and

Fortinbras, the men of action; Horatio, the "true Roman" friend; and Ophelia, the courtly love heroine.

The historical critic in looking at *Hamlet* might be expected to ask, "What do we need to know about eleventh-century Danish court life or about Elizabethan England to understand this play?" Similar questions are more or less relevant to the traditional interpretive approach to any literary work, but they are particularly germane to analysis of *Hamlet*. For one thing, most twentieth-century American students, largely unacquainted with the conventions, let alone the subtleties, of monarchical succession, wonder (unless they are aided by notes) why Hamlet does not automatically succeed to the throne after the death of his father. He is not just the oldest son; he is the only son. Such students need to know that in Hamlet's day the Danish throne was an elective one. The royal council, composed of the most powerful nobles in the land, named the next king. The custom of the throne's descending to the oldest son of the late monarch had not yet crystallized into law.

As true as this may be in fact, however, Dover Wilson maintains that it is not necessary to know it for understanding *Hamlet*, because Shakespeare intended his audiences to think of the entire situation—characters, customs, and plot—as English, which he apparently did in most of his plays, even though they were set in other countries. Wilson's theory is based upon the assumption that an Elizabethan audience could have but little interest in the peculiarities of Danish government, whereas the problems of royal succession, usurpation, and potential revolution in a contemporary English context would be of paramount concern. He thus asserts that Shakespeare's audience conceived Hamlet to be the lawful heir to his father and Claudius to be a usurper and the usurpation to be one of the main factors in the play, important to both Hamlet and Claudius. Whether one accepts Wilson's theory or not, it is certain that Hamlet thought of Claudius as a usurper, for he describes him to Gertrude as

A cutpurse of the empire and the rule,
That from a shelf the precious diadem stole
And put it in his pocket! [III, iv]

and to Horatio as one

... that hath killed my king and whored my mother,
Popped in between th' election and my hopes. ... [V, ii]

This last speech suggests strongly that Hamlet certainly expected to succeed his father by election if not by primogeniture.

Modern students are also likely to be confused by the charge of incest against the queen. Although her second marriage to the brother of her deceased husband would not be considered incestuous today by many civil and religious codes, it was so considered in Shakespeare's day. Some dispensation or legal loophole must have accounted for the popular acceptance of Gertrude's marriage to Claudius. That Hamlet considered the union incestuous, however, cannot be emphasized too much, for it is this repugnant character of Gertrude's sin, perhaps more than any other factor, that plunges Hamlet into the melancholy of which he is a victim. And here it is necessary to know what "melancholy" was to Elizabethans and to what extent it is important in understanding the play. A. C. Bradley tells us that it meant to Elizabethans a condition of the mind characterized by nervous instability, rapid and extreme changes of feeling and mood, and the disposition to be for the time absorbed in a dominant feeling or mood, whether joyous or depressed. If Hamlet's actions and speeches are examined closely, they seem to indicate symptoms of this disease. He is by turns cynical (I, ii), idealistic (II, ii), hyperactive, lethargic, averse to evil, disgusted at his uncle's drunkenness and his mother's sensuality, convinced he is rotten with sin. To appreciate his apparent procrastination, his vacillating from action to contemplation, and the other superficially irreconcilable features in his conduct, readers need to realize that at least a part of Hamlet's problem is that he is a victim of extreme melancholy. (For more detailed discussions of Hamlet's melancholy, see A. C. Bradley's *Shakespearean Tragedy* [London: Macmillan, 1914], J. Dover Wilson's *What Happens in "Hamlet"* [London: Cambridge University Press, 1935], and Weston Babcock's *"Hamlet," A Tragedy of Errors* [Lafayette, Ind.: Purdue University Press, 1961].)

One reason for *Hamlet's* popularity with Elizabethan audiences was that it dealt with a theme they were familiar with and fascinated by—revenge. *Hamlet* is in the grand tradition of revenge tragedies and contains virtually every stock device observable in vastly inferior plays of this type. Thomas Kyd's *The Spanish Tragedy* (ca. 1585) was the first successful English adaptation of the Latin tragedies of Seneca. The typical revenge tragedy began with a crime (or the recital of it); continued with an injunction by some agent (often a ghost) to the next of kin to avenge the crime; grew complicated by various impediments to the revenge, such as identifying the criminal and hitting upon the proper time, place, and mode of the revenge; and concluded with the death of the criminal, the avenger, and frequently all the principals in the drama.

One additional fact about revenge may be noted. When Claudius asks Laertes to what lengths he would go to avenge his father's death, Laertes answers that he would "cut [Hamlet's] throat i' th' church" (IV, vii). It is probably no accident that Laertes is so specific about the method by which he would willingly kill Hamlet. In Shakespeare's day it was popularly believed that repentance had to be vocal to be effective. By cutting Hamlet's throat, presumably before he could confess his sins, Laertes would deprive Hamlet of this technical channel of grace. Thus Laertes would destroy both Hamlet's soul and his body and would risk his own, a horrifying illustration of the measure of his hatred. Claudius's rejoinder that

> No place indeed should murder sanctuarize;
> Revenge should have no bounds.

indicates the desperate state of the king's soul. He is condoning murder in the church, traditionally a haven of refuge, protection, and legal immunity for murderers.

Elizabethan audiences were well acquainted with these conventions. They thought there was an etiquette, almost a ritual, about revenge; they believed that it was in fact a fine art and that it required a consummate artist to execute it.

4. MORAL-PHILOSOPHICAL CONSIDERATIONS

Any discussion of *Hamlet* should acknowledge the enormous body of excellent commentary that sees the play as valuable primarily for its moral and philosophical insights. Little more can be done here than to summarize the most famous of such interpretations. They naturally center on the character of Hamlet. Some explain Hamlet as an idealist temperamentally unsuited for life in a world peopled by fallible creatures. He is therefore shattered when he discovers that some humans are so ambitious for a crown that they are willing to murder for it and that others are so highly sexed that they will violate not only the laws of decorum (for example, by remarrying within a month of a spouse's death) but also the civil and ecclesiastical laws against incest. He is further crushed when he thinks that his fiancée and his former schoolfellows are tools of his murderous uncle. Other critics see Hamlet's plight as that of the essentially moral and virtuous intellectual man, certainly aware of the gentlemanly code that demands satisfaction for a wrong, but too much the student of philosophy and the Christian religion to believe in the morality or the logic of revenge. Related to this is the view of Hamlet as a kind of transitional figure, torn between the demands and the values of the Middle Ages and those of the modern world. The opposed theory maintains that Hamlet *is* a man of action, thwarted by such practical obstacles as how to kill a king surrounded by a bodyguard. Many modern critics emphasize what they term Hamlet's psychoneurotic state, a condition that obviously derives from the moral complexities with which he is faced.

Hamlet fulfills the technical requirements of the revenge play as well as the salient requirements of a classical tragedy; that is, it shows a person of heroic proportions going down to defeat under circumstances too powerful for him to cope with. For most readers and audiences the question of Hamlet's tragic flaw will remain a moot one. But this will not keep them from recognizing the play as one of the most searching artistic treatments of the problems and conflicts that form so large a part of the human condition.

C. Traditional Approaches to *Adventures of Huckleberry Finn*

There are few works of literature that lend themselves to so many interpretive analyses as *Huckleberry Finn*. Bernard De Voto has written that the novel contains "God's plenty"; in that verdict lies the key to the traditional critical approach. The phrase "God's plenty" was also applied by Dryden to Chaucer's *Canterbury Tales;* so we should remember those attributes of Chaucer's art that elicited such praise—narrative and descriptive power, keen knowledge of human nature, high comedy, biting satire, and lofty morality. All of these are also in *Huckleberry Finn*.

1. DIALECT AND TEXTUAL MATTERS

To Twain's good ear and appreciation of the dramatic value of dialect we owe not only authentic and subtle shadings of class, race, and personality, but also, as Lionel Trilling has said, a "classic prose" that moves with "simplicity, directness, lucidity, and grace" ("Introduction," *The Adventures of Huckleberry Finn* [New York: Holt, Rinehart and Winston, 1948], p. xvii). T. S. Eliot called this an "innovation, a new discovery in the English language," an entire book written in the natural prose rhythms of conversation ("Introduction" to *The Adventures of Huckleberry Finn* [London: Cresset Press, 1950] in *Adventures of Huckleberry Finn*, ed. Sculley Bradley, Richmond Croom Beatty, and E. Hudson Long [New York: Norton, 1962], p. 323). This linguistic innovation is certainly one of the features to which Ernest Hemingway referred when he said that "all modern American literature comes from one book by Mark Twain called *Huckleberry Finn*" (*Green Hills of Africa* [New York: Scribner, 1935], p. 22). If we agree with Hemingway, therefore, we can think of Twain as the "father of modern American literature."

Huckleberry Finn has an interesting textual history that space will allow us only to touch on here. Writing a frontier dialect, Twain was trying, with what success we have just seen, to capture in both pronunciation and vocabulary the spirit of the times from the lips of contemporary people. Nevertheless, some of his editors (for example, Richard Watson Gilder of the *Century Magazine*, William Dean Howells, and especially Twain's wife Livvie) bowdlerized and prettified those passages they thought "too coarse or vulgar" for Victorian ears, in certain cases with Twain's full consent. It is a minor miracle that this censoring, though it has taken something from the verisimilitude of the novel, seems not to have harmed it materially. (Hamlin Hill and Walter Blair, *The Art of "Huckleberry Finn"* [New York: Intext, 1962] is an excellent succinct treatment of the textual history of this novel.)

2. THE GENRE AND THE PLOT OF THE NOVEL

Huckleberry Finn is a novel, that is, an extended prose narrative dealing with characters within the framework of a plot. Such a work is usually fictitious, but both characters and situations or events may be drawn from real life. It may emphasize action or adventure (for example, *Treasure Island* or mystery stories); or it may concentrate on character delineation (that is, the way people grow or deteriorate or remain static in the happenings of life—*The Rise of Silas Lapham* or *Pride and Prejudice*); or it may illustrate a theme either aesthetically or propagandistically (*Wuthering Heights* or *Uncle Tom's Cabin*). It can, of course, do all three of these, as *Huckleberry Finn* does, a fact that accounts for the multiple levels of interpretation.

Huckleberry Finn is not only a novel; it is also a direct descendant of an important subgenre: the Spanish picaresque tale that arose in the sixteenth century as a reaction against the chivalric romance. In the latter type, pure and noble knights customarily rescued virtuous and beautiful heroines from enchanted castles guarded by fire-breathing dragons or wicked knights. In an attempt to debunk the artificiality and insipidity of such tales, Spanish writers of the day (notably the anonymous author of *Lazarillo de Tormes*) introduced into fiction as a central figure a kind of antihero, the picaro—a rogue or rascal of low birth who lived by his wits and his cunning rather than by exalted chivalric ideals. (Although not a pure picaro, Cervantes's Don Quixote is involved in a plot more rambling and episodic than unified and coherent.) Indeed, except for the fact that the picaro is *in* each of the multitude of adventures, all happening "on the road," the plot is negligible by modern standards. In these stories we simply move with this new type of hero from one wild and sensational experience to another, involving many pranks and much trenchant satire. Later treatments of the picaro have occasionally minimized and frequently eliminated his roguish or rascally traits. Dickens's picaros, for example, are usually model little poor boys.

Many of the classics of world literature are much indebted to the picaresque tradition, among them René Le Sage's *Gil Blas,* Henry Fielding's *Tom Jones,* and Charles Dickens's *David Copperfield,* to mention only a few. *Huckleberry Finn* is an obvious example of the type. The protagonist is a thirteen- or fourteen-year-old boy living in the American antebellum South. He is a member by birth of the next to the lowest stratum of Southern society, white trash—one who has a drunkard father who alternately abandons him and then returns to persecute him, no mother, no roots, and no background or breeding in the conventionally accepted sense. He is the town bad boy who smokes, chews, plays hooky, and stays dirty, and

Huck as anti-hero

whom two good ladies of St. Petersburg, Missouri, have elected to civilize.

The narrative moves onto "the road" when Huck, partly to escape the persecution of his drunken father and partly to evade the artificially imposed restrictions and demands of society, decides to accompany Nigger Jim, the slave of his benefactors, in his attempt to run for his freedom. The most immediate reason for Jim's deciding to run away is the fact that Miss Watson, his owner, has decided to sell him "down the river"—that is, into the Deep South, where instead of making a garden for nice old ladies or possibly being a house servant, he will surely become a field hand and work in the cane or cotton fields. These two, the teen-aged urchin and the middle-aged slave, defy society, the law, and convention in a daring escape on a raft down the dangerous Mississippi River.

Continually in fear of being captured, Huck and Jim travel mostly at night. They board a steamboat that has run onto a snag in the river and has been abandoned; on it they find a gang of robbers and cutthroats, whom they manage to elude without detection. In a vacant house floating down the river they discover the body of a man shot in the back, who, Jim later reveals, is Huck's father. They become involved in a blood feud between two aristocratic pioneer families. They witness a cold-blooded murder and an attempted lynching on the streets of an Arkansas village. They acquire two disreputable traveling companions who force them to render menial service and to take part in burlesque Shakespearean performances, bogus revival meetings, and attempted swindles of orphans with newly inherited wealth. Finally, after some uneasy moments when Jim is captured, they learn that Jim has been freed by his owner, and Huck decides to head west—away from civilization.

3. HISTORICAL-BIOGRAPHICAL CONSIDERATIONS

At the surface narrative level, *Huckleberry Finn* is something of a thriller. The sensationalism may seem to make the story improbable, if not incredible, but we should consider its historical and cultural context. This was part of frontier America in the 1840s and 1850s, a violent and bloody time. It was the era of Jim Bowie and his murderous knife, of gunslingers like Jack Slade, of Indian fighters like Crockett and Houston. Certainly there is a touch of the frontier, South or West, in the roughness, the cruelty, the lawlessness, and even the humor of *Huckleberry Finn*. Indeed, Mark Twain was very much in the tradition of such Southwestern humorists as Thomas Bangs Thorpe and such professional comedians as Artemus Ward and Josh Billings; in various writings he employed dialect for comedy, burlesque, the "tall tale," bombast, the frontier brag. *Huckleberry Finn*, of course, far transcends the examples of early American humor.

Furthermore, we know from Mark Twain's autobiographical writings and from scholarly studies of him, principally those of Bernard De Voto, A. B. Paine, and Dixon Wecter, that the most sensational happenings and colorful characters in *Huckleberry Finn* are based on actual events and persons Twain saw in Hannibal, Missouri, where he grew up, and in other towns up and down the Mississippi. For example, the shooting of Old Boggs by Colonel Sherburn is drawn from the killing of one "Uncle Sam" Smarr by William Owsley on the streets of Hannibal on January 24, 1845. The attempted lynching of Sherburn is also an echo of something that Mark Twain saw as a boy, for he declared in later life that he once "saw a brave gentleman deride and insult a [lynch] mob and drive it away." During the summer of 1847 Benson Blankenship, older brother of the prototype of Huck, secretly aided a runaway slave by taking food to him at his hideout on an island across the river from Hannibal. Benson did this for several weeks and resolutely refused to be enticed into betraying the man for the reward offered for his capture. This is undoubtedly the historical source of Huck's loyalty to Jim that finally resulted in his electing to "go to Hell" in defiance of law, society, and religion rather than turn in his friend.

A point about Jim's escape that needs clarification is his

attempt to attain his freedom by heading *south*. Actually, however, Cairo, Illinois, free territory and Jim's destination, is farther south on the river than St. Petersburg, Missouri, where he is escaping from. Thus when the fugitives miss Cairo in the fog and dark, they have lost their only opportunity to free Jim by escaping southward. Still another point is that if it had been Jim's object simply to get to *any* free territory, he might as easily have crossed the river to Illinois right at St. Petersburg, his home. But this was not his aim. Although a free state, Illinois had a law requiring its citizens to return runaway slaves. Jim therefore wanted particularly to get to Cairo, Illinois, a junction of the underground railroad system where he could have been helped on his way north and east on the Ohio River by abolitionists.

underground railroad

The obscene performance of the "Royal Nonesuch" in Bricksville, Arkansas, where the King prances about the stage on all fours as the "cameleopard," naked except for rings of paint, was based on some of the bawdier male entertainments of the old Southwest. This particular type featured a mythical phallic beast called the "Gyascutus." There were variations, of course, in the manner of presentation, but the antics of the King illustrate a common version. (Both Mark Twain and his brother Orion recorded performances of this type, Orion in an 1852 newspaper account of a Hannibal showing, Mark in a notebook entry made in 1865 while he was in Nevada.)

The detailed description of the Grangerford house with its implied yet hilarious assessment of nineteenth-century culture may be traced to a chapter from *Life on the Mississippi* entitled "The House Beautiful." Here may be observed the conformity to the vogue of sentimentalism, patriotism, and piousness in literature and painting and the general garishness in furniture and knickknacks.

One pronounced theme in *Huckleberry Finn* that has its origin in Twain's personality is his almost fanatical hatred of aristocrats. Indeed, aristocracy was one of his chief targets. *A Connecticut Yankee in King Arthur's Court* is less veiled than *Huckleberry Finn* in its attack on the concept. But it was not only British aristocracy that Twain condemned; elsewhere he made his most vitriolic denunciations of the American "Southern aristocrat." Though more subtle, *Huckleberry Finn* nevertheless is the more searching criticism of aristocracy. For one thing, aristocracy is hypocritical. Aristocrats are not paragons of true gentleness, graciousness, courtliness, and selflessness. They are trigger-happy, inordinately proud, implacable bullies. But perhaps Twain's antipathy to aristocracy, expressed in virtually all his works, came from the obvious misery caused to all involved, perpetrators as well as victims. The most significant expression of this in *Huckleberry Finn* is, of course, in the notion of race superiority. Clinging as they did to this myth, aristocrats—as Alex Haley has portrayed them in *Roots*—could justify any kind of treatment of blacks. They could separate families, as in the case of Jim and the Wilks slaves; they could load them with chains, forget to feed them, hunt them like animals, curse and cuff them, exploit their labor, even think of them as subhuman, and then rationalize the whole sordid history by affirming that the slaves ought to be grateful for any contact with civilization and Christianity.

Moreover, not only aristocrats but every section of white society subscribed to this fiction; thus a degenerate wretch like pap Finn could shoulder a free Negro college professor off the sidewalk and later deliver an antigovernment, racist tirade to Huck replete with the party line of the Know-Nothings, a semisecret, reactionary political group that flourished for a brief period in the 1850s. (Its chief tenet was hostility to foreign-born Americans and the Roman Catholic church. It derived its name from the answer its oath-bound members made to any question about it, "I don't know.") We thus sense the contempt Twain felt for Know-Nothingism when we hear its chief doctrines mouthed by a reprobate like pap Finn. (Indeed, it may be more than coincidental that Twain never capitalizes the word "pap" when Huck is referring to his father.)

Closely related to this indictment of aristocracy and racism and their concomitant evils are Twain's strictures on romanticism, which he thought largely responsible for the harmful myths and cultural horrors that beset the American South of his day. In particular, he blamed the novels of Sir Walter Scott and their idealization of a feudal society. In real life this becomes on the adult level the blood feud of the Grangerfords and Shepherdsons and on the juvenile level the imaginative "high jinks" of Tom Sawyer with his "robber gang" and his "rescue" of Jim.

There are many other examples of historical and biographical influences on the novel. Years spent as a steamboat pilot familiarized Mark Twain with every snag, sandbar, bend, or other landmark on the Mississippi, as well as with the more technical aspects of navigation—all of which provide vivid authenticity to the novel. His vast knowledge of Negro superstitions was acquired from slaves in Hannibal, Missouri, and on the farm of his beloved uncle, John Quarles, prototype of Silas Phelps. Nigger Jim himself is modeled after Uncle Dan'l, a slave on the Quarles place. These superstitions and examples of folklore are not mere local color, devoid of rhyme or reason, but, as Daniel Hoffman has so clearly pointed out in *Form and Fable in American Fiction* (New York: Oxford University Press, 1961), they are "of signal importance in the thematic development of the book and in the growth toward maturity of its principal characters" (p. 321). Huck was in real life Tom Blankenship, a boyhood chum of Twain's who possessed most of the traits Twain gave him as a fictional character. Although young Blankenship's real-life father was ornery enough, Twain modeled Huck's father on another Hannibal citizen, Jimmy Finn, the town drunk.

Like *The Canterbury Tales*, where Dryden found "God's plenty," *Huckleberry Finn* gives its readers a portrait gallery of the times. Scarcely a class is omitted. The aristocracy is represented by the Grangerfords, the Shepherdsons, and Colonel Sherburn. They are hardly Randolphs and Lees of tidewater Virginia, and their homes reveal that. The Grangerford parlor, for example, shows more of philistinism and puritanism than of genuine culture. These people are, nevertheless, portrayed as recognizable specimens of the traditional aristocrat, possessed of dignity, courage, devotion to principle, graciousness, desire to preserve ceremonious forms, and Calvinistic piety. Colonel Sherburn in particular illustrates another aspect of the "traditional" aristocrat—his contempt for the common man, which is reflected in his cold-blooded shooting of Old Boggs, his cavalier gesture of tossing the pistol on the ground afterward, and his single-handedly facing down the lynch mob.

The towns of any size contain the industrious, respectable, conforming bourgeoisie. In this class are the Widow Douglas and her old maid sister Miss Watson, the Peter Wilks family, and Judge Thatcher. The Phelpses too, although they own slaves and operate a "one-horse cotton plantation," belong to this middle class. Mrs. Judith Loftus, whose canniness undoes Huck when he is disguised as a girl, is, according to De Voto, the best-drawn pioneer wife in any of the contemporary records. The host of anonymous but vivid minor characters reflects and improves upon the many eyewitness accounts. These minor characters include the ferryboat owner, the boatmen who fear smallpox as they hunt Jim, the raftsmen heard from a distance joking in the stillness of the night. The Bible Belt poor white, whether whittling and chewing and drawling on the storefront benches of an Arkansas village or caught up in the fervor of a camp meeting or joining his "betters" in some sort of mob action, is described with undeniable authenticity.

Criminals like the robbers and cutthroats on the "Walter Scott" and those inimitable confidence men, the King and the Duke, play their part. Pap Finn is surely among the earliest instances of Faulkner's Snopes types—filthy, impoverished, ignorant, disreputable, bigoted, thieving, pitifully sure of only one thing, his superiority as a white man. Then we observe the Negroes themselves, convincing because they include not just stereotyped minstrel characters or "moonlight and magnolia good darkies," but interesting human beings, laughable, sullen, honorable, trifling, dignified, superstitious, illiterate, wise, pathetic, loyal, victimized. Most make only brief appearances, yet we feel that we have known almost firsthand a group of engaging, complex, and gifted people.

4. MORAL-PHILOSOPHICAL CONSIDERATIONS

Important as are its historical and biographical aspects, the chief impact of *Huckleberry Finn* derives from its morality. This is, indeed, the *meaning* of the novel. All other aspects are subservient to this one. "Man's inhumanity to man" (as Huck says, "Human beings *can* be awful cruel to one another") is the major theme of this work, and it is exemplified in both calm and impassioned denunciation and satire. Almost all the major events and most of the minor ones are variations on this theme. The cruelty may be manifested in attempts to swindle young orphans out of their inheritance, to con village yokels with burlesque shows, to fleece religion-hungry frontier folk with camp meetings, or to tar and feather malefactors extralegally. Cruelty can and often does have more serious consequences: for example, the brutal and senseless slaughter of the aristocratic Grangerfords and Shepherdsons and the murder of a harmless old windbag by another arrogant aristocrat.

The ray of hope that Mark Twain reveals is Huck himself, whose ultimate salvation comes when of his own choice he rejects the values of the society of his time (he has all along had misgivings about them) and decides to treat Jim as a fellow human being. The irony is that Huck has made the right decision by scrapping the "right" reasons (that is, the logic of conventional theology) and by following his own conscience. He is probably too young to have intellectualized his decision and applied it to the Negro race as a whole. Doubtless it applies only to Jim as an individual. But this is a tremendous advance for a boy of Huck's years. It is a lesson that is stubbornly resisted, reluctantly learned. But it is the lesson of *Huckleberry Finn*.

Huckleberry Finn is a living panorama of a country at a given time in history. It also provides insights, and it makes judgments that are no less valid in the larger sense today than they are about the period Mark Twain chronicled. This fidelity to life in character, action, speech, and setting; this personal testament; this encyclopedia of human nature; this most eloquent of all homilies—all of these are what cause this book to be not only a supreme artistic creation, but also, in the words of Lionel Trilling, "one of the central documents of American culture" (p. 6).

D. Traditional Approaches to "Young Goodman Brown"

"Young Goodman Brown," universally acclaimed as one of Hawthorne's best short stories, presents the student searching out its meaning with not only several possibilities but several rather ambiguous ones. D. M. McKeithan, in an article entitled " 'Young Goodman Brown': An Interpretation" (*Modern Language Notes*, 67 [1952], 93), has listed the suggestions that have been advanced as "the theme" of the story: "the reality of sin, the pervasiveness of evil, the secret sin and hypocrisy of all persons, the hypocrisy of Puritanism, the results of doubt or disbelief, the devastating effects of moral scepticism . . . the demoralizing effects of the discovery that all men are sinners and hypocrites." Admittedly, these themes are not as diverse as they might at first appear. They are, with the possible exception of the one specifically mentioning Puritanism, quite closely related. But meaning is not restricted to theme, and there are other ambivalences in the story that make its meanings both rich and elusive. After taking into account some matters of text and genre, we shall look at "Young Goodman Brown" from our traditional approaches.

1. THE TEXT OF THE STORY

Textually, "Young Goodman Brown," first published in

1835 in the *New England Magazine*, presents relatively few problems. Obsolete words in the story like "wot'st" (know), "Goody" (Goodwife, or Mrs.), "Goodman" (Mr.) are defined in most desk dictionaries, and none of the other words has undergone radical semantic change. Nevertheless, as we have seen, although a literary work may have been written in a day when printing had reached a high degree of accuracy, a perfect text is by no means a foregone conclusion. With Hawthorne, as with other authors, scholars are constantly working on more accurate texts.

For example, the first edition of this handbook used a version of "Young Goodman Brown" that contained at least two substantive variants. About three-fourths of the way through the story the phrase "unconcerted wilderness" appeared. David Levin, in an article entitled "Shadows of Doubt: Specter Evidence in Hawthorne's 'Young Goodman Brown'" (*American Literature,* 34 [November 1962], 346, n. 8) points out that nineteen years after Hawthorne's death, an edition of the story by George P. Lathrop printed "unconcerted" for the first time: Every version before that, including Hawthorne's last revision, had had "unconverted." In that same paragraph the first edition of this handbook printed "figure" as opposed to "apparition," the word that Levin tells us, occurred in the first published versions of the story. Obviously, significant interpretive differences could hinge on which words are employed in these contexts.

2. THE GENRE AND THE PLOT OF THE STORY

"Young Goodman Brown" is a short story; that is, it is a relatively brief narrative of prose fiction (ranging in length from 500 to 20,000 words) characterized by considerably more unity and compression in all its parts—theme, plot, structure, character, setting, mood—than the novel. In the story we are considering, the situation is this: One evening near sunset sometime in the late seventeenth century, Goodman Brown, a young man who has been married only three months, prepares to leave his home in Salem, Massachusetts, and his pretty young bride, Faith, to go into the forest and spend the night on some mission that he will not disclose other than to say that it must be performed between sunset and sunrise. Although Faith has strong forebodings about his journey and pleads with him to postpone it, Brown is adamant and sets off. His business is evil by his own admission; he does not state what it is specifically, but it becomes apparent to the reader that it involves attending a witches' Sabbath in the forest, a remarkable action in view of the picture of Brown, drawn early in the story, as a professing Christian who admonishes his wife to pray and who intends to lead an exemplary life after this one night.

The rising action begins when Brown, having left the village, enters the dark, gloomy, and probably haunted forest. He has not gone far before he meets the Devil in the form of a middle-aged, respectable-looking man whom Brown has made a bargain to meet and accompany on his journey. Perhaps the full realization of who his companion is and what the night may hold in store for him now dawns on Brown, for he makes an effort to return to Salem. It is at best a feeble attempt, however, for, though the Devil does not try to detain him, Brown continues walking with him deeper into the forest.

As they go, the Devil shocks Goodman Brown by telling him that his (Brown's) ancestors were religious bigots, cruel exploiters, and practitioners of the black art—in short, full-fledged servants of the Devil. Further, the young man is told that the very pillars of New England society, church, and state are witches (creatures actually in league with the Devil), lechers, blasphemers, and collaborators with the Devil. Indeed, he sees his childhood Sunday School teacher, now a witch, and overhears the voices of his minister and a deacon of his church as they ride past conversing about the diabolical communion service to which both they and he are going.

Clinging to the notion that he may still save himself from this breakup of his world, Goodman Brown attempts to pray, but stops when a cloud suddenly darkens the sky. A babel of voices seems to issue from the cloud, many recognizable to Brown as belonging to godly persons, among them his wife. After the cloud has passed, a pink ribbon such as Faith wears in her cap flutters to the ground. Upon seeing it, Goodman Brown is plunged into despair and hastens toward the witches' assembly. Once there, he is confronted with a congregation made up of the wicked and those whom Brown had always assumed to be righteous. As he is led to the altar to be received into this fellowship of the lost, he is joined by Faith. The climax of the story comes just before they receive the sacrament of baptism: Brown cries to his wife to look heavenward and save herself. In the next moment he finds himself alone.

The dénouement (resolution, unraveling) of the plot comes quickly. Returning the next morning to Salem, Goodman Brown is a changed man. He now doubts that anyone is good—his wife, his neighbors, the officials of church and state—and he remains in this state of cynicism until he dies.

The supernaturalism and horror of "Young Goodman Brown" mark the story as one variant of the Gothic tale, a type of ghost story originating formally in late eighteenth-century England and characterized by spirit-haunted habitations, diabolical villains, secret doors and passageways, terrifying and mysterious sounds and happenings, and the like. Obviously, "Young Goodman Brown" bears some resemblance to these artificial creations, the aesthetic value of most of which is negligible. What is much more significant is that here is a variation of the Faust legend, the story of the man who makes a bargain with the Devil (frequently the sale of his soul) in exchange for some desirable thing. In this instance Goodman Brown did not go nearly so far in the original indenture, but it was not necessary from the Devil's point of view. One glimpse of evil unmasked was enough to wither the soul of Brown forever.

3. HISTORICAL-BIOGRAPHICAL CONSIDERATIONS

So much for textual matters, paraphrasable content, and genre. What kind of historical or biographical information do we need in order to get the full impact of this story, aesthetically and intellectually? Obviously, some knowledge of Puritan New England is necessary. We can place the story in time easily, because Hawthorne mentions that it takes place in the days of King William (that is, William III, who reigned from 1688 to 1702). Other evidences of the time of the story are the references to persecution of the Quakers by Brown's grandfather (the 1660s) and King Philip's War (primarily a massacre of Indians by colonists [1675-1676]), in which Brown's father participated. Specific locales like Salem, Boston, Connecticut, and Rhode Island are mentioned, as are terms used in Puritan ecclesiasticism and government, such as ministers, elders, meetinghouses, communion tables, saints (in the Protestant sense of *any* Christian), selectmen, and lecture days.

But it is not enough for us to visualize a sort of "First Thanksgiving" picture of Pilgrims with steeple-crowned hats, Bibles, and blunderbusses. For one thing, we need to know something of Puritan religion and theology. This means at least a slight knowledge of Calvinism, a main source of Puritan religious doctrine. A theology as extensive and complex as Calvinism and one that has been the subject of so many misconceptions cannot be described adequately in a handbook of this type. But at the risk of perpetuating some of these misconceptions, let us mention three or four tenets of Calvinism that will illuminate to some degree the story of Goodman Brown. Calvinism stresses the sovereignty of God—in goodness, power, and knowledge. Correspondingly, it emphasizes the helplessness and sinfulness of man. Man has been, since the Fall of Adam, innately and totally depraved. His only hope is in the grace of God, for God alone is powerful enough (sovereign enough) to save him. And the most notorious, if not the chief, doctrine is predestination, which includes the belief that God has, before their creation, selected certain people for eternal salvation, others for eternal damnation. Appearances are therefore misleading; an outwardly godly man might not be one of the elect. Thus it is paradoxical that Goodman Brown is so shocked to learn that there is evil among the apparently righteous for this was one of the most strongly implied teachings of his church.

In making man conscious of his absolute reliance on God alone for salvation, Puritan clergymen dwelt long and hard on the pains of hell and powerlessness of mere men to escape them. Brown mentions to the Devil that the voice of his pastor "would make me tremble both Sabbath day and lecture day." This was a typical reaction. In Calvinism, nobody "had it made." Introspection was mandatory. Christians had to search their hearts and minds constantly to purge themselves of sin. Goodman Brown is hardly expressing a Calvinistic concept when he speaks of clinging to his wife's skirts and following her to Heaven. Calvinists had to work out their own salvation in fear and trembling, and they were often in considerable doubt about the outcome. The conviction that sin was an ever-present reality that destroyed the unregenerate kept it before them all the time and made its existence an undoubted, well-nigh tangible fact. We must realize that aspects of the story like belief in witches and an incarnate Devil, which until the recent upsurge of interest in demonism and the occult world have struck modern readers as fantastic, were entirely credible to New Englanders of this period. Indeed, on one level, "Young Goodman Brown" may be read as an example of Satanism. Goody Cloyse and the Devil in the story even describe at length a concoction with which witches were popularly believed to have anointed themselves and a satanic worship attended by witches, devils, and lost souls.

It is a matter of historical record that a belief in witchcraft and the old pagan gods existed in Europe side by side with Christianity well into the modern era. (The phenomenon recurred—how genuinely is questionable—in the

1960s and 1970s, ballyhooed by the popular press as well as the electronic media.) There was an analogous prevalent belief in Puritan New England. Clergymen, jurists, statesmen—educated people generally, as well as uneducated folk—were convinced that witches and witchcraft were realities. Cotton Mather, one of the most learned men of the period, attests eloquently to his own belief in these phenomena in *The Wonders of the Invisible World,* his account of the trials of several people executed for witchcraft. Some of the headings in the table of contents are instructive: "A True Narrative, collected by Deodat Lawson, related to Sundry Persons afflicted by Witchcraft, from the 19th of March to the 5th of April, 1692" and "The Second Case considered, viz. If one bewitched be cast down with the look or cast of the Eye of another Person, and after that recovered again by a Touch from the same Person, is not this an infallible Proof that the party accused and complained of is in Covenant with the Devil?"

Hawthorne's great-grandfather, John Hathorne (Nathaniel added the "w"), was one of the judges in the infamous Salem witch trials of 1692, during which many people were tortured and hanged and one was crushed to death. (A legal technicality was responsible for this special form of execution.) Commentators have long pointed to "Young Goodman Brown," *The Scarlet Letter,* and many other Hawthorne stories to illustrate his obsession with the guilt of his Puritan forebears for their part in these crimes. In "The Custom House," his introduction to *The Scarlet Letter,* Hawthorne wrote of these ancestors who were persecutors of Quakers and witches and of his feeling that he was tainted by their crimes. The Devil testified that he helped young Goodman Brown's grandfather, a constable, lash a "Quaker woman . . . smartly through the streets of Salem," an episode undoubtedly related to Hawthorne's "Custom House" reference to his great-grandfather's "hard severity towards a woman of [the Quaker] sect."

Hawthorne's notebooks are also a source in interpreting his fiction. They certainly shed light on his preoccupation with the "unpardonable sin" and his particular definition of that sin. It is usually defined as blasphemy against the Holy Ghost, or continued conscious sin without repentance, or refusing to acknowledge the existence of God even though the Holy Spirit has actually proved it. The notebooks, however, and stories like "Ethan Brand," "Young Goodman Brown," and The Scarlet Letter make it clear that for Hawthorne, the Unpardonable Sin was to probe, intellectually and rationally, the human heart for depravity without tempering the search by a "human" or "democratic" sympathy. Specifically in the case of "Young Goodman Brown," Brown's obduracy of heart cuts him off from all, so that "his dying hour [is] gloom."

4. MORAL-PHILOSOPHICAL CONSIDERATIONS

The terror and suspense in the Hawthorne story function as integral parts of the allegory that defines the story's theme. In allegory (a narrative containing a meaning beneath the surface one), there is usually a one-to-one relationship; that is, one idea or object in the narrative stands for only one idea or object allegorically. A story from the Old Testament illustrates this. The pharaoh of Egypt dreamed that seven fat cows were devoured by seven lean cows. Joseph interpreted this dream as meaning that seven years of plenty (good crops) would be followed by seven years of famine. "Young Goodman Brown" clearly functions on this level of allegory (while at times becoming richly symbolic). Brown is not just one Salem citizen of the late seventeenth century, but rather seems to typify mankind, to be in a sense Everyman, in that what he does and the reason he does it appear very familiar to most people, based on their knowledge of others and on honest appraisal of their own behavior.

For example, Goodman Brown, like most people, wants to experience evil, not perpetually, of course, for he is by and large a decent chap, a respectably married man, a member of a church, but he desires to "taste the forbidden fruit" ("have one last fling") before settling down to the business of being a solid citizen and attaining "the good life." He feels that he can do this because he means to retain his religious faith, personified in his wife, who, to reinforce the allegory, is even named Faith. But in order to encounter evil, he must part with his Faith at least temporarily, something he is either willing or compelled to do. It is here that he makes his fatal mistake, for evil turns out to be not some abstraction nor something that can be played with for a while and then put down, but the very pillars of Goodman Brown's world—his ancestors, his earthly rulers, his spiritual overseers, and finally his Faith. In short, so overpowering is the fact and the universality of evil in the world that Goodman Brown comes to doubt the existence of any good. By looking upon the very face of evil, he is transformed into a cynic and a misanthrope whose "dying hour was gloom."

Thomas E. Connolly, in "Hawthorne's 'Young Goodman Brown': An Attack on Puritanic Calvinism" (*American Literature*, 28 [November 1956], 370–375), has remarked that Goodman Brown has not *lost* his faith; he has *found* it. That is, Goodman Brown believes that he understands the significance of the Calvinistic teaching of the depravity of man; this realization makes him doubt and dislike his fellow man and in effect paralyzes his moral will so that he questions the motivation of every apparently virtuous act. But this is surely a strange conclusion for Brown to reach, for he has violated the cardinal tenets of Calvinism. If Calvinism stressed anything, it stressed the practical and spiritual folly of placing hope or reliance on human beings and their efforts, which by the very nature of things are bound to fail, whereas God alone never fails. Therefore all trust should be reposed in Him. It is just this teaching that Brown has not learned. On the practical plane, he cannot distinguish between appearance and reality. He takes things and people at face value. If a man *looks* respectable and godly, Brown assumes that he is. And if the man turns out to be a scoundrel, Brown's every standard crumbles. He is in a sense guilty of a kind of idolatry: Human institutions in the forms of ministers, church officers, statesmen, and wives have, as it were, been his god. When they are discredited, he has nothing else to place his trust in and thus becomes a cynic and a misanthrope.

Thus, rather than making a frontal attack on Calvinism, Hawthorne indicted certain reprehensible aspects of Puritanism—the widespread "holier-than-thou" attitude; the spiritual blindness that led many Puritans to mistake a pious front for genuine religion; the latent sensuality in the apparently austere and disciplined soul (the very capstone of hypocrisy, because sins of the flesh were particularly odious to Puritan orthodoxy).

It will perhaps be argued that Calvinism at its most intense, with its dim view of human nature, is quite likely to produce cynicism and misanthropy. But historically, if paradoxically, Calvinists have been dynamic and full of faith; they have been social and political reformers, educators, enterprisers in business, explorers, foes of tyranny. The religious furnace in which these men's souls were tempered, however, is too hot for Goodman Brown. He is of a weaker breed, and the sum of his experience with the hard realities of life is disillusion and defeat. He has lost his faith. Whether because his faith was false or because he wished for an objectively verifiable certainty that is the antithesis of faith, Hawthorne does not say. He does not even say whether the whole thing was a dream or reality. Actually, it does not matter. The result remains: Faith has been destroyed and supplanted by total despair because Brown is neither a good Calvinist, a good Christian, nor, in the larger sense, a good man.

As we have seen in our discussions of these works, the traditional approach in literary interpretation is neither rigidly dogmatic nor unaesthetic. It is eclectic. And although it has its rationale in the methods discussed in this chapter, it does not eschew insights from any other critical approach; it does however, insist on its own fundamental validity. Those other critical approaches, however, do provide insights not stressed in the traditional, such as the appreciation of form, to which we now turn.

CHAPTER 2

THE FORMALISTIC APPROACH

I. The Nature of Formalistic Criticism

As its name suggests, "formalistic" criticism has for its sole object the discovery and explanation of *form* in the literary work. This approach assumes the autonomy of the work itself and thus the relative unimportance of extraliterary considerations—the author's life; his times; sociological, political, economic, or psychological implications. Hawthorne's obsession with his family's role in colonial New England; the real-life identity of Huckleberry Finn or Silas Phelps; the possible origin of Shakespeare's Polonius in Elizabeth's Lord Treasurer Burghley; or Marvell's training in classical logic and polemics may all intrigue the scholar of literary history, as we have learned in Chapter 1, but seldom do we read and reread a great novel, a Shakespearean tragedy, a tale by Hawthorne, or Marvell's poem because of such information. The heart of the matter for the formalist critic is quite simply: What *is* the literary work, what are its *shape* and *effect*, and *how* are these achieved? All relevant answers to these questions ought to come from the text itself.

A. Two "Parables" of Form

At the end of Virginia Woolf's *To the Lighthouse* (New York: Harcourt Brace Jovanovich, 1927) an artist-figure named Lily Briscoe is struggling to complete a painting she had started ten years before. She has realized earlier that a painter is always being called away from the "fluidity of life for the concentration of painting," but somehow her picture's completion has remained stubbornly elusive, although it has been teasing her mind all those years. Resolving to make one more attempt to finish it, she recalls the remarkable Mrs. Ramsay, a woman who before her death had given shape and form to the lives of her family and her friends and whose presence as she had sat knitting one day ten years before had been the unifying element of the scene Lily tried to paint. In her longing for the departed Mrs. Ramsay, Lily has an insight that relates her struggle as artist to Mrs. Ramsay's genius for establishing moments of order and shape out of human discords and the relentless flow of time. She recalls

> Mrs. Ramsay making of the moment something permanent (as in another sphere Lily herself tried to make of the moment something permanent) — this was of the nature of a revelation. In the midst of chaos there was shape; this eternal passing and flowing (she looked at the clouds going and the leaves shaking) was struck into stability. Life stand still here, Mrs. Ramsay said. "Mrs. Ramsay! Mrs. Ramsay!" she repeated. She owed it all to her. [p. 241]

As Lily begins to make strokes with her brush, she achieves a "rhythm" whose origin cannot be placed, but form is about to emerge on the canvas:

> There it was—her picture. Yes, with all its greens and blues, its lines running up and across, its attempt at something. It would be hung in the attics, she thought; it would be destroyed. But what did that matter? she asked herself, taking up her brush again. She looked at the steps; they were empty; she looked at her canvas; it was blurred. With a sudden

> intensity, as if she saw it clear for a second, she drew a line there, in the centre. It was done; it was finished. Yes, she thought, laying down her brush in extreme fatigue, I have had my vision. [pp. 309–310]

Out of intense concentration had come *vision*, which in turn supplied *form*: the meaning of the dead woman's life and presence within the scene and the artist's craftsmanship had merged to make the finished painting. Idea and line are forever one in what Henry James called the "figure in the carpet." The episode becomes a little parable of formalistic search and discovery.

Keats's "Ode on a Grecian Urn" is another eloquent assertion of what can be called the "aesthetic moment," a celebration of the triumphant imagination's total revelation of form and its meaning. After the speaker's attempts to define the urn through a series of epithets: "bride of quietness," "foster-child of silence and slow time," "Sylvan historian," "Attic shape," "Cold Pastoral," the urn starts to speak a language not heard but intensely felt by the rapt beholder. In his mounting excitement, he perceives in the urn a unity of images and ideas. That unity of the vase's shape, the sequence of images of Greek pastoral life, and the consequent impressions upon the speaker (and the reader) become a simultaneously solidified and boundless amalgam of the whole spirit of classicism that unifies religion, art, and passion. Thus the urn becomes a model for any successful work of art—succesful in achievement of a form that can be perceived by a sensibility other than the creator's.

B. Backgrounds of Formalistic Theory

Classical art and aesthetics amply testify to a preoccupation with form. Plato exploits dialectic and shapes movement toward Socratic wisdom by his imagery, metaphor, dramatic scenes, characterization, setting, and tone. Aristotle's *Poetics* recommends an "orderly arrangement of parts" that form a beautiful whole or "organism." Horace admonishes the would-be poet: "In short, be your subject what it will, let it be simple and unified." And some awareness of "formalism" is at least implicit in many other classical, medieval, and Renaissance treatises on art or poetics.

But the Romantic movement in Europe in the late eighteenth and nineteenth centuries intensified speculations about form in literature, especially in the generation of concepts of "organicism," analogies between the "life-principle" of a work of art and that of living organisms. Perhaps because of the Romantics' infatuation with nature, the analogy usually likened the internal life of a painting or poem to the quintessential unity of parts within a tree, flower, or plant: As the seed determines, so the organism develops and lives. Samuel Taylor Coleridge (1772–1834) brought to England (and thus to America) the conception of a dynamic *imagination* as the shaping power and unifier of vision—a conception he had acquired from his studies of the German philosophical idealists: Kant, Hegel, Fichte, and Schelling. Such a conception encouraged discrimination between a poem and other forms of discourse by stressing the poem's power to elicit delight as a "whole" and "distinctive gratification from each component *part.*" In a *"legitimate* poem," Coleridge declared, the parts "mutually support and explain each other; all in their proportion harmonizing with, and supporting the purpose and known influences of metrical arrangement." In America Edgar Allan Poe (1809–1849), extending Coleridge's theory, asserted the excellence of short lyric poems and short tales because they can maintain and transmit a single, unitary "effect" more successfully than can long works like *Paradise Lost.* In "The Philosophy of Composition" Poe demonstrated how the parts of his "The Raven" allegedly developed from the single "effect" he desired. Poe also reprimanded certain contemporary poets like Longfellow for their apostasy to what he called the "heresy of the didactic" because they tacked on obtrusive (thus inorganic) moral lessons and accordingly violated the lyric effects of their poems.

Later in the nineteenth century and on into the twentieth, Henry James (1843–1916), in "The Art of Fiction" and the prefaces to his tales and novels, argued for the right of fiction to be considered as a "fine art" and for the intricate, necessary interrelationships of parts and the whole:

> There are bad and good novels, as there are bad pictures and good pictures; but that is the only distinction in which I can see any meaning, and I can as little imagine speaking of a novel of character as I can imagine speaking of a picture of character. When one says picture one says of character, when one says novel one says of incident, and the terms seem to be transposed at will. What is character but the determination of incident? What is incident but the illustration of character? What is either a picture or a novel that is *not* of character? What else do we seek in it and find in it? It is an incident for a woman to stand up with her hand resting on a table and look at you in a certain way; or if it be not an incident, I think it will be hard to say what it is.

James implies the same interdependence and kinship for all other aspects of a work of fiction—setting, theme, scene and narrative, image and symbol. When the artist is attending to his craft, nothing that goes into the work will be wasted, and form will be present: "Form alone *takes*, and holds and preserves, substance—saves it from the welter of helpless verbiage that we swim in as in a sea of tasteless tepid pudding." When the work achieves "organic form," everything will count.

C. The "New Criticism"

Although there were antecedents from Plato through James, a systematic and methodological formalistic approach to literary criticism appeared only with the rise of what came to be called the New Criticism in the 1930s. Coming together originally at Vanderbilt University in the years following World War I, the New Critics included a teacher-scholar-poet, John Crowe Ransom, and some bright students—Allen Tate, Robert Penn Warren, and Cleanth Brooks. Associated at first in an informal group that discussed literature, they in time adopted the name of

"Fugitives" and published an elegant literary magazine called *The Fugitive* in Nashville from 1922 to 1925. When the poetry and critical essays of T. S. Eliot came to their attention, they found sturdy reinforcement for ideas that were emerging from their study and writing of lyric poetry. Ideas thus shared and promoted included literature viewed as an organic "tradition," the importance of strict attention to form, a conservatism related to classical values, the ideal of a society that encourages order and tradition, a preference for ritual, and the rigorous and analytical reading of literary texts. Eliot was particularly influential in his formulation of the "objective correlative" ("a set of objects, a situation, a chain of events which shall be the formula of [a] *particular* emotion; such that when the external facts, which must terminate in sensory experience, are given, the emotion is immediately invoked"), and in his endorsement of the English "metaphysical poets" of the seventeenth century for their success in blending "states of mind and feeling" in a single "verbal equivalent." Such developments strengthened the emergent New Criticism, which by the 1950s had become the dominant critical system in such influential journals as *The Sewanee Review, Kenyon Review,* and *Hudson Review* and in college and university English departments.

The New Critics sought precision and structural tightness in the literary work; they favored a style and tone that tended toward irony; they insisted on the presence within the work of everything necessary for its analysis; and they called for an end to a concern by critics and teachers of English with matters outside the work itself—the life of the author, the history of his times, or the social and economic implications of the literary work. In short, they turned the attention of teachers, students, critics, and readers to the essential matter: *what* the work says and *how* it says it as inseparable issues. To their great credit they influenced at least one generation of college students to become more careful and serious readers than they otherwise would have been.

Members and disciples of the group advanced their

critical theory and techniques through a series of brilliant college textbooks on literary analysis: *Understanding Poetry* (1st ed., 1939) and *Understanding Fiction* (1943), by Brooks and Warren; *Understanding Drama* (1945), by Brooks and Robert B. Heilman; *The Art of Modern Fiction*, by Ray B. West, Jr., and Robert W. Stallman; and *The House of Fiction* (1950), by Caroline Gordon and Allen Tate. Since 1942, *The Explicator*, a monthly publication during the academic year, has published hundreds of short textual explications of great varieties of literary works; and most of the prestigious literary journals and quarterlies still publish articles that show the continuing influence of the New Criticism.

D. The Process of Formalistic Analysis

Intensive reading begins with a sensitivity to the words of the text and all their denotative and connotative values and implications. An awareness of multiple meanings, even the etymologies of words, as traced in dictionaries will offer significant guidelines to what the work says. Usually adequate for most readers is one of the standard "collegiate" dictionaries.

For expanded information on meanings and origins of words, one occasionally may need to check one of the huge "unabridged" dictionaries such as *Webster's Third New International Dictionary of the English Language* (G. & C. Merriam Co.). Details and examples of historical changes in word meanings are recorded in the ten volumes of and a supplement to *The Oxford English Dictionary*. Most of these larger dictionaries are usually available in college and public libraries.

To repeat a point made in Chapter 1, the reader sees, for example, that much of the concrete imagery of Shakespeare's song on winter is lost unless we know that "keel" in the line "While greasy Joan doth keel the pot" means "to cool, by skimming." Moreover, he must be alert to any allusion to mythology, history, or literature. *The Waste Land,* Pound's *Cantos,* and Joyce's *Ulysses* are scarcely comprehensible (or at least might seem hardly worth the trouble) without some understanding of the many rich allusions in them.

After one has mastered the individual words in the literary text, he looks for *structures* and *patterns*, interrelationships of the words. If a reader studies those verbal relationships, ideally as intensively as Keats contemplated the Grecian urn, he will begin to see relationships of *reference* (pronouns to nouns, a voice to a speaker, an appositive to a name or place, time to a process, etc.), of *grammar* (sentence patterns and their modifiers, parallel words and phrases, agreement of subjects and verbs, etc.), of *tone* (choice of words, manner of speaking, attitudes toward subject and audience, etc.), and of *systems* (related metaphors, symbols, myths, images, allusions, etc.). Such internal relationships gradually reveal a *form*, a principle by which all subordinate patterns can be accommodated and accounted for. When all the words, phrases, metaphors, images, and symbols are examined in terms of each other and of the whole, any literary text (most obviously, a short lyric poem) will display what the American poet Hart Crane once called the "logic of metaphor": "images, themselves totally dissociated [i.e, in terms of scientific or ordinary logic], when joined in the circuit of a particular emotion located with specific relation to both of them, conduce to great vividness and accuracy of statement in defining that emotion" ("Letter to Harriet Monroe," in *The Complete Poems and Selected Letters and Prose of Hart Crane*, ed. Brom Weber [Garden City, N.Y.: Doubleday (Anchor Books), 1966], p. 238). When that "internal logic" has been established, the reader is very close to identifying the overall form of the work.

The *context* (for example, the nature and personality of the speaker in a poem) must be identified also. In Browning's "My Last Duchess" one must understand not only the personality of the Duke, who is speaking, but also something of the nature of the man to whom he addresses his remarks. Only to the extent that the reader understands

77

that *what* the Duke is saying is revealed largely by *how* he says it can he really fathom the full implications of the Duchess' story. One of the beautiful ironies of the poem, after all, is the reader's awareness of implications that the Duke does not consciously intend. In Eliot's *The Waste Land* one must constantly remember the presence of the Tiresias figure, from whom all other characters in the poem take their being, as the ironically disposed observer-participant-commentator of each episode or context. When the intricate links of the many shards of experience drawn from both the ancient and the modern worlds (and they are linked by the pervasive Tiresias) are perceived, the form of the poem is becoming apparent.

E. Form in Poetry

In systems of the past, the word *form* usually meant what we would call *external form*. Thus when we identify a poem with fourteen lines of iambic pentameter, a conventional pattern of rhymes, and a conventional division into two parts, as a sonnet, we are defining its external form. The same kind of description takes place when we talk about couplets, tercets, *ottava rima*, quatrains, Spenserian stanzas, blank verse, or even free verse. But the formalistic critic is only moderately interested in external forms (in fact, only when external form is related to the work's total form, when stanzaic or metrical pattern is integral to internal relationships, reverberations, patterns, and systems). The process of formalistic analysis is complete only when everything in the work has been accounted for in terms of its overall form.

Statements that follow discovery of form must embrace what Ransom called "local texture" and "logical structure" (*The World's Body* [New York: Scribner, 1938], p. 347). The "logical structure" refers to the argument or the concept within the work; "local texture" comprises the particular details and devices of the work (for example, specific metaphors and images). However, such a dualistic view of a literary work has its dangers, for it might encourage the reduction of "logical structure" to précis or summary—what Brooks has called the "heresy of paraphrase." In *Understanding Poetry*, Brooks and Warren simply include "idea," along with rhythm and imagery, as a component of form: "the form of a poem is the organization of the material . . . for the creation of the total effect" (3d ed. [New York: Holt, Rinehart and Winston, 1960], p. 554). The emphasis, in any case, is upon accounting for all aspects of the work in seeking to name or define its form and effect. Mark Schorer pressed the distinction further between the critic's proper concentration on *form* and an improper total concern with *content only*: "Modern [i.e., formalistic] criticism has shown that to speak of content as such is not to speak of art at all, but of experience; and that it is only when we speak of the *achieved* content, the form, the work of art as a work of art, that we speak as critics. The difference between content, or experience, and achieved content, or art, is technique" ("Technique as Discovery," *Hudson Review*, 1 [Spring 1948], 67). He goes on to say that "technique is the only means [an author] has of discovering, exploring, developing his subject, of conveying its meaning, and, finally, of evaluating it."

Such a concept of form stresses the analogy developed by the Romantic poets of the literary work (or any other art form, for that matter) to a living organism like a plant rather than to a dead thing like a wall, a candle mold, or a packed trunk. The writer's imagination, perhaps starting out with only an idea, an image, or even a feeling, simply supplies, as the work grows, all the constituent elements validated by the imagination as germane or organic to that starting point (what Henry James called the artist's *donné* or the "given"). The creating imagination shapes the work into stanza patterns, a system of imagery or symbols, a sequence of events (plot) or sensations or feelings (lyric poetry). Walt Whitman, disdaining the practice of adding ornaments to the poem in the interests of mere conventional prettiness, proclaimed: "The rhyme and uniformity of perfect poems show the free growth of metrical laws and bud from them as unerringly and loosely as lilacs or roses on a bush, and take shapes as compact as the shapes of chestnuts and oranges and melons and pears, and shed the perfume impalpable to form" ("Preface" to the 1855 edition of *Leaves of Grass*).

F. Formalistic Approach to Fiction and Drama

Obviously the relatively short lyric poem has been the favored genre for formalistic analyses, largely for reasons that remind us of Poe's preference. Classic instances like Cleanth Brooks's famous treatment of Keats's "Ode on a Grecian Urn" (in *The Well Wrought Urn: Studies in the Structure of Poetry* [New York: Reynal and Hitchcock, 1947]) are the showpieces of the New Criticism, just as Brooks and Warren's *Understanding Poetry* made much more of an impact than the later books on fiction and drama. The short poem can be held in the mind as a whole much more successfully than can a novel, a three-act play, or even a short story. Moreover, one can look back over it as often as he likes while he works out his analysis. Even its shape on the printed page and its typically precise and formal language make the relatively short lyric poem highly amenable to the approach of the formalistic critic.

However, there *were* textbooks on the analysis of fiction and drama, and certainly the recognition of form in those genres is important too. For example, Robert B. Heilman's *This Great Stage: Image and Structure in* King Lear (Baton Rouge: Louisiana State University Press, 1948) expertly demonstrated that a formalist approach to one of the most powerful and complex dramas in the English language could be illuminating. And in "Toward a Formalist Criticism of Fiction" William Handy argued that "Form in fiction is an embodiment of meaning just as in poetry, not merely a framework for content" (*Texas Studies in Literature and Language*, 3 [Spring 1961], 81–88).

More recently, the idea of the chapter as the "novel in miniature" has been advanced by Philip Stevick (*The*

Chapter in Fiction: Theories of Narrative Division [Syracuse, N.Y.: Syracuse University Press, 1970]): "If art, in general, demands in creator and observer a heightening of the gestalt perception which organizes experience itself, then the writer of extended narrative is obliged to make his work out of subordinate, distinguishable parts, each of which can be seen in relation to the whole work and each of which can be seen as a form in itself" (p. 15). Obviously, similar claims can be made for the relationships of acts and scenes to the whole drama.

Recent interest in what Frank Kermode calls the "sense of an ending" and others call "closure" (the technical means by which a work of fiction is ended to give the reader a sense of "completeness") also promises to extend the perimeters of formalistic criticism of fiction. In older structures (the eighteenth-century novel, for example) closure is usually more easily seen and evaluated than it is with much recent "open-ended" fiction. For example, people get married and satisfy society that their youthful recklessness or their "prejudice" will be curbed (as in Fielding's *Tom Jones* or Jane Austen's *Pride and Prejudice*). Even so, the "open form" of some recent fiction achieves in its "open end" the corollary of new knowledge and new ways of evaluating experience. New modes of closure presumably correspond to new states of consciousness. What is true of the fiction of John Barth, Kurt Vonnegut, or Joseph Heller is also true of the plays of Edward Albee or Samuel Beckett.

In fiction one must look for the *point of view* established by the author: (1) the narrator who tells the story (Huck in *Adventures of Huckleberry Finn*, Marlow in *Lord Jim*, Nick Carraway in *The Great Gatsby*, Jake Barnes in *The Sun Also Rises*, Bob Slocum in Heller's *Something Happened*); (2) a character from whose vantage point the story is told in the third person (Strether in James's *The Ambassadors*, Charley Wales in Fitzgerald's "Babylon Revisited"); or (3) the omniscient narrator (the familiar pattern of narrative told by the all-knowing author in the third person, such as we find in *War and Peace, Vanity Fair, Oliver Twist,* or Faulkner's *Sanctuary*). Although these three modes of viewpoint account for nearly all fiction, there have been experiments with other possibilities. Michel Butor, for instance, uses the formal second-person *vous* in his novel *A Change of Heart,* and the French novelist Alain Robbe-Grillet has tried to turn his protagonist into a roving camera eye that sees but does not allow any authorial intrusion or analysis.

In Melville's *Moby-Dick* the personality of Ishmael, who at least starts the telling of the story, colors the events of the *Pequod's* journey by framing it within the sensibility of an outcast who longs to be reinstated within the human race and to explore the most dangerous and profound dimensions of truth. Holden Caulfield, the narrator of Salinger's *The Catcher in the Rye,* supplies the angle from which the "phonies" of his world can be viewed and judged; that world can be understood only in terms of Holden's attitude toward it, the impact of incidents and people on him, the kind of language he brings to his narrative, and his age and consequent limitations. On the other hand, Gene Forrester of John Knowles's *A Separate Peace* recalls in his thirties a traumatic experience he had at prep school during World War II. In Fitzgerald's *The Great Gatsby* the impact of Gatsby's decline and fall would be completely different if it were told by someone other than the curiously complex, somewhat naive narrator, Nick Carraway, who, like Gatsby himself, is not always all that he seems to be or should be. Nick's Midwestern roots qualify his responses to experience, just as Huck's frontier background determines his speech, his ironic turn of mind, his frequent use of the tall tale with all its buoyant hyperbole and romantic inventiveness, and his realistic appraisal of detail. Telling the story of *The Ambassadors* from the limited viewpoint of Lambert Strether (this restricted use of the third person is sometimes called "central intelligence"), James can produce for the reader a depth of moral discrimination and intricate analysis of character

and situation because of Strether's New England conscience and determination to "live" intensively while he is
in Paris. As Wayne Booth reminds us in *The Rhetoric of
Fiction* (Chicago: University of Chicago Press, 1961), however, narrators may be either "reliable" (if they support the
explicit or implicit moral norms of the author) or "unreliable" (if they do not). Thus Jake Barnes in *The Sun Also
Rises* is a completely "reliable narrator," for he is the very
embodiment of what is often called the "Hemingway
code"; on the other hand, the lawyer in Melville's *Bartleby
the Scrivener* is "unreliable" in his early evaluations of
himself because he is not involved with humanity. Whatever the point of view we encounter, it has to be recognized as a basic means of control over the area or scope of
the action, the quality of the fictional world offered to the
reader, and even the reactions of the reader.

In drama, also, the characters comment upon themselves
and others so that we can establish a *tone* peculiar to each
and can evaluate speeches and actions by a kind of
yardstick established by the play as a whole. The way the
playwright poses his characters against each other (the
kind of conflict established is the essence of any dramatic
situation) and the sorts of dialogue he puts into their
mouths become keys to his attitude. Early in *Hamlet,* for
example, we discover Hamlet's tendencies toward poetic
comment upon his situation, the world, and the possibility
of human vision and toward thought rather than action.

Another important facet of context is the "world" of the
work. Each author, of course, must imagine and create a
world in which his characters move and have their being.
It may bear little resemblance to the empirical world, as in
most of Poe's fiction. It may have its existence authorized
only in terms of fantasy, as in much science fiction or in
fairy tales. On the other hand, the author may desire a
fictional world that closely mirrors the actual world with
which his readers can relatively easily identify; any realist
(for example, William Dean Howells, Willa Cather, or John
Steinbeck) labors to give us what Henry James called the

"solidity of specification," a texture of details that we recognize as faithful and accurate resemblances to the world we know. Sometimes a work of fiction, such as Shirley Jackson's "The Lottery," establishes a fictional world that borrows from real life as well as from the fantastic. To account for the world of a literary work, we must ask what the "laws" are that control and define the behavior of the characters. Do they permit frequent violations of probability (as in the easy coincidences of melodrama and sentimental novels)? Do they justify or proceed from some idea of a deity, or do they merely reflect the disordered state of an isolated mind (for example, in the stories of Kafka)? Are there recognizable links between causes and effects or merely inexplicable series of incidents that seem to have little or no necessary connections? Is the world highly restricted in time and space (as in Hawthorne's *The Scarlet Letter*), expansive in space (Shakespeare's *Antony and Cleopatra*) or time (Faulkner's *The Sound and the Fury*), or timeless (as in most myths or even a modern play like Jean Anouilh's *Antigone*)? Is there a highly structured society (as in Jane Austen's novels) or are anarchy and chaos prevalent (as in Heller's *Catch-22*)? Such questions transcend the merely superficial identity of setting, for they require the reader to analyze the world presented by a work in terms of every implication, innuendo, and viewpoint he can discover.

But having thus mentioned generally some of the things one can look for as handles by which form may be grasped, we should now proceed to specific applications of these guidelines.

II. THE FORMALISTIC APPROACH IN PRACTICE

A. A Formalistic Reading of "To His Coy Mistress"

The obvious concentration by the New Critics and their followers on lyric poetry in both precept and example suggests that we look first at Andrew Marvell's "To His Coy Mistress." Here even the title helps somewhat (it often does!), for it tells the reader that the poem is probably an address by a male speaker to a reluctant (or as a standard dictionary defines "coy"—"shy, bashful, retiring, demure") female for whom he has more than merely friendly feelings. We can forget about trying to discover the identity of the woman or doing research on seventeenth-century standards of courtship or seduction; instead we can concentrate on *what* this poem says and *how* it says it. We need not even know that the poem belongs to the classical tradition of *carpe diem* (literally, "seize the day"; more freely, "Make hay while the sun shines, baby!"), although if we have the *schemata* of other poems within the mode in mind, so much the better.

A first reading of the poem justifies the hint of the title; the male speaker importunes his mistress (today's equivalent term is probably closer to "girl friend") to cease being "coy," or reluctant toward his offered love. Poems, said Ransom, are "little dramas, exhibiting actions in complex settings" (*The World's Body* [New York: Scribner, 1938], p. 249). Here the lover's urgency obviously conflicts with the lady's reservations in a very dramatic context.

Certain key words call attention to themselves in this first reading and may be underlined for easy recall when a more intensive second or third reading takes place. Thus words like "time," "love's long day," references to an event in Biblical history ("the Flood"), the "slow" growth of "vast" empires (line 12), "an hundred years" and "two hundred [years]" and "thirty thousand [years]," "an age," "the last age," "lower rate [of time]," "time's wingèd chariot hurrying near," "deserts of vast eternity," images of the inevitable death of the lady (a process of time) in lines 25–30, "now," "at once," "our time," "the iron gates of life," and the final references to the movement of the sun—all suggest an insistent preoccupation of the speaker with the passing of time, the consequent brevity of youth and life, and the urgency of experiencing all the delights of young love in the proper season. A verbal system of interconnected words, phrases, and images can quickly be established.

There are also some rhetorical features of the poem that deserve consideration. The first twenty lines present a series of conditions ("Had we but world enough and time," "if you please") and use only the subjunctive mood ("this coyness, lady, *were* no crime") and the closely related conditional verb forms of *should* and *would*. The emphasis is rather obviously placed upon the qualification *if things were somehow or other different* or, more specifically, *if men and women were not imprisoned within fleeting time.*

The elaborate conditions attached to the lady's coyness are yoked rather grotesquely and scathingly with vast exaggerations, a device known as *hyperbole.* Thus the speaker and the lady *could* be separated by the distance between the Ganges River of India and the Humber River of England (a dictionary's gazetteer section will identify references to places); the speaker's love *would* extend from before the Biblical flood in the story of Noah (the beginnings of orthodox Hebraic-Christian chronology) to the conversion of the Jews (which presumably will not take place until just before the Last Judgment)—in effect, throughout all time. His love is compared to a vast vegetable that would grow as large and as slowly as empires; he would expend 100 years in praising her eyes and gazing raptly at her forehead, 200 years in adoration of each of her breasts, and 30,000 years for the celebration of the rest of her body. After these rather specific periods of time, he adds, "an age at least" should be devoted to the celebration of each physical part, the last of which ages should reveal the lady's heart (that is, she would now presumably be ready to return his love after he had conducted such an elaborate and virtually endless courtship). This section (the first twenty lines) is summed up by the concluding and apparently courtly compliment:

> For, Lady, you deserve this state,
> Nor would I love at lower rate.

Probably we must search the dictionary for a fairly uncommon meaning of the word "state" in these lines, because the usual twentieth-century meanings are not quite suitable. Here the rare or obsolete meaning of "high rank or position" (which has been attributed to her by the apparently tireless lover of the hypothetical situation suggested by "Had we but world enough, and time") makes for a better reading. Because these first twenty lines postulate a series of extravagantly impossible situations, all of which are connected grammatically with the opening conditional clause (line 1), we can see that the speaker is no irresponsible romantic dreamer who would prefer to exchange the limited human state for a condition unrestricted by clock and calendar; he is instead a militant realist who recognizes and accepts the brevity of life and who, through the force of his extravagant conditional situations, points up the folly of unnatural coyness by the lady in the face of the even greater brevity of youth and its compelling sexuality.

With the beginning of the next twelve lines the tone (attitude of the speaker or *persona* as conveyed by the language and its artful arrangement) seems to shift from the seemingly expansive, genial, more nearly conventional, and exaggerated praise of the lady. Now the speaker turns away from idle concern with "what might be if human life were not so inexorably limited" to say the kind of thing totally foreign to conventional love songs, love letters, or declarations of eternal devotion. He now confronts the lady with the inescapable fact of hastening time and the shocking certainty of death and the flesh's decay. His honesty, thus, by implication and by shrewd strategy, makes the lady's reluctance to enjoy fully the pleasures of love in their allotted season seem foolish, illogical, perhaps even perverse. His impatience with her unrealistic coyness is held in check by the outward politeness and understatement of lines 31–32, in which, like a schoolmaster lecturing a not-so-bright pupil, he says, by way of clinching the logic of his argument:

> The grave's a fine and private place,
> But none, I think, do there embrace.

That the whole poem has been moving in the direction of tightly reasoned argument is suggested by the summing-up word "therefore" in the third and final section of the poem (the last fourteen lines). Having made the lady's conventional shrinking from surrender to an ardent lover seem grotesque and unnatural in the first twenty lines and having employed scathing irony at her expense in the second section, the speaker now adopts a tone of blunt and brutal honesty. In view of the relatively sharp realism of the second section (with its emphasis on what worms do to the body in the grave), the speaker can now afford to assume and to ask the lady to admit tacitly that she is as eager for the experience as he is (her "willing soul transpires/At every pore with instant fires"; that is, her inner and true self obviously, even physically, betrays what she cannot bring her face or her voice to consent to—that she is as strongly impelled toward sexual gratification as he is). Because he refuses to accept as a suitable substitute for love's consummation the idle and unsatisfactory composition of plaintive and complimentary love songs, he now discards all pretense and asks her to join with him in the violent, animalistic, physical enactment of love:

> Now let us sport us while we may,
> And now, like amorous birds of prey,
> Rather at once our time devour
> Than languish in his slow-chapped power.

This insistence upon a frank acceptance of sexual love is carried forward by "Let us roll all our strength and all/Our sweetness up into one ball" and "tear our pleasures with rough strife/ Thorough the iron gates of life."

But the poem is more than a witty and realistic confrontation with a conventionally coy lady. Intricately woven into the brisk, seemingly comic argument is a melancholy awareness of the brevity of youth and life, of mutability and mortality. The lover is ever mindful of life's hastening toward an inevitable end:

> But at my back I always hear
> Time's wingèd chariot hurrying near;
> And yonder all before us lie
> Deserts of vast eternity.

In such an overlapping context much of what the speaker says takes on a new dimension. Something more than mere gratification of the physical appetites is involved. For as the poem moves along toward its end, it becomes plain that the speaker is stressing the importance of living fully each moment in a heroic defiance of Time's "slow-chapped power." The apparently playful approach to love may be seen as a kind of witty or ironic defense against human limitation; and the sophisticated realism, as a foil to genuine feelings. The savage dismissal of the lady's negative attitude is not diminished, but the ultimately more pervasive theme of defiance toward mortality constitutes a second motif that plays against the first theme.

Although much of the foregoing may sometimes appear to be mere prose paraphrase, actually the emphasis has consistently been on *how* the language of the poem is used, the artful arrangement of words, an *"achieved content."* But what of rhyme and meter in this artful arrangement? The four-stress lines (notice that a perfectly natural reading of the line tells us where to place the beat or *accent:* "Had' we but world' enough' and time' ") suggest precision by the lecturing *persona*, a precision in which key words, simple as they are in general, get the emphasis of stress. Often each thought unit or syntactical pattern is completed within the two lines of a rhyming couplet. Thus the succession of thoughts is kept basically simple and straightforward as the speaker concentrates on the simplicity and directness of his argument, an argument addressed to a reluctant woman who has denied logic and reality in her zeal for conventional coyness. The seeming flippancy of the speaker's approach and his underlying seriousness are effectively merged in the final couplet, whose *spondees* (metrical feet with two stressed syllables) underscore the terse, blunt, sudden close:

> Thus, though we cannot make our sun
> Stand still, yet we will make him run.

The adverb "thus" emphasizes that this couplet is to be a formal conclusion to the argument, and the whole burden of the previous steps in the argument—living fully and vitally in the face of man's inevitable end—is wittily telescoped into the figure of the busy lovers forcing the sun, the image of time, into a brisk trot. If they cannot really control time, they can at least, with their determined pace, make it race by and thus seem to be controlled. The wit, the irony, the playfulness avoid any effect of sentimentality (a stock emotional response beyond what a situation actually deserves).

B. The Short Story as Formal Structure: Juxtaposition in "Young Goodman Brown"

In short fiction one can look, as in a poem, for the telling word or phrase, the recurring or patterned imagery, the symbolic object or character, the hint of or clue to meaning greater than that of the action alone (that is, the *plot*). Because we can no more justify stopping with a mere summary of what outwardly happens in the story than we can with a mere prose paraphrase of a lyric poem's "content," we must look for the key to a story's form in a balanced juxtaposition of plot or "content" with theme or "larger implication." In short, we seek a point at which the structure of the story coincides with and illuminates its meaning. Once more we must look at the various parts before we can evaluate the whole.

1. THE STORY AS FORM

As we have seen, the lyric poem generally embraces a dramatic stiuation: A speaker (who need not be the poet at all, though often we can suppose it is) reacts to an experience, a feeling, an idea, or even a physical sensation. Only one voice is present usually in the lyric poem, but in the other literary genres there usually is a group of characters. In fiction the story is told by the author, by one of the characters in the story, or by someone who has heard of an episode. The major difference between the short story and the novel—the important fictional types—is one of length and complexity of plot. The novel contains more characters; its plot, a number of situations. The short story is characteristically concerned with relatively few characters (sometimes really only one, as in Poe's "William Wilson" or "The Black Cat") and with only one major situation, which achieves its climax and solution and thus tidily comes to an end. Like a news story, the short story is restricted in scope, but unlike the news story, the short story possesses balance and design—the polish and finish, the completeness that we associate with the work of art. A principle of unity operates throughout to give that single "effect," which Poe emphasized as necessary. In short, like any other imaginative literary work, the short story possesses *form*.

2. ALLEGORY AND SYMBOLISM

Hawthorne characteristically uses a combination of "allegorical" and "symbolic" methods. The allegorical bent, with its normal one-to-one relationships, can be sensed in the first paragraph of "Young Goodman Brown," for the very names of the title character and his wife Faith immediately identify their roles in the tale by suggesting associations beyond those of a historical character or a John Doe or Mary Jones. Although "Goodman" was a commonplace honorific for persons below the class of gentleman in both England and the colonies ("Goody" is a contraction of the comparable feminine title of "Goodwife"), the use of "Young" with it and its constant repetition throughout the narrative hint at something more than mere title—Brown's youth, his innocence, his simple and unquestioned attachment to abstract Faith. Yet his last name, Brown, points just as surely to the young man's affinities with the gloomy and dark forest where most of the story takes place, that strange world outside the settled, comfortable village of untested goodness and Faith. The forest itself is not just a simply allegorical entity, but a complex symbol in which nature, sin, and danger are ambiguously and richly combined.

The urgency of the dark journey from home, security, and commitment is emphasized by the conversation of Brown and Faith as he prepares to leave. Faith implores him to stay at home and "put off" the journey "until sunrise." But Brown feels compelled to go, or wills to go, despite the claims and premonitions of Faith. Brown himself seems to be quite clear about the nature of the night's errand, for he says to Faith: "My journey, *as thou callest it,* forth and back again, *must needs be done* 'twixt now and sunrise" (our italics, to emphasize his apparent certainty about what he is doing). Into the dark and ambiguous forest, whose dimensions are only dimly suspected but whose attractions are irresistible, he will go; and the irony of his position is revealed by his asking Faith: "What, my sweet, pretty wife, dost thou doubt me already, and we but three months married?" We stress this irony because Brown is poised somewhere between superficial attachment to Faith and deep doubts about the kind of reality he will encounter in the forest. This initial contest between the will of Brown and the tug of Faith thus establishes early the formal level of the journey and the issues involved in it. Not only is the willful voyager at odds with the innocent Faith, but also the simple values of the safe, familiar, ordered village are economically and immediately set against those equivocal and, as we shall see, unordered forces that lurk outside. It is an unequal contest, for Faith cannot summon any strong argument—only uneasy questions about possible consequences of the voyages—to forestall Brown's departure.

And off he goes, with only a passing pang of regret for his Faith. That he has some idea of what will take place in the forest is clearly suggested by his thought that perhaps

Faith has had some idea of "what work is to be done to-night" and that, moreover, " 'twould kill her to think it." Evidently Brown's object in the forest is inimical to Faith (or faith); he suspects the kind of risk he is taking and accepts that risk, although he promises himself that "after this one night" in darkness "I'll cling to her [Faith's] skirts and follow her to heaven." The largely allegorical functions of Faith and Brown, as well as the import of the journey, are clearly set forth. The formal linking of Faith, the village, light, and unquestioned certainty, on the one hand, and Brown, the forest, darkness, ambiguity, perhaps even skepticism, on the other, has been established.

Although, as we have pointed out in Chapter 1, some knowledge of conflicting Puritan superstition about the wilderness and the savages who lurked there and Puritan assurance about the inevitable victory of God's "saints" in any contest with Satan may be helpful here, Hawthorne's story really contains all the necessary hints about Brown's ambivalence, the journey, and the forest. The formal nexus of place, time, atmosphere, dialogue (often question and answer), and carefully stylized action really offers us everything we need for a significant reading.

The journey begins at sundown, Brown hastens on "his present evil purpose," the road is "dreary, darkened by all the gloomiest trees of the forest," the solitude is complete, there are the traveler's apprehensions about fearful creatures that may lurk behind the trees, and Brown returns to the familiar world only at sunrise. The circular pattern of withdrawal and return provides a narrative structure with a generally Gothic context.

But the mystery transcends the conventional melodrama that we associate with Gothic romance, in which typically all the mysterious events turn out to have completely rational *raisons d'être*. For as Brown asks himself, "What if the devil himself should be at my very elbow!" that elderly figure instantly appears to chide Brown for being late. That the older man is no earthly being in disguise is suggested by his timetable: Even in a prejet day he has made his way from Boston to the outskirts of Salem in fifteen minutes! That Brown is neither surprised to see him nor ignorant of his powers is manifest in his explanation that "Faith kept me back a while."

Of course, Brown's reply is true on two levels—both that of the young husband and that of the simple man of faith. And just as that response admits a double interpretation, so on a formal level the world of the forest is seemingly juxtaposed to that of the village at every turn in the narrative from that point. The characters who begin to appear (including Brown himself, who aspires to inhabiting both worlds) seem to be basically the same as those of the village. Brown recognizes them by the names, mannerisms, and clothes they use in Salem. Outwardly they seem to be going about their accustomed affairs. The difference is, of course, that trees have replaced homes and meetinghouse and the people have simply taken on the values of the forest without any outward change in person and demeanor. As in Alice's journey into the world of the looking glass, the values of the village are reversed in the forest but without any apparent change in the "saints" as they romp gleefully into darkness.

Hawthorne's comments on the relationships between Satan and Brown bear some close reading too. The older man resembles Brown and is "apparently in the same rank of life"; as if to emphasize the relationship, Hawthorne adds that "they might have been taken for father and son." Of course, they are father and son: The younger man, as are all men in the village and the great world, is the child of Satan. And Satan, though he may wear the clothes of Brown's class at this point, "had an indescribable air of one who knew the world, and would not have felt abashed at the governor's dinner table or in King William's court." This authorial interpolation is merely another way of saying that the principle of evil is at home everywhere or that wherever men are, there is Satan. All this is communicated to us by the formal juxtaposition of the world Brown has left with the world he has now entered.

If we yet have doubts about the supernatural identity of the older man, Hawthorne now ends them when he mentions the staff, which seems to "twist and wriggle itself like a live serpent." Lest this appear too suddenly heavy-handed, Hawthorne seems to retreat a little when he says that the living movements of the snake-staff may have been caused by an "ocular deception, assisted by the uncertain light." But such a coy tactic actually emphasizes the difficulty of "seeing" the manifestations of evil. Any alternative to identification of the older man has already been closed by the revelation that he and Brown had arranged the tryst in the forest and that the older man had traveled from Boston to Salem in record time. Nevertheless, in the forest the light is "uncertain," and "ocular deception" makes difficult the empirical tests used in the village.

The traveler's identity and the nature of the rendezvous are further confirmed when Brown halfheartedly tries to back out of his commitment to the night journey, offering as weak explanation that neither his ancestors nor the "good" people of New England in general have ever ventured on such a perilous trip. Again the "elder person" has a ready answer: Not only has he been the intimate and active associate of Brown's father and grandfather, but he has also enjoyed a "very general acquaintance here in New England." As Brown goes deeper into the forest with his amiable guide, he encounters one by one all the sober church officials of Salem and the people who he had thought were completely incorruptible—Goody Cloyse, from whom he had learned his catechism, the minister, and Deacon Gookin. Each encounter for young Goodman Brown is a step toward disillusionment and a further breach between him and his faith. Moving farther into darkness and density, Brown finds the upside-down world of the forest irresistible. Yet after each encounter, he recalls his Faith and believes that he can yet return to the safety and assurance of home.

However, his commitment to the forces of darkness is

sealed when from a "cloud of night" sweeping overhead
he thinks he hears, mingled with the voices of his Salem
neighbors, the sound of Faith's voice. The suspicion is
confirmed when the ambiguously pink ribbon, the only
specific detail given us by Hawthorne to associate with
Faith, flutters down from above. In that moment, of course,
Brown comes to know what he had suspected all along
about the depravity of mankind. This is an important point:
If he had not suspected the truth of what he now discovers,
he would never have made the journey. Though the
theological content of his knowledge comes from the world
of the village (even in the catechism), it is in the forest that
he is able to articulate it eloquently and dramatically:
" 'My Faith is gone!' cried he, after one stupefied moment.
'There is no good on earth; and sin is but a name. Come,
devil; for to thee is this world given.' " But such a recognition scene would seem superficially mechanical if it were
not for Hawthorne's careful juxtaposition of the gloom of
the forest against the now uncertain light of the village.

Thus he rushes off, with the supersonic aid of the staff
thoughtfully left him by Satan, toward a midnight assigna-
tion in the heart of the dark forest and the confirmation of
his knowledge of evil, diabolism, and depravity. The rendezvous, we discover, is the Puritan equivalent of a Black
Mass—a solemn meeting at which hymns strangely like
those of the choir in the Salem meetinghouse are sung and
the form of the Puritan sermon is maintained. The members of the congregation are clad in familiar drab garb and
display their customary solemnity. Once again we see the
careful juxtaposition of the forms and appearances of the
village and the meetinghouse with those of the forest and
satanic orgy. The familiar world of fact and certainty has
become one with the hitherto unknown world of fantasy
and doubt. The people are the same, and the urgency of
forms and ritual has a similarity too obvious to miss. The
only unusual elements are the roaring fire, the presence of
the socially and politically prominent personages of the
colony, the easy mingling of the dissolute with the saintly,

and the "Indian priests, or powwows, who had often scared their native forest with more hideous incantations than any known to English witchcraft." Otherwise, in detail after detail, the likeness of the meeting to the godly services Brown has known all his life is emphasized. But in the forest the meaning and purpose of ritual are reversed, for the object of this meeting is to admit converts to the communion of the damned; the special converts are revealed to be Brown and Faith.

What Brown has learned is stated for him in the introduction to the confirmation service by Satan (who now "bore no slight similitude, both in garb and manner, to some grave divine of the New England churches"): All men are evil, all engage compulsively in evil, and all sanctity is merely appearance. At just the moment when the "mark of baptism" by blood is about to be placed on their heads by the "shape of evil," Brown cries out to save himself and Faith.

Once again Hawthorne engages in a deliberate withdrawal from a verdict on what happened. He tells the reader that Brown did not know whether Faith obeyed his anguished cry to "look up to heaven, and resist the wicked one." This authorial retreat from unequivocal statement is followed by the strongest of all the equivocations strewn throughout the tale: "Had Goodman Brown fallen asleep in the forest and only dreamed a wild dream of a witch meeting?" Hawthorne then gravely says he will allow the reader to accept the possibility of a dream if the reader is so inclined, but dream or fact, the effect is to change Brown's life forever—to change it so drastically that Brown is never able again to accept as valid the goodness of man. The result of the experience is to take Brown beyond the point of return. His belief in the basic goodness of man is gone forever, and with the loss of that belief comes virtual alienation from human kind. Having perceived the depths of evil to which all men are prone, he is never able for the rest of his life to rise above that perception. In the morning light he returns physically to the serene village, but he is a far different man from the mildly skeptical young husband who had departed the previous evening. In the intervening night he has replaced the perspective of the village with that of the forest, for he has been exposed to the tragic view of the discrepancy between reality and appearance.

Hawthorne's strategy is important for perceiving the form and thus the meaning in the form of his allegory. In his now classic study of the tale, Richard Harter Fogle (*Hawthorne's Fiction: The Light & The Dark* [Norman: University of Oklahoma Press, 1952], Chap. 2) calls to our attention the quality of stylistic tone as a key to meaning:

> The satisfaction one feels in the clean line of the story's structure is enhanced by Hawthorne's steady detachment from his materials, an attitude which deepens the impression of classic balance, which in turn stands against the painful ambiguity of the theme. Even the full tone of the most intense scenes . . . is tempered by restraint. The participant is overweighted by the calm, impartial (though not unfeeling) spectator; Hawthorne does not permit himself to become identified with his hero. He displays young Goodman Brown not in and for the hero himself, but always in relation to the whole situation and set of circumstances. This detachment of attitude is plainest in the almost continuous irony, unemphatic but nonetheless relentless: an irony organically related to the ever-present ambiguities of the situation, but most evident in sustained tone. . . .
>
> This detachment is implicit in the quiet, the abstractness, and the gravity of Hawthorne's style, which is everywhere formal and exactly, though subtly, cadenced. It throws a light and idealizing veil over the action and maintains an aesthetic distance, while hinting at the ugliness it covers. The difference between the saying and the thing said provides dramatic tension. [pp. 30–31]

Juxtaposition of manner and meaning, of idealization and ugliness, thus reinforces form.

But most important of all for seeing Hawthorne's formal control of his materials is his location of the narrative halfway between the relatively prosaic world of a young, newlywed man, beset by doubts about the world he has always known and taken at face value, and the shadowy world of dream and myth. Thus our author can lend to his narrative an equivocal quality that straddles the borderline between fact and dream. In short, Hawthorne refuses to identify either level as the province of real knowing; whichever carries the greater impact for a man, therein lies the reality to which he commits the shaping of his life. The point is that the two poles are constantly being juxtaposed throughout the story. Perhaps young Goodman Brown did dream all the horrifying stages of the journey into the forest, but he had deliberately set out upon the journey against the pleas of Faith and even his own better judgment. It was a journey toward which his skeptical disposition had always been tending, and whether it took place in a way that could be measured by distance traveled or only in ways that the heart and soul can traverse becomes finally irrelevant. By the careful ordering of the experience, equivocal though it may be, Hawthorne has delineated very sharply and clearly the crucial pathway by which a young man, already suspicious about the nature of mankind, comes to a totally pessimistic, even cynical, conclusion. Another man might have arrived at a Rousseauesque commitment to the natural goodness of man, but Brown, a child of the Puritans, arrived, not surprisingly, at a conviction of the innate depravity of man and is unable to rise above that conviction. Therefore when he died, his family and neighbors "carved no hopeful verse upon his tombstone, for his dying hour was gloom."

The formal stages by which Hawthorne managed the difficult problem of an allegorical exposure to the hard fact of evil in man might be likened to a dramatic situation (the adventures in the forest) that has both prologue (Brown's farewell to the village) and epilogue (his return). Full circle moves the narrative from sunset through nightmare to sunrise; but only in the careful, systematic juxtaposition of village and forest, style and matter, fact and dream does

Hawthorne achieve formal mastery over the seemingly dual but actually inseparable worlds of good and evil.

C. Form and Structure in the Novel: *Adventures of Huckleberry Finn*

Earlier in this chapter the importance of point of view in fiction was stressed. Even the most common point of view (especially in nineteenth-century fictions), that of the omniscient, omnipresent author, who tells the story in the third person, has its impact on the force of the narrative: We look at the characters from the Olympian heights of their creator and judge, primarily from what he explicitly says of them, what kind of people they are and what attitude we are to take toward their involvement in the circumstances of the plot. The author may interrupt his narrative to make moral judgments or to editorialize to his reader. With the completely unrestricted omniscient point of view, the author may jump back and forth from one group of widely separated characters to another; he can see into the minds and hearts of all his characters equally well. The reader's judgments of character and responses to situations are utterly dependent on what the characters are allowed to say and do or on the authorial pronouncements inserted between chunks of narrative. Some of the greatest English and American novelists (Jane Austen and James Fenimore Cooper, for example) have made the omniscient-author technique serve their purposes. Even more, the typically unsophisticated "western" novel, with its formula of "Meanwhile, back at the ranch . . . ," displays the omniscient author at his baldest lack of pretense about point of view.

But in *Huckleberry Finn*, Twain abandoned the simpler omniscient-author point of view he had very successfully used for *The Adventures of Tom Sawyer* for a relatively sophisticated technique: He allowed the central character to relate his "adventures" in his own way (the point of view called *first-person narrator*). T. S. Eliot refers to the difference in points of view as indicative of the major qualitative distinction between *Tom Sawyer* and *Huckleberry Finn:* Tom's story is told by an adult looking at a boy and his gang, whereas Huck's narrative requires that "we see the world through his eyes" (Eliot, introduction to *The Adventures of Huckleberry Finn* [London: Cresset Press, 1950]; reprinted in *Adventures of Huckleberry Finn: An Annotated Text, Backgrounds and Sources, Essays in Criticism,* ed. Sculley Bradley, Richmond Croom Beatty, and E. Hudson Long [New York: Norton, 1962], p. 321). Granted that Twain sometimes allows us to see beyond Huck's relatively simple narrative manner some dimensions of meaning not apparent to Huck, the point of view has been so contrived (and controlled) that we do not see anything that is not at least implicit in Huck's straightforward narration.

Several questions can be raised. What is the character of Huck like? How does his manner of telling his story control our responses to that story? Finally, how does this point of view assist us in perceiving the novel's form?

To begin with, Huck is an objective narrator. He is objective about himself, even when that objectivity tends to reflect negatively upon himself. He is objective about the society he repeatedly confronts, even when, as he often fears, that society possesses virtues and sanctions to which he must ever remain a stranger. He is an outcast, he knows that he is an outcast, and he does not blame the society that has made and will keep him an outcast. He always assumes in his characteristic modesty that he must somehow be to blame for the estrangement. His deceptions, his evasions, his lapses from conventional respectability are always motivated by the requirements of a given situation; he is probably the first thoroughgoing, honest pragmatist in American fiction. When he lies or steals, he assumes that society is right and that he is simply depraved. He does not make excuses for himself, and his conscience is the stern voice of a pietistic, hypocritical backwoods society asserting itself within that sensitive and wistful psyche. We know that he is neither depraved nor dishonest, because we judge that society by the damning clues that emerge from the naive account of a boy about thirteen years old who has been forced to lie in order to get out of trouble but who never lies to himself or to his reader. In part, his lack of subtlety is a measure of his reliability as narrator: He has mastered neither the genteel speech of "respectable" folks nor their deceit, evasions of truth, and penchant for pious platitudes. He is always refreshingly himself, even when he is telling a "tall tale" or engaging in one of his ambitious masquerades to get out of a jam.

Thus the point of view Twain carefully establishes from the first words of the narrative offers a position from which the reader must consider the events of the narrative. That position never wavers from the trustworthy point of view of the hero-narrator's clear-eyed gaze. He becomes at once the medium and the norm for the story that unfolds. By him (although he never overtly does it himself) we can measure the hypocrisy of Miss Watson, perceive the cumulative contrast between Huck and the incorrigible Tom Sawyer, and finally judge the whole of society along the river. Eliot makes this important discrimination: "Huck has not imagination, in the sense in which Tom has it; he has, instead, vision. He sees the real world; and he does not judge it—he allows it to judge itself" (ibid.).

Huck's characteristic mode of speech is ironic and self-effacing. Although at times he can be proud of the success of his tall tales and masquerades, in the things that matter he is given to understatement. Of his return to "civilized" life with the Widow Douglas, he tersely confides, "Well, then, the old thing commenced again." Of the senseless horror with which the Grangerford-Shepherdson feud ends, Huck says with admirable restraint: "I ain't a-going to tell all that happened—it would make me sick again if I was to do that. I wished I hadn't ever come ashore that night to see such things. I ain't ever going to get shut of them—lots of times I dream about them." And in one of the most artfully conceived, understated but eloquent endings in all fiction, Huck bids his reader and "civilization" goodbye simultaneously: "But I reckon I got to light out for the Territory ahead of the rest, because Aunt Sally she's going to adopt me and civilize me, and I can't stand it. I been there before."

The movement of the novel likewise has an effect on the total shape of the work. The apparently aimless plot with its straightforward sequence—what happened, what happened next, and then what happened after that, to paraphrase Gertrude Stein—is admirably suited to the personality of Huck as narrator. In the conventional romantic novel, of course, we expect to find a more or less complex central situation, in which two lovers come together by various stratagems of the novelist, have their difficulties (they disagree about more or less crucial matters or they must contend against parents, a social milieu, deprivations of war or cattle rustlers or dozens of other possible impediments to their union), resolve their problems, and are destined to live happily ever afterward. Even in such a classic novel as Jane Austen's *Pride and Prejudice*, the separate chapters and the pieces of the plot concern the manifestations, against the background of early nineteenth-century English provincial life, of the many facets of Mr. Darcy's insuperable pride and Elizabeth Bennet's equally tenacious prejudice, but everything works toward the happy union of two very attractive young people.

In *Huckleberry Finn*, however, there is no real center to the plot as such. Instead we have what Kenneth Burke has called "repetitive form"—"the consistent maintaining of a principle under new guises . . . a restatement of the same thing in different ways. . . . A succession of images, each of them regiving the same lyric mood; a character repeating his identity, his 'number,' under changing situations; the sustaining of an attitude as in satire . . . " (*Counter-Statement* [Los Altos, Calif.: Hermes, 1953], p. 125). The separate situations or episodes are loosely strung together by the presence of Huck and Jim as they make their way down the Mississippi River from St. Petersburg, while the river flows through all, becoming really a vast highway across

[margin handwritten note:] man's inhumanity to man theme

backwoods America. In the separate episodes there are new characters who, after Huck moves on, usually do not reappear. There are new settings and always new situations. At the beginning, there are five chapters about the "adventures" of Huck and Tom and the gang in St. Petersburg; at the end, there are twelve chapters centering around the Phelps farm that chronicle the high jinks of the boys in "freeing" Jim; in between, there are twenty-six chapters in which Huck and Jim pursue true freedom and in which Tom Sawyer does not appear. This large midsection of the book includes such revealing experiences as Jim and Huck's encounter with the "house of death" (chap. 9); the dual masquerades before the perceptive Mrs. Judith Loftus (chap. 11); the terror of being aboard the *Walter Scott* (chap. 12 and 13); Huck's life with the Grangerfords (chap. 17 and 18); the performance of the Duke and Dauphin at Parkville (chap. 20); the Arkansas premiere of Shakespeare and the shooting of Boggs by Colonel Sherburn (chap. 21 and 22); and, finally, the relatively lengthy involvement with the Wilks family (chap. 24-29).

Despite changes in settings and *dramatis personae*, the separate episodes share a cumulative role (their "repetitive form"): Huck learns bit by bit about the depravity hiding beneath respectability and piety. He learns gradually and unwillingly that society or "civilization" is vicious and predatory and that the individual has small chance to assert himself against a monolithic mass. Harmless as the sentimental tastes of the Grangerfords or their preference for the conventionally pretty may seem, Twain's superb sense for the "objective correlative" allows us to *realize* (without being *told*) that conventional piety and sentimentality hide depravity no more effectually than the high coloring of the chalk fruit compensates for the chips that expose the underlying chalk. Likewise, elaborate manners, love of tradition, and "cultivated" tastes for "graveyard school" poetry and lugubrious drawings are merely genteel facades for barbarism and savagery. Mrs. Judith Loftus, probably the best-developed minor character in the entire novel, for all her sentimental response to the hackneyed story of a mistreated apprentice, sees the plight of the runaway slave merely in terms of the cash reward she and her husband may win. Even the Wilks girls, as charming as they seem to Huck, are easily taken in by the grossest sentimentality and pious clichés. A review of the several episodes discloses that for all their apparent differences they are really reenactments of the same insistent revelation: The mass of humanity is hopelessly depraved, and the genuinely honest individual is constantly being victimized, betrayed, and threatened.

The framework of the plot is, then, a journey—a journey from north to south, and a journey from relative innocence to horrifying knowledge. Huck tends to see people for what they are, but he does not suspect the depths of evil and the pervasiveness of sheer meanness, of man's inhumanity to man, until he has completed his journey. The relative harmlessness of Miss Watson's lack of compassion and her devotion to the letter rather than the spirit of religious law or of Tom's incurable romanticism does not become really sinister until Huck reenters the seemingly good world at the Phelps farm, a world that is really the same as the "good" world of St. Petersburg— a connection that is stressed by the kinship of Aunt Sally and Aunt Polly. Into that world the values of Tom Sawyer are once more injected, but Huck discovers that he has endured too much on his journey down the river to become Tom's foil again.

Much has been written about the end of the novel. In *The Green Hills of Africa* Hemingway complained that the section about the Phelps farm is "cheating," that the novel should have ended with Huck and Jim floating down the river to an inevitable and tragic end. But precisely because Huck has come full circle, back into the world of St. Petersburg, comes his shocking realization that "you can't go home again." Therefore Huck must set off on another flight from an oppressive "civilization" into the temporary freedom of the Territory.

closure

The characters, except for Huck and Jim, are stereotypes. The women, except perhaps for Mrs. Judith Loftus, are flat—either "humor" characters like the elderly women or incorrigibly pure virgins like Sophia Grangerford or Mary Jane Wilks. The men represent the frontier types Twain knew—the braggart, the superman like Colonel Sherburn, the vagrant actors like the Duke and the Dauphin, the lawyers, the itinerant preachers, and backwoodsmen generally. But distinction in characterization is another formal suggestion that the stereotype is another integer of the anti-individualism that pervades the society represented in this novel.

One can imagine something like a descending scale of viciousness operating in the dramatis personae of the novel. The relatively harmless "good" people like the Widow Douglas, the Wilks girls, and Aunt Sally and Uncle Silas rank near the top. Somewhere along the middle are the Grangerfords, whose basic kindness and devotion to what they suppose is an aristocratic tradition of manners and forms must be set aginst their overweening sentimentality, their canting theological commitments, and their single-minded obsession with a senseless and brutal blood feud whose origin has long before been lost to memory. Alongside the Grangerfords is Mrs. Judith Loftus, with her paradoxical combination of sympathy and generosity for the homeless, ostensibly mistreated white waif, and unmitigated avarice and indifference to the humanity of the miserable runaway slave. And the bottom of the scale is crowded with animalistic, predatory characters like the Duke and Dauphin, pap Finn, and the mob that pursues Colonel Sherburn.

Even such a simple classification of the characters enables us to see a significance in the arrangement of episodes. Huck's flight into freedom, although its origin lies in his need to escape, both the "civilization" of Miss Watson and possible death at the hands of pap, starts out as a kind of lark—even a Tom Sawyer type of "adventure." But the "adventures" become increasingly sinister for Huck, as he and Jim drift down the river, involvements with society take on a darker and darker cast. By the time he and Jim arrive at Pikesville and have been victimized by the Duke and Dauphin, they have seen every kind of depravity possible on the frontier, once the sanctuary of the seekers after freedom.

Thus the narrative moves in a circular pattern. Huck has left St. Petersburg to escape from conventional gentility and morality. But he sees the same conventions shaping life at the Phelps farm. Tom Sawyer returns to play more of his tricks, this time with Jim as victim. Although Huck has "gone home again" (back to the world of St. Petersburg), he knows now that there is really no home for him as men define "home." He was merely a social outcast before; now he is a moral outcast because he cannot accept conventional morality, which is after all part of the texture of "civilization." At the end of the novel, then, he is preparing to set forth once again, on another journey that time and history will probably defeat. Huck had been subjected to the same kind of cruel, senseless captivity at the hands of pap that Jim must endure under Tom Sawyer at the Phelps farm. Now Huck realizes, finally and tragically, that all of society is constantly arranging to "capture" the individual in one way or another—that, indeed, all members of society are really captives of an oppressive sameness that destroys any mode of individualism. Huck and Jim alone have a capacity to pursue freedom.

Only the great, flowing river defines the lineaments of otherwise elusive freedom; that mighty force of nature opposes and offers the only possible escape from the blighting tyranny of towns and farm communities. The Mississippi is the novel's major symbol. It is the one place where one does not need to lie to himself or to others. Its ceaseless flow mocks the static, stultifying society on its banks. There are those lyrical passages in which Huck communicates, even with all his colloquial limitations, his feelings about the river, its symbolic functions, as in the image-packed description that follows the horrors of the Grangerford-Shepherdson carnage (chap. 19). In that memorable passage Huck extols the freedom and contemplation that the river encourages. In contrast to the oppressive places on land, the raft and the river promise release: "We said there warn't no home like a raft, after all. Other places do seem so cramped up and smothery, but a raft don't. You feel mighty free and easy and comfortable on a raft."

Like the river, Huck's narrative flows spontaneously and ever onward. Around each bend lies a possible new adventure; in the eddies, a lyrical interlude. But the river always carries Huck and Jim out of each adventure toward another uncertain try for freedom. That freedom is never really achieved is a major irony, but the book's structure parallels the river's flow. The separate adventures become infinite variations upon ("repetitive forms" of) the quest for freedom. That the final thwarting of freedom is perpetrated by the forces of St. Petersburg, of course, is no fault of the river or its promise of freedom; it simply seems that membership in humanity generates what we have elsewhere called the circular pattern of flight and captivity.

D. Dialectic as Form in *Hamlet*

Of all Shakespeare's plays, *The Tragedy of Hamlet, Prince of Denmark,* has generated the greatest amount of commentary and criticism. No period since Shakespeare's day, least of all our own, has been able to ignore the play. Fashions in criticism and scholarship come and go, but always this great monument of the English Renaissance remains, like Keats's Grecian urn, to "tease us out of thought/As doth Eternity." But it has also teased many of the best critical minds *into* thought. As questions about stagecraft and the dramatic unities have come to seem somewhat secondary, new questions about poetic texture and form have arisen. For we now have ample testimony and example that the play can be examined much as we would analyze any lengthy poetic structure. Certainly in the process of regarding the play's formal qualities, the patterns of which move together to encourage interpretation, we lose nothing of its force as a play.

We can begin interpretation by characterizing once

again the world of the work. The setting, we know, is the castle of Elsinore in medieval Denmark. But what is this Denmark? It is, to be sure, largely a Denmark of Shakespeare's imagination—an imaginatively apprehended Denmark that has only tenuous relationships to a historical Denmark. It is a world, however, peopled by Shakespeare's characters that takes on definition from what happens and what is said in the play and that in turn determines what can be done and said. We need go no further than the first scene of Act I to realize that it is a disturbed world, that a sense of mystery and deep anxiety preoccupies the soldiers of the watch. The ghost has appeared already and is expected to appear again. The guards instinctively assume that the apparition of the former king has more than passing import, and in their troubled questions to Horatio about the mysterious preparations for war, the guards show how closely they regard the connection between the unnatural appearance of the dead king and the welfare of the state. The guards have no answers for the mystery, their uncertainty, or their premonitions; their quandary is mirrored in abundant questions and minimal answers—a rhetorical phenomenon that recurs throughout the play, even in the soliloquies of Hamlet. The sense of cosmic implication in the special situation of Denmark emerges strongly in the exchange between Hamlet and his friends Rosencrantz and Guildenstern:

> *Hamlet.* Denmark's a prison.
> *Rosencrantz.* Then is the world one.
> *Hamlet.* A goodly one; in which there are many confines, wards, and dungeons, Denmark being the one o' th' worst.
> [II, ii]

These remarks recall the assertion of Marcellus as Hamlet and the ghost go offstage: "Something is rotten in the state of Denmark" (I, iv, 90). Indeed, Hamlet's obsession is both the product and the cure of the rottenness of Denmark, but the rottenness, he acknowledges, pervades all of nature: ". . . this goodly frame the earth seems to me a sterile promontory; this most excellent canopy, the air, look you, this brave o'erhanging firmament, this majestical roof fretted with golden fire—why, it appeareth nothing to me but a foul and pestilent congregation of vapors" (II, ii). Much earlier, before his encounter with the Ghost, Hamlet has expressed his extreme pessimism at man's having to endure earthly existence within nature's unwholesome realm:

> How weary, stale, flat and unprofitable
> Seem to me all the uses of this world!
> Fie on't, ah, fie, 'tis an unweeded garden
> That grows to seed. Things rank and gross in nature
> Possess it merely. [I, ii]

As he speaks these lines, Hamlet apparently has no idea of the truth of his father's death but is dismayed over his mother's hasty marriage to the new King. He has discovered a seeming paradox in being: the fair, in nature and humanity, inevitably submits to the dominion of the foul. His obsession with the nature and cause of the paradox focuses his attention on Denmark as the model of nature and human frailty. Thus a pattern of increasing parallels of Denmark to the cosmos, of man to nature, develops. Question and answer, dialogue and soliloquy, become a verbal unity of repeated words and phrases, looking forward to larger thematic assertion and backward to early adumbration.

The play constitutes a vast poem in which speculation about nature, man's nature, the health of the state, and human destiny intensifies into a passionate dialectic. Mystery, riddle, enigma, and metaphysical question complicate the dialogue. Particularly in his soliloquies does Hamlet confront questions that have obsessed protagonists from Oedipus to Yossarian. What begins with the relatively simple questions of the soldiers of the watch in Act I is magnified and complicated as the play moves on. Increasingly tenuous and rarified probes of the maddening gulf between reality and appearance proliferate. Moreover, the contrast between what the simple man cheerfully accepts at face value and what the thoughtful man is driven to question calls into doubt every surface of utterance, act, or thing. In the world of *Hamlet* the cosmic implications of myriad distinctions between "seem" and "be" confront us at every hand.

An index to form looms in the crucial qualitative differences between Hamlet's mode of speech and that of the other inhabitants of his strange world. Because Hamlet's utterances and manners are characteristically unconventional, the other major characters (except Horatio, of course) assume that he is mad or at least temporarily deranged. Conversely, because they *do* speak the simple, relatively safe language of ordinary existence, he assumes that they are hiding or twisting the truth. No one who easily settles for "seeming" is quite trustworthy to the man obsessed with the pursuit of "being." Even the ghost's nature and origin (he may be a diabolical agent, after all) must be tentative to Hamlet until he can settle the validity of the ghost's revelations by the "play within the play." Even Ophelia must be treated as the possible tool of Claudius and Polonius. The presence of Rosencrantz and Guildenstern, not to mention their mission on the journey to England, arouses Hamlet's deepest suspicions. Only Horatio is exempt from distrust, and even to him Hamlet cannot divulge the full dimension of his subversion. Yet though Hamlet seems to speak only in riddle and to act solely with evasion, his utterances and acts always actually bespeak the full measure of his feelings and his increasingly single-minded absorption with his inevitable mission. The important qualification of his honesty lies in his full knowledge that others do not (or cannot) comprehend his real meanings and that they are hardly vitally concerned with deep truths about the state, mankind, or themselves.

MEANING IN FORM

For our purposes, of course, the important fact is that these contrasting levels of knowledge and understanding achieve formal expression. When the king demands some explanation for his extraordinary melancholy, Hamlet replies, "I am too much in the sun" (I, ii). The reply thus establishes, although Claudius does not perceive it, Hamlet's judgment of and opposition to the easy acceptance of "things as they are." And when the queen tries to reconcile him to the inevitability of death in the natural scheme and asks, "Why seems it so particular with thee?" he responds with a revealing contrast between the seeming evidences of mourning and real "woe"—an unequivocal condemnation of the queen's apparently easy acceptance of his father's death as opposed to the vindication of his refusal to view that death as merely an occasion for ceremonial "mourning duties." To the joint entreaty of Claudius and Gertrude that he remain in Denmark, he replies only to his mother: "I shall in all my best obey you, madam" (I, ii). But in thus disdaining to answer the king, he has promised really nothing to his mother, although she takes his reply for complete submission to the royal couple. Again we see that every statement of Hamlet is dialectic: that is, it tends toward double meaning—a kind of countermeaning for the world of Denmark and subtler meaning for Hamlet and the reader.

As we have observed, Hamlet's overriding concern, even before he knows of the ghost's appearance, is the frustration of living in a world attuned to imperfection. He sees, wherever he looks, the pervasive blight in nature, especially human nature. Man, outwardly the acme of creation, is susceptible to "some vicious mole of nature," and no matter how virtuous he otherwise may be, the "dram of evil" or the "stamp of one defect" adulterates nobility (I, iv). Hamlet finds that "one may smile and smile, and be a villain" (I, v). To the uncomprehending Guildenstern, Hamlet emphasizes his basic concern with the strange puzzle of corrupted and corrupting man:

> What a piece of work is a man, how noble in reason, how infinite in faculties, in form and moving how express and admirable, in action how like an angel, in apprehension how

like a god: the beauty of the world, the paragon of animals!
And yet to me what is this quintessence of dust? Man
delights not me—no, nor woman neither, though by your
smiling you seem to say so. [II, ii]

This preoccupation with the paradox of man, recurring as
it does throughout the play, obviously takes precedence
over the revenge ordered by the ghost. From the beginning
of Hamlet's inquiry into the world that surrounds him—
whether he is considering his father's death, his mother's
remarriage, the real or supposed defection of his friends,
or the fallen state of man—we see a developing pattern of
meaning in which man's private world of marriage bed
and lust for power becomes part and parcel of the larger
dimension of identity and worth.

Reams have been written about Hamlet's reasons for the
delay in carrying out his revenge; for our purpose, however, the delay is not particularly important, except as it
emphasizes Hamlet's greater obsession with the pervasive
blight within the cosmos. From almost every bit of verbal
evidence we have he considers as paramount the larger
role of investigator and punitive agent of all mankind (for
example, his bristling verbal attack on the queen, his
accidental—but to his mind quite justifiable—murder of
Polonius, his indignation about the state of the theater and
his instructions to the players, his bitter castigation of
Ophelia, his apparent delight not only in foiling Rosencrantz and Guildenstern but also in arranging their destruction, his fight with Laertes over the grave of Ophelia).
Hamlet, in living up to what he conceives to be a higher
role than that of mere avenger, recurrently broods about
his self-imposed mission, although he characteristically
avoids naming it. In his warfare against bestiality, however, he asserts his allegiance to heaven-sent reason and
its dictates:

What is a man,
If his chief good and market of his time
Be but to sleep and feed? A beast, no more.

> Sure he that made us with such large discourse,
> Looking before and after, gave us not
> That capability and godlike reason
> To fust in us unused. Now, whether it be
> Bestial oblivion, or some craven scruple
> Of thinking too precisely on th'event—
> A thought which, quartered, hath but one part wisdom
> And ever three parts coward—I do not know
> Why yet I live to say, "This thing's to do,"
> Sith I have cause, and will, and strength, and means
> To do't. [IV,iv]

With some envy he regards the active competence of Fortinbras as opposed to his own "craven scruple/Of thinking too precisely on th'event" (that is, his obligation to act to avenge his father's death). Although he promises himself to give priority to that obligation, he goes off to England on what he suspects to be a ruse, presumably because for the moment he prefers outwitting Rosencrantz, Guildenstern, and the king. In short, almost from his first appearance in the play, Hamlet obviously is convinced that to him is given a vast though somewhat general (even ambiguous) task:

> The time is out of joint. O cursèd spite
> That ever I was born to set it right! [I, v]

The "time," like the place of Denmark, has been corrupted by men vulnerable to natural flaws. And once again Hamlet's statement (this time in the philosophic, lyrical mode of *soliloquy*) offers formal reinforcement for the dialectic of the play—the opposition of two attitudes toward human experience that must achieve resolution or synthesis before the play's end.

To the ideal of setting things right, then, Hamlet gives his allegiance. The order he supports transcends the expediency of Polonius, the apostle of practicality, or of Claudius, the devotee of power and sexuality. Again and again we see Hamlet's visionary appraisal of an order so remote from the ken of most people that he appears at times to be inhuman in his refusal to be touched by the scales of ordinary joy or sorrow. He will set straight the political and social order by ferreting out bestiality, corruption (of state, marriage bed, or theater), trickery, and deceit. He is obsessed throughout the play by the "dusty death" to which all must come, and his speeches abound in images of sickness and death. But if he has finally gotten the king, along with his confederates, "Hoist with his own petard" (III, iv), Hamlet also brings himself through his own trickery, deceit, perhaps even his own ambitions, to the fate of Yorick.

Thus does the play turn upon itself. It is no simple morality play. It begins in an atmosphere of mourning for the late king and apprehensions about the appearance of the ghost, and it ends in a scene littered with corpses. The noble prince, like his father before him, is, despite his best intentions, sullied by the "foul crimes done in my days of nature" (I, v). All men apparently are, as Laertes says of himself, "as a woodcock to mine own springe" (V, ii) (that is, like a fool caught in his own snare). And although all beauty and aspiration (a counterpoint theme) are reduced ultimately to a "quintessence of dust," it is in Hamlet's striving, however imperfectly and destructively, to bend the order of nature to a higher law that we must see the play's tragic assertion in the midst of an otherwise pervasive and unrelieved pessimism.

The design of the play can be perceived in part by the elaborate play upon the words "see" and "know" and their cognates. Whereas the deity can be understood as "Looking before and after" (IV, iv), the player king points out to his queen that there is a hiatus between what man intends and what he does: "Our thoughts are ours, their ends none of our own" (III, ii). Forced by Hamlet to consider the difference between her two husbands, Gertrude cries out in anguish against having to see into her own motivations:

> O Hamlet, speak no more.
> Thou turn'st mine eyes into my very soul,

> And there I see such black and grainèd spots
> As will not leave their tinct. [III, iv]

But she does not see the ghost of her former husband, nor can she see the metaphysical implications of Hamlet's reason in madness. The blind eye sockets of Yorick's skull once "saw" their quota of experience, but most people in Denmark are quite content with the surface appearances of life and refuse even to consider the ends to which mortality brings all men. The intricate weavings of images of sight thus become a kind of tragic algebra for the plight of a man who "seemed to find his way without his eyes" (II, i) and who found himself at last "placed to the view" of the "yet unknowing world" (V, ii).

The traveling players had acted out the crime of Denmark on another stage, but their play seemed to most of the audience only a diversion in a pageant of images designed to keep men from really knowing themselves or their fellows as corrupted by nature and doomed at last to become "my Lady Worm's, chapless and knocked about the mazzard with a sexton's spade" (V, i). The contexts of these words assert a systematic enlargement of the play's tragic pronouncement of man's ignorance in the midst of appearances. Formally, the play progresses from the relatively simple speculations of the soldiers of the watch to the sophisticated complexity of metaphysical inquiry. There may not be final answers to the questions Hamlet ponders, but the questions assume a formal order as their dimensions are structured by speech and action—in miniature, by the play within the play; in extension, by the tragedy itself.

Ophelia, in her madness, utters perhaps the key line of the play: "Lord, we know what we are, but we know not what we may be" (IV, v). Hamlet has earlier said that if the king reacts as expected to the play within the play, "I know my course" (II, ii). But he is not sure of his course, nor does he even know himself—at least not until the final act. In the prison of the world he can only pursue his destiny, which, as he realizes before the duel, inevitably leads to the grave. The contest between aspiring man and natural order in which Hamlet finds himself is all too unequal: Idealism turns out to be a poor match for the prison walls of either Denmark or the grave.

III. Limitations of the Formalistic Approach

By the 1950s, dissent was in the air. Still outraged by the award of the Bollingen Prize for Poetry to Ezra Pound in 1949, some voices thought they detected a pronounced elitism, if not more sinister rightist tendencies, in the New Critics, their disciples, and the poets to whom they had granted the favor of their attention. All the details of this political argument need not compel our attention here. What does concern us is the realization that by 1955, some doubters were pointing to the formalistic critics' absorption with details, their greater success with intensive than with extensive criticism, their obvious preference for poets like Eliot and Yeats, and their lack of success with the novel and the drama (C. Hugh Holman, "The Defense of Art: Criticism Since 1930," *The Development of American Literary Criticism*, ed. Floyd Stovall [Chapel Hill: University of North Carolina Press, 1955], pp. 238–239).

Less general caveats have emphasized the restriction of formalistic criticism to a certain kind of literature simply because that kind proved itself especially amenable—lyric poetry generally but especially English poetry of the seventeenth century and the "modernist" poetry that stems from Pound and Eliot, and some virtually self-selecting fiction that significantly displays poetic textures (for example, *Moby-Dick* and *Ulysses*). New Critics tended to ignore or undervalue some poetry and other genres that do not easily respond to formalistic approaches (for example, the poetry of Wordsworth and Shelley, philosophical and didactic verse generally, and the essay). Apparently the problems increase whenever the language of the literary work tends to approach that of the philosopher, or even the critic himself. The formalistic approach sometimes seems to lapse into a "treasure hunt" for "objective correlatives," conceits, "the image," or ironic turns of phrase. It has not seemed to work particularly well for most American poetry written since 1950; as students often point out, it tends to overlook "feeling" and appears heartless and cold in its absorption with form.

More recently, Robert Langbaum has pronounced the New Criticism "dead—dead of its very success." For, says he, "We are all New Critics nowadays, whether we like it or not, in that we cannot avoid discerning and appreciating wit in poetry, or reading with close attention to words, images, ironies, and so on" (*The Modern Spirit: Essays on the Continuity of Nineteenth and Twentieth Century Literature* [New York: Oxford University Press, 1970], p. 11). There is more to criticism than "understanding the text, [which] is where criticism begins, not where it ends" (p. 14). Langbaum believes that the New Criticism took us for a time outside the "main stream of criticism" (Aristotle, Coleridge, Arnold), but now we should return, with the tools of explication and analysis given us by the New Critics, to that "main stream." That is, instead of insisting upon its autonomy, we must resume relating literature to life and ideas.

CHAPTER 3

THE PSYCHOLOGICAL APPROACH

I. AIMS AND PRINCIPLES

Having discussed two of the basic approaches to literary understanding, the traditional and the formalistic, we now examine a third interpretive perspective, the "psychological." Of all the critical approaches to literature, this is perhaps the most controversial, the most abused, and—for most readers—the least appreciated. Yet, for all the difficulties involved in its proper application to interpretive analysis, the psychological approach can be fascinating and rewarding. Our purpose in this chapter is threefold: (1) to account briefly for the misunderstanding of psychological criticism, (2) to outline the psychological theory most commonly used as an interpretive tool by modern critics, and (3) to show by examples how the reader may apply this mode of interpretation to enhance his understanding and appreciation of literature.

The idea of *enhancement* must be underscored as a preface to our discussion. It is axiomatic that no single approach can exhaust the manifold interpretive possibilites of a worthwhile literary work; each approach has its own peculiar limitations. As we have already discovered, the limitations of the traditional approach lie in its tendency to overlook the structural intricacies of the work. The formalistic approach, on the other hand, often neglects historical and sociological contexts that may provide important insights into the meaning of the work. In turn, the crucial limitation of the psychological approach is its aesthetic inadequacy: Psychological interpretation can afford many profound clues toward solving a work's thematic and symbolic mysteries, but it can seldom account for the beautiful symmetry of a well-wrought poem or of a fictional masterpiece. Though the psychological approach is an excellent tool for "reading beneath the lines," the interpretive craftsman must often use other tools, such as the traditional and the formalistic, for a proper rendering of the lines themselves.

A. Abuses and Misunderstandings of the Psychological Approach

In the general sense of the word there is nothing new about the psychological approach. As early as the fourth century B.C., Aristotle used this approach in setting forth his classic definition of tragedy as combining the emotions of pity and terror to produce catharsis. The "compleat gentleman" of the English Renaissance, Sir Philip Sidney, with his statements about the moral effects of poetry, was "psychologizing" literature, as were such Romantic poets as Coleridge, Wordsworth, and Shelley with their theories of the imagination. In this sense, then, virtually every literary critic has been concerned at some time with the psychology of writing or responding to literature.

During the twentieth century, however, psychological criticism has come to be associated with a particular school of thought; the psychoanalytic theories of Sigmund Freud (1852–1939) and his followers. From this association have derived most of the abuses and misunderstandings of the modern psychological approach to literature. Abuses of the approach have resulted from an excess of enthusiasm, which has been manifested in several ways. First, the practitioners of the Freudian approach often push their critical theses too hard, forcing literature into a Procrustean bed of psychoanalytic theory at the expense of other relevant considerations (for example, the work's total thematic and aesthetic context). Second, the literary criticism of the psychoanalytic extremists has at times degenerated into a special occultism with its own mystique and jargon exclusively for the "in-group." Third, many critics of the "psychological school" have been either literary scholars who have understood the principles of psychology imperfectly or professional psychologists who have had little feeling for literature as art: The former have abused Freudian insights through oversimplification and distortion; the latter have bruised our literary sensibilities.

These abuses have given rise to a widespread mistrust of the psychological approach as a tool for critical analysis. Conservative scholars and teachers of literature, often shocked by such terms as "anal eroticism," "phallic symbol," and "Oedipal complex" and confused by the clinical diagnoses of literary problems (for example, the interpretation of Hamlet's character as a "severe case of hysteria on a cyclothymic basis"—that is, a manic-depressive psychosis), have rejected all psychological criticism, other than the commonsense type, as pretentious nonsense. In some quarters this reaction goes so far as to brand the Freudian approach as not only invalid but even indecent. By explaining a few of the principles of Freudian psychology that have been applied to literary interpretation and by providing some cautionary remarks, we hope to introduce the reader to a balanced critical perspective that will enable him or her to appreciate the instructive possibilities of the psychological approach but to avoid the pitfalls of either extremist attitude.

B. Freud's Theories

The foundation of Freud's contribution to modern psychology is his emphasis on the unconscious aspects of the human psyche. A brilliant creative genius, Freud provided convincing evidence, through his many carefully recorded case studies, that most of our actions are motivated by psychic forces over which we have very limited control. He demonstrated that, like the iceberg, the human mind is structured so that its great weight and density lie beneath the surface (below the level of consciousness). In "The Anatomy of the Mental Personality, Lecture XXI," *New Introductory Lectures on Psychoanalysis* [New York: Norton, 1964], Freud discriminates between the levels of conscious and unconscious mental activity:

> The oldest and best meaning of the word "unconscious" is the descriptive one; we call "unconscious" any mental process the existence of which we are obligated to assume— because, for instance, we infer it in some way from its effects—but of which we are not directly aware. . . . If we want to be more accurate, we should modify the statement by saying that we call a process "unconscious" when we have to assume that it was active *at a certain time,* although *at that time* we knew nothing about it. [pp. 99–100]

Freud further emphasizes the importance of the unconscious by pointing out that even the "most conscious processes are conscious for only a short period; quite soon they become *latent,* though they can easily become conscious again" (p. 100). In view of this, Freud defines two kinds of unconscious:

> one which is transformed into conscious material easily and under conditions which frequently arise, and another in the case of which such a transformation is difficult, can only come about with a considerable expenditure of energy, or may never occur at all. . . . We call the unconscious which is only latent, and so can easily become conscious, the "preconscious," and keep the name "unconscious" for the other. [p. 101]

That most of the individual's mental processes are unconscious is thus Freud's first major premise. The second (which has been rejected by a great many professional psychologists, including some of Freud's own disciples— for example, Carl Jung and Alfred Adler) is that all human behavior is motivated ultimately by what we would call sexuality. Freud designates the prime psychic force as libido, or sexual energy. His third major premise is that because of the powerful social taboos attached to certain sexual impulses, many of our desires and memories are repressed (that is, actively excluded from conscious awareness).

Starting from these three premises, we may examine several corollaries of Freudian theory. Principal among these is Freud's assignment of the mental processes to three psychic zones: the *id*, the *ego*, and the *superego*. An explanation of these zones may be illustrated with Freud's own diagram:

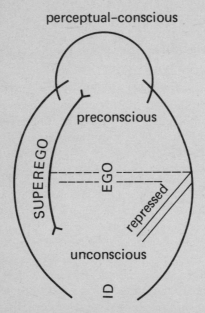

The diagram reveals immediately the vast portion of the mental apparatus that is not conscious. Furthermore, it helps to clarify the relationship between ego, id, and superego, as well as their collective relationship to the conscious and the unconscious. We should note that the id is entirely unconscious and that only a small portion of the ego and superego is conscious. With this diagram as a guide, we may define the nature and functions of the three psychic zones.

1. The id is the reservoir of libido, the primary source of all psychic energy. It functions to fulfill the primordial life principle, which Freud considers to be the *pleasure principle*. Without consciousness or semblance of rational order, the id is characterized by a tremendous and amorphous vitality. Speaking metaphorically, Freud explains this "obscure inaccessible part of our personality" as "a chaos, a cauldron of seething excitement [with] no organization and no unified will, only an impulsion to obtain satisfaction for the instinctual needs, in accordance with the pleasure principle" (pp. 103–104). He further stresses that the "laws of logic—above all, the law of contradiction—do not hold for processes of the id. Contradictory impulses exist side by side without neutralizing each other or drawing apart. . . . Naturally, the id knows no values, no good and evil, no morality" (pp. 104–105).

The id is, in short, the source of all our aggressions and desires. It is lawless, asocial, and amoral. Its function is to gratify our instincts for pleasure without regard for social conventions, legal ethics, or moral restraint. Unchecked, it would lead us to any lengths—to destruction and even self-destruction—to satisfy its impulses for pleasure. Safety for the self and for others does not lie within the province of the id; its concern is purely for instinctual gratification, heedless of consequence. For centuries before Freud, this force was recognized in human nature but often attributed to supernatural and external rather than to natural and internal forces: The id as defined by Freud is identical in many respects to the Devil as defined by theologians. Thus there is a certain psychological validity in the old saying that a rambunctious child (whose id has not yet been

125

brought under proper control by ego and superego) is "full of the devil." We may also see in young children (and neurotic adults) certain uncontrolled impulses toward pleasure that often lead to excessive self-indulgence and even to self-injury.

2. In view of the id's dangerous potentialities, it is necessary that other psychic agencies function to protect the individual and society. The first of these regulating agencies, that which protects the individual, is the ego. This is the rational governing agent of the psyche. Though the ego lacks the strong vitality of the id, it is needed to regulate the instinctual drives of the id so that these energies may be released in nondestructive behavioral patterns. And though a large portion is unconscious, the ego nevertheless comprises what we ordinarily think of as the conscious mind. As Freud points out, "In popular language, we may say that the ego stands for reason and circumspection, while the id stands for the untamed passions." Whereas the id is governed solely by the pleasure principle, the ego is governed by the *reality principle*. Consequently, the ego serves as intermediary between the world within and the world without.

3. The other regulating agent, that which primarily functions to protect society, is the superego. Largely unconscious, the superego is the moral censoring agency, the repository of conscience and pride. It is, as Freud says in "The Anatomy of the Mental Personality," the "representative of all moral restrictions, the advocate of the impulse toward perfection, in short it is as much as we have been able to apprehend psychologically of what people call the 'higher' things in human life" (p. 95). Acting either directly or through the ego, the superego serves to repress or inhibit the drives of the id, to block off and thrust back into the unconscious those impulses toward pleasure that society regards as unacceptable, such impulses as overt aggression, sexual passions, and the Oedipal instinct. Freud attributes the development of the superego to the parental influence that manifests itself in terms of punishment for

what society considers to be bad behavior and reward for what is considered good behavior. An overactive superego creates an unconscious sense of guilt (hence the familiar term "guilt complex" and the popular misconception that Freud advocated the relaxing of all moral inhibitions and social restraints). Whereas the id is dominated by the pleasure principle and the ego by the reality principle, the superego is dominated by the *morality principle*. We might say that the id would make us devils, that the superego would have us behave as angels (or, worse, as creatures of absolute social conformity), and that it remains for the ego to keep us healthy human beings by maintaining a balance between these two opposing forces. It was this balance that Freud advocated—not a complete removal of inhibiting factors.

One of the most instructive applications of this Freudian tripartition to literary criticism is the well-known essay "In Nomine Diaboli" by Henry A. Murray (*New England Quarterly*, 24 [1951], 435–452), a knowledgeable psycho-analyst and a sensitive literary critic as well. In analyzing Herman Melville's masterpiece *Moby-Dick* with the tools provided by Freud, Murray explains the White Whale as a symbolic embodiment of the strict conscience of New England Puritanism (that is, as a projection of Melville's own superego). Captain Ahab, the monomaniac who leads the crew of the *Pequod* to destruction through his insane compulsion to pursue and strike back at the creature who has injured him, is interpreted as the symbol of a rapacious and uncontrollable id. Starbuck, the sane Christian and first mate who struggles to mediate between the forces embodied in Moby Dick and Ahab, symbolizes a balanced and sensible rationalism (that is, the ego).

Though many scholars are reluctant to accept Freud's tripartition of the human psyche, they have not reacted against this aspect of psychoanalytic criticism so strongly as against the application of his sexual theories to the symbol-ic interpretation of literature. Let us briefly examine the highlights of such theories. Perhaps the most controversial (and, to many persons, the most offensive) facet of psychoanalytic criticism is its tendency to interpret imagery in terms of sexuality. Following Freud's example in his interpretation of dreams, the psychoanalytic critic tends to see all concave images (ponds, flowers, cups or vases, caves, and hollows) as female or womb symbols, and all images whose length exceeds their diameter (towers, mountain peaks, snakes, knives, lances, and swords) as male or phallic symbols. Perhaps even more objectionable to some is the interpretation of such activities as dancing, riding, and flying as symbols of sexual pleasure: For example, in *The Life and Works of Edgar Allan Poe: A Psycho-Analytic Interpretation* (London: Imago, 1949), Princess Marie Bonaparte interprets the figure of Psyche in "Ulalume" as an ambivalent mother figure, both the longed-for mother and the mother as superego who shields her son from his incestuous instincts, concluding with the following startling observation: "Psyche's drooping, trailing wings in this poem symbolise in concrete form Poe's physical impotence. We know that flying, to all races, unconsciously symbolises the sex act, and that antiquity often represented the penis erect and winged." For the skeptical reader Bonaparte provides this explanation:

> Infinite are the symbols man has the capacity to create, as indeed, the dreams and religions of the savage and civilized well show. Every natural object may be utilised to this end yet, despite their multiple shapes, the objects and relations to which they attach are relatively few: these include the beings we loved first, such as mother, father, brothers or sisters and their bodies, but mainly our own bodies and genitals, and theirs. Almost all symbolism is sexual, in its widest sense, taking the word as the deeply-buried primal urge behind all expressions of love, from the cradle to the grave. [p. 294]

Although such observations as these may have a sound psychoanalytic basis, their relevance to sound critical analysis has been questioned by many scholars. We may sympathize with their incredulousness when we encounter

the Freudian essay that interprets even a seemingly innocent fairy tale like "Little Red Riding Hood" as an allegory
of the age-old conflict between male and female in which
the plucky young virgin, whose red cap is a menstrual
symbol, outwits the ruthless, sex-hungry "wolf" (Erich
Fromm, *The Forgotten Language* [New York: Grove Press,
1957], pp. 235–241).

Somewhat less controversial than Freudian dream symbolism are Freud's theories concerning child psychology.
Contrary to traditional beliefs, Freud found infancy and
childhood a period of intense sexual experience, sexual in
a sense much broader than is commonly attached to the
term. During the first five years of his life, the child passes
through a series of phases in his erotic development, each
phase being characterized by emphasis on a particular
erogenous zone (that is, a portion of the body in which
sexual pleasure becomes localized). Freud indicated three
such zones: the *oral,* the *anal,* and the *genital.* (Note that
the uninitiated layman, unfamiliar with the breadth of
Freud's term, generally restricts the meaning of "sexuality"
to "*genital* sexuality.") These zones are associated not only
with pleasure in stimulation but also with the gratification
of our vital needs: eating, elimination, and reproduction. If
for some reason the individual is frustrated in gratifying
these needs during childhood, his adult personality may be
warped accordingly (that is, his development may be ar-
rested or *fixated*). For example, adults who are compulsively fastidious may suffer, according to the psychoanalyst, from an anal fixation traceable to overly strict toilet
training during early childhood. Likewise, compulsive
cigarette smoking may be interpreted as a symptom of oral
fixation traceable to premature weaning. Even among
"normal" adults, sublimated responses occur when the
individual is vicariously stimulated by images associated
with one of the major erogenous zones. In his *Fiction and
the Unconscious* (Boston: Beacon Press, 1957), Simon O.
Lesser suggests that the anal-erotic quality in *Robinson
Crusoe* (manifested in the hero's scrupulous record keep-

ing and orderliness) accounts at least partially for the unconscious appeal of Defoe's masterpiece (p. 306).

According to Freud, the child reaches the stage of "genital primacy" around the age of five years, at which time the Oedipus complex manifests itself. In simple terms, the Oedipus complex derives from the boy's unconscious rivalry with his father for the love of his mother. Freud borrowed the term from the classic Sophoclean tragedy in which the hero unwittingly murders his father and marries his mother. In *The Ego and the Id* (New York: Norton, 1962), Freud describes the complex as follows:

> the boy deals with his father by identifying himself with him. For a time these two relationships [the child's devotion to his mother and identification with his father] proceed side by side, until the boy's sexual wishes in regard to his mother become more intense and his father is perceived as an obstacle to them; from this the Oedipus complex originates. His identification with his father then takes on a hostile colouring and changes into a wish to get rid of his father in order to take his place with his mother. Henceforward his relation to his father is ambivalent; it seems as if the ambivalence inherent in the identification from the beginning had become manifest. An ambivalent attitude to his father and an object-relation of a solely affectionate kind to his mother make up the content of the simple positive Oedipus complex in a boy. [pp. 21–22]

Further ramifications of the Oedipus complex are a fear of castration and an identification of the father with strict authority in all forms; subsequent hostility to authority is therefore associated with the Oedipal ambivalence to which Freud refers. A story like Nathaniel Hawthorne's "My Kinsman, Major Molineux," for instance, has been interpreted by Lesser as essentially a symbolic rebellion against the father figure. And with this insight we may find meaning in the young hero's curious laughter as he watches the cruel tarring and feathering of his once-respected relative: The youth is expressing his unconscious joy in being released from parental authority. Now he is free, as the friendly stranger suggests, to make his own way in the adult world without the help (and restraint) of his kinsman.

II. THE PSYCHOLOGICAL APPROACH IN PRACTICE

A. *Hamlet:* The Oedipus Complex

Although Freud himself made some applications of his theories to art and literature, it remained for an English disciple, psychoanalyst Ernest Jones, to provide us with the first full-scale psychoanalytic treatment of a major literary work. Jones's *Hamlet and Oedipus,* originally published as an essay in *The American Journal of Psychology* in 1910, was later revised and enlarged in a paperback edition (Garden City, N.Y.: Doubleday [Anchor Books], 1949).

Jones bases his argument on the thesis that Hamlet's much debated delay in killing his uncle, Claudius, is to be explained in terms of internal rather than external circumstances and that the "play is mainly concerned with a hero's unavailing fight against what can only be called a disordered mind." In his carefully documented essay Jones builds a highly persuasive case history of Hamlet as a psychoneurotic suffering from manic-depressive hysteria combined with an *abulia* (an inability to exercise will power and come to decisions)— all of which may be traced to the hero's severely repressed Oedipal feelings. Jones points out that no really satisfying argument has ever been substantiated for the idea that Hamlet avenges his father's murder as quickly as practicable. Shakespeare makes Claudius's guilt as well as Hamlet's duty perfectly clear from the outset—if we are to trust the words of the ghost and the gloomy insights of the hero himself. The fact is, however, that Hamlet does not fulfill this duty until absolutely forced to do so by physical circumstances—and even then only after Gertrude, his mother, is dead. Jones also elucidates the strong misogyny that Hamlet displays

131

throughout the play, especially as it is directed against Ophelia, and his almost physical revulsion from sex. All of this adds up to a classic example of the neurotically repressed Oedipus complex.

The ambivalence that typifies the child's attitude toward his father is dramatized in the characters of the ghost (the good, lovable father with whom the boy identifies) and Claudius (the hated father as tyrant and rival), both of whom are dramatic projections of the hero's own conscious-unconscious ambivalence toward the father figure. The ghost represents the conscious ideal of fatherhood, the image that is socially acceptable:

> See, what a grace was seated on this brow:
> Hyperion's curls, the front of Jove himself,
> An eye like Mars, to threaten and command,
> A station like the herald Mercury
> New-lighted on a heaven-kissing hill,
> A combination and a form indeed,
> Where every god did seem to set his seal,
> To give the world assurance of a man:
> This was your husband. [III, iv]

His view of Claudius, on the other hand, represents Hamlet's repressed hostility toward his father as a rival for his mother's affection. This new king-father is the symbolic perpetrator of the very deeds toward which the son is impelled by his own unconscious motives: murder of his father and incest with his mother. Hamlet cannot bring himself to kill Claudius becuase to do so he must, in a psychological sense, kill himself. His delay and frustration in trying to fulfill the ghost's demand for vengeance may therefore be explained by the fact that, as Jones puts it, the "thought of incest and parricide combined is too intolerable to be borne. One part of him tries to carry out the task, the other flinches inexorably from the thought of it" (pp. 78–79).

One of the leading contemporary Freudian critics, Norman N. Holland, has neatly summed up the reasons both for Hamlet's delay and also for our 300-year delay in comprehending Hamlet's true motives:

> Now what do critics mean when they say that Hamlet cannot act because of his Oedipus complex? The argument is very simple, very elegant. One, people over the centuries have been unable to say why Hamlet delays in killing the man who murdered his father and married his mother. Two, psychoanalytic experience shows that every child wants to do just exactly that. Three, Hamlet delays because he cannot punish Claudius for doing what he himself wished to do as a child and, unconsciously, still wishes to do: he would be punishing himself. Four, the fact that this wish is unconscious explains why people could not explain Hamlet's delay. (*The Shakespearean Imagination* [Bloomington: Indiana University Press, 1968], p. 158.)

A corollary to the Oedipal problem in *Hamlet* is the pronounced misogyny in Hamlet's character. Because of his mother's abnormally sensual affection for her son, an affection that would have deeply marked Hamlet as a child with an Oedipal neurosis, he has in the course of his psychic development repressed his incestuous impulses so severely that this repression colors his attitude toward all women: "The total reaction culminates in the bitter misogyny of his outburst against Ophelia, who is devastated at having to bear a reaction so wholly out of proportion to her own offense and has no idea that in reviling her Hamlet is really expressing his bitter resentment against his mother" (Jones, p.96). The famous "Get thee to a nunnery" speech has even more sinister overtones than are generally recognized, explains Jones, when we understand the pathological degree of Hamlet's condition and read "nunnery" as Elizabethan slang for "brothel."

> The underlying theme relates ultimately to the splitting of the mother image which the infantile unconscious effects into two opposite pictures: one of a virginal Madonna, an inaccessible saint towards whom all sensual approaches are

unthinkable, and the other of a sensual creature accessible to everyone. . . . When sexual repression is highly pronounced, as with Hamlet, then both types of women are felt to be hostile: the pure one out of resentment at her repulses, the sensual one out of the temptation who offers to plunge into guiltiness. Misogyny, as in the play, is the inevitable result. [pp. 97–98]

Although it has been attacked by the anti-Freudians and occasionally disparaged as "obsolete" by the neo-Freudians, Jones's critical *tour de force* has nevertheless attained status as a modern classic. "Both as an important seminal work which led to a considerable re-examination of *Hamlet,* and as an example of a thorough and intelligent application of psychoanalysis to drama," writes Claudia C. Morrison, "Jones's essay stands as the single most important Freudian study of literature to appear in America prior to the present decade" (*Freud and the Critic* [Chapel Hill: University of North Carolina Press, 1968], p. 175).

B. Rebellion Against the Father in *Huckleberry Finn*

Mark Twain's great novel has this in common with Shakespeare's masterpiece: Both are concerned with the theme of rebellion—with a hostile treatment of the father figure. (It is interesting to note that in both works the father is finally slain and that knowledge of this death brings a curious sense of relief—and release—for the reader.) As we have seen, from the psychoanalytic viewpoint all rebellion is in essence a rejection of parental, especially paternal, authority. Sociologically speaking, Huck rebels against the unjust, inhumane restrictions of a society that condones slavery, hypocrisy, and cruelty. However, Mark Twain showed a remarkable pre-Freudian insight when he dramatized this theme of rebellion in the portrayal of Huck's destestable father as the lowest common denominator of social authority. The main plot of the novel is launched with Huck's escape from "pap" (whose name, in keeping with the reductive treatment of this father figure, is not captialized), a flight that coincides with Jim's escape from Miss Watson.

Symbolically, Huck and Jim, in order to gain freedom and to regain prelapsarian bliss (the happiness enjoyed by Adam before the Fall), must escape whatever is represented by Miss Watson and pap (who reminds Huck of Adam all covered with mud, that is, Adam after the Fall). Despite their superficial and rather melodramatic differences, Miss Watson and pap have much in common. They represent extremes of authority: authority at its most respectable and at its most contemptible. What is more, they both represent social and legal morality, again in the extremes of the social spectrum. Notwithstanding his obvious worthlessness, pap is still Huck's sole guardian by law and holds the power of life and death, an authority condoned by society, over his son—just as Miss Watson has a similar power over Jim. In the light of such authority both Miss Watson and pap may be said to represent the superego (for example, when Huck goes against his conscience by refusing to turn Jim in to the authorities, it is the letter to Miss Watson that he tears up). In this sense, then, it is to escape the oppressive tyranny and cruel restraints of the superego that Huck and Jim take flight on the river.

Huckleberry Finn cannot by any means be read as a psychological allegory, and it would be foolish to set up a strict one-to-one ratio of characters and events to ideas, particularly because Mark Twain wrote the book with no notion of Freudian concepts. But like most great writers, Twain knew human nature and from the psychoanalytic perspective, a "linked analogy" can be seen between the structure of his novel and the Freudian structure of the human psyche. Water in any form is generally interpreted by the psychoanalysts as a female symbol, more specifically as a maternal symbol. From the superegoistic milieu of society Huck and Jim flee to the river, where they find freedom. Except when invaded by men, the river is characterized by a strange, fluid, dreamlike peacefulness; Huck's most lyrical comments are those describing the beauty of the river:

> Two or three days and nights went by; I reckon I might say they swum by, they slid along so quiet and smooth and

lovely. . . . Not a sound anywheres—perfectly still—just like
the whole world was asleep. . . . [Then] the nice breeze
springs up, and comes fanning you from over there, so cool
and fresh and sweet to smell on account of the woods and
flowers; but sometimes not that way, because they've left
dead fish laying around, gars and such, and they do get
pretty rank. . . . [And] we would watch the lonesomeness of
the river, and kind of lazy along, and by and by lazy off to
sleep. . . . It's lovely to live on a raft. We had the sky up there,
all speckled with stars, and we used to lay on our backs and
look up at them, and discuss about whether they was made
or only just happened. . . . Jim said the moon could 'a' *laid*
them; well, that looked kind of reasonable, so I didn't say
nothing against it, because I've seen a frog lay most as many,
so of course it could be done. [Chap. 19]

The foregoing passage is redolent with female-maternal
imagery; it also suggests the dark, mysterious serenity
associated with the prenatal state, as well as with death, in
psychoanalytic interpretation. The tension between land
and water may be seen as analogous to that between the
conscious and the unconscious in Freudian theory. Lacking
a real mother, Huck finds his symbolic mother in the river;
in Freudian terms, he returns to the womb. From this
matrix he undergoes a series of symbolic deaths and
rebirths, punctuated structurally by the episodes on land.
As James M. Cox *Sewanee Review*, 62 [1954], 389–405) has
pointed out, Huck's fake murder in escaping from pap is
crucial to our understanding the central informing pattern
of death and rebirth: "Having killed himself, Huck is
'dead' throughout the entire journey down the river. He is
indeed the man without identity who is reborn at almost
every river bend, not because he desires a new role, but
because he must re-create himself to elude the forces
which close in on him from every side. The rebirth theme
which began with pap's reform becomes the driving idea
behind the entire action." Enhancing this pattern is the
hermaphroditic figure of Jim, Huck's adopted friend and

parent, whose blackness coincides with the darkness associated with death, the unconscious, and the maternal. (We are reminded of Whitman's celebration of death as the Dark Mother in such famous poems as "Out of the Cradle Endlessly Rocking" and "When Lilacs Last in the Dooryard Bloom'd.") Jim's qualities are more maternal than paternal. He possesses the gentleness, unquestioning loyalty, and loving kindness that we traditionally ascribe to the mother, in sharp contrast to the brutal authoritarianism of pap.

Viewed from a slightly different psychological angle, *Huckleberry Finn* is a story of the child as victim, embodying the betrayal-of-innocence theme that has become one of the chief motifs in American fiction. Philip Young, in *Ernest Hemingway* (New York: Holt, Rinehart and Winston, 1952), has detected similarities between Huck's plight and that of the Hemingway hero. Young sees Huck as the wounded child, permanently scarred by traumas of death and violence; he has counted thirteen separate corpses in the novel and observes that virtually every major episode in the book ends with violence or death. Young makes explicit the causal relationship between the traumatic experiences suffered by Huck (and later by Hemingway's protagonists) and the growing preoccupation with death that dominates much modern literature.

> [Huck] is a wounded and damaged boy. He will never get over the terror he has seen and been through, is guilt-ridden and can't sleep at night for his thoughts. When he is able to sleep he is tortured with bad dreams. . . . This is a boy who has undergone an unhappy process of growing up, and has grown clean out of his creator's grasp. . . . Precisely as Clemens could never solve his own complications, save in the unmitigated but sophomoric pessimism of his last books, so he could not solve them for Huck, who had got too hot to handle and was dropped. What the man never realized was that in his journey by water he had been hinting at a solution all along: an excessive exposure to violence and death

produced first a compulsive fascination with dying, and finally an ideal symbol for it. [pp. 200-201]

This "ideal symbol" is the dark river itself, which is suggestive of the Freudian death instinct, the unconscious instinct in all living things to return to the inorganic state and thereby achieve permanent surcease from the pain of living. Our recognition of these symbolic implications does not, by any means, exhaust the interpretive potential of Twain's novel, nor does it preclude insights gained from other critical approaches. Such recognition should enhance our appreciation of the greatness of *Huckleberry Finn* by revealing that Mark Twain produced a masterwork that, intentionally or not, has appealed in a profound psychological way to many generations of readers.

C. "Young Goodman Brown": Id Versus Superego

The theme of innocence betrayed is also central to Nathaniel Hawthorne's "Young Goodman Brown," the tale of the young bridegroom who leaves his wife Faith to spend a night with Satan in the forest. The events of that terrifying night are a classic "traumatic experience" for the youth. At the center of the dark wilderness he discovers a witches' Sabbath involving all the honored teachers, preachers, and friends of his village. The climax is reached when his own immaculate bride is brought forth to stand by his side and pledge eternal allegiance to the Fiend of Hell. Following this climactic moment in which the hero resists the diabolical urge to join the fraternity of evil, he wakes to find himself in the deserted forest wondering if what has happened was dream or reality. Regardless of the answer, he is a changed man. He returns in the morning to the village and to his Faith, but he is never at peace with himself again. Henceforth he can never hear the singing of a holy hymn without also hearing echoes of the anthem of sin from that terrible night in the forest. He shrinks even from the side of Faith. His dying hour is gloom and no hopeful epitaph is engraved upon his tombstone.

Aside from the clearly intended allegorical meanings discussed elsewhere in this book, it is the story's underlying psychological implications that attract us. We start with the assumption that, through symbolism and technique, "Young Goodman Brown" means more than it says. In this respect our task is one of extrapolation, an inferring of the unknown from the known. Our first premise is that Brown's journey is more than a physical one; it is a psychological one as well. To see what this journey means in psychological terms, we need to examine the setting, the time and place. Impelled by unmistakably libidinal force, the hero moves from the village of Salem into the forest. The village is a place of light and order, both social and spiritual order. Brown leaves Faith behind in the town at sunset and returns to Faith in the morning. The journey into the wilderness is taken in the night: "My journey ... forth and back again," explains the young man to his wife, "must needs be done 'twixt now and sunrise." It is in the forest, a place of darkness and unknown terrors, that Brown meets the Devil. On one level, then, the village may be equated with consciousness, the forest with the dark recesses of the unconscious. But, more accurately, the village, as a place of social and moral order (and inhibition) is analogous to Freud's superego, conscience, the morally inhibiting agent of the psyche; the forest, as a place of wild, untamed passions and terrors, has the attributes of the Freudian id. As mediator between these opposing forces, Brown himself resembles the poor ego, which tries to effect a healthy balance and is shattered because it is unable to do so.

Why can't he reconcile these forces? Is his predicament that of all men, as is indicated by his name? If so, are all men destined to die in gloom? Certainly, Hawthorne implies, men cannot remain always in the village, outside the forest. And sooner or later, all men must confront Satan. Let us examine this diabolical figure for a moment. When we first see him (after being prepared by Brown's expressed fear, "What if the devil himself should be at my very elbow!"), he is "seated at the foot of an old tree"—an allusion to the "old tree" of forbidden fruit and the knowledge of sin. He is described as "bearing a considerable resemblance" to the hero himself. He is, in short, Brown's own alter ego, the dramatic projection of a part of Brown's psyche, just as Faith is the projection of another part of that psyche. The staff Satan is carrying, similar to the maple stick he later gives to Brown, is like a "great black snake . . . a living serpent"—a standard Freudian symbol for the uncontrollable phallus. As he moves on through the forest, Brown encounters other figures, the most respected of his moral tutors: old Goody Cloyse, Deacon Gookin, and, at last, even Faith herself, her pink ribbon reflecting the ambiguity that Brown is unable to resolve (for pink is the mixture of white for purity and red for passion). Thoroughly unnerved, then maddened, by disillusionment, Brown capitulates to the wild evil in this heart of darkness and becomes "himself the chief horror of the scene, [shrinking] not from its other horrors." That the whole lurid scene may be interpreted as the projection of Brown's formerly repressed impulses is indicated in Hawthorne's description of the transformed protagonist:

> In truth, all through the haunted forest there could be nothing more frightful than the figure of Goodman Brown. On he flew among the black pines, brandishing his staff with frenzied gestures, now giving vent to an inspiration of horrid blasphemy, and now shouting forth such laughter as set all the echoes of the forest laughing like demons around him. *The fiend in his own shape is less hideous than when he rages in the breast of man.* [Our italics]

Though Hawthorne implies that Brown's problem is that of Everyman, he does not suggest that all men share Brown's gloomy destiny. Like Freud, Hawthorne saw the dangers of an overactive suppression of libido and the consequent development of a tyrannous superego (though he thought of the problem in his own terms as an imbalance of head versus heart). Goodman Brown is the tragic victim of a society that has shut its eyes to the inevitable "naturalness" of sex as a part of man's physical and mental constitution, a society whose moral system would suppress too severely man's natural impulses. Among Puritans the word "nature" was virtually synonymous with "sin." In Hawthorne's *The Scarlet Letter,* little Pearl, illegitimate daughter of Hester Prynne and the Reverend Mr. Arthur Dimmesdale, is identified throughout as the "child of nature." In his speech to the General Court in 1645, Governor John Winthrop defined "natural liberty"—as distinguished from "civil liberty"—as a "liberty to do evil as well as good . . . the exercise and maintaining of [which] makes men grow more evil, and in time to be worse than brute beasts . . . ." Hawthorne, himself a descendant of Puritan witch hunters and a member of the New England society whose moral standards had been strongly conditioned by its Puritan heritage, was obsessed with the nature of sin and with the psychological results of violating the taboos imposed by this system. Young Goodman Brown dramatizes the neurosis resulting from such a violation.

After his night in the forest he becomes a walking guilt complex, burdened with anxiety and doubt. Why? Because he has not been properly educated to confront the realities of the external world or of the inner world, because from the cradle on he has been indoctrinated with admonitions against tasting the forbidden fruit, and because sin and Satan have been inadvertently glamorized by prohibition, he has developed a morbid compulsion to taste thereof. He is not necessarily evil; he is, like most young people, curious. But because of the severity of Puritan taboos about "natural" impulses, his curiosity has become an obsession. His dramatic reactions in the forest are typical of what happens in actual cases of extreme repression. Furthermore, the very nature of his wilderness fantasy substantiates Freud's theory that our repressed desires express themselves in our dreams, that dreams are symbolic forms of wish fulfillment. Hawthorne, writing more than a generation before Freud, was a keen enough psychologist to be aware of many of the same phenomena Freud was to systematize through clinical evidence.

D. *The Turn of the Screw*: The Consequences of Sexual Repression

Perhaps the most famous story dealing with the theme of sexual repression is Henry James's *The Turn of the Screw*. One of the most celebrated ghost stories of our literature, this many-faceted gem has been the focus of critical controversy since 1924, when Edna Kenton published her Freudian analysis of the tale, "Henry James to the Ruminant Reader: The Turn of the Screw" (*The Arts*, 6 [1924], 245–255). This interpretation was buttressed ten years afterward by the highly respected critic Edmund Wilson in his "The Ambiguity of Henry James" (*Hound and Horn*, 7 [1934], 385–406). It was exhaustively reinforced a generation later by Thomas M. Cranfill and Robert L. Clark, Jr., in *An Anatomy of "The Turn of the Screw"* (Austin: The University of Texas Press, 1965).

Briefly, *The Turn of the Screw* is the story of a young English governess who takes a position as tutor and protectress of two beautiful children living in a magnificent old country mansion. The children's parents are dead, and their legal guardian is a debonair bachelor uncle who lives in London and does not want to be bothered with looking after his wards. He hires the young governess-narrator with the provisions that she is to be in complete charge at Bly, his country estate, and that she will under no circumstances disturb him with appeals of complaints about her problems there. Though she is only twenty years old, she is to become governess of the estate as well as of the children, and the uncle is to be left alone, disburdened of worries about the welfare of his wards. The children, Miles and Flora, are two perfectly well-mannered youngsters with whom the governess falls in love at first sight.

All seems to be well at Bly, except for the ugly mystery surrounding the relationship between the governess's predecessor, Miss Jessel, and the uncle's former valet, Peter

Quint, both of whom are now dead. Also, there is the puzzling dismissal of little Miles from his school on the grounds that he "was an injury" to his fellow students. As best the governess can discover from rumor and from the scanty information given her by the housekeeper, Mrs. Grose, there had been "an affair" between Miss Jessel and Quint, carried on in the presence of the children, which had left some subtle mark of corruption on Miles and Flora. On several occasions after her arrival at Bly the governess sees the ghosts of Miss Jessel and Quint and deduces that they are somehow after the children, diabolically intent upon ensnaring their young souls. The actions of the children themselves, though superficially normal, suggest to the governess that her apprehensions are not without foundation. At the end of the narrative, little Flora turns against the governess and is taken off to the city by Mrs. Grose, as a means, presumably, of preserving her from further corruption by Miss Jessel. The governess stays at Bly with Miles and fights for his soul against the apparition of Peter Quint. In this final climactic struggle the governess seems to triumph in driving off the evil spirit, but the little boy dies from the terrible ordeal of being dispossessed.

No brief summary can do justice to the complexities and the exquisite horror of James's tale; our primary concern here is with its interpretive possibilities. In his preface to Vol. XII of the New York Edition of his collected works, James himself disavows all psychical implications in *The Turn of the Screw,* designating it as a pure and simple *amusette* intended "to catch those not easily caught (the 'fun' of the capture of the merely witless being ever but small), the jaded, the disillusioned, the fastidious"—a "Christmas-tide toy" designed "to rouse the dear old sacred terror."

Two questions may be asked about James's statements. Is he serious in disavowing a "clinical" intent? And does it really matter whether or not he "intended" the story to be no more than a simple *amusette?* The first question is unanswerable. We cannot be sure about his stated purpose; perhaps it, too, is designed to "catch" the literal-minded reader. To the second question we must answer a qualified no. In the strictest interpretive sense, James's conscious intentions are not directly relevant to our critical analysis of his story. Because the mind of the artist is structured essentially like other human minds and is therefore influenced by a welter of unconscious forces, the author may write more profoundly than he realizes. The important thing is not so much what the writer "intended" as what we as careful, informed readers find in his work. The fact is, a very strong case can be made for the "clinical" implications in the story.

In his essay on *The Turn of the Screw* (revised for *The Triple Thinkers* [New York: Oxford University Press, 1948]), Edmund Wilson pointed out that no one except the governess ever admits to seeing the ghosts of Peter Quint and Miss Jessel. We assume that the children see them, as we infer this from their curious behavior, but in truth we have only the governess's word. Mrs. Grose, the simple, illiterate housekeeper whose name signifies her down-to-earthness, never apprehends either ghost, despite several opportunities to do so. She, too, relies only upon the word of the highly sensitive governess.

What, then, is the significance of the ghosts, and why does only the young governess see them? To the psychoanalytic observer, the answer if fairly obvious. The governess is suffering from hallucinations, the result of a severe case of sexual repression; the ghosts are dramatic projections of her own unconscious sexual desires. As James's narrator informs us at the beginning of the story, she has been reared as the "youngest of several daughters of a poor country parson." We may therefore infer that, in such a sheltered, feminine world, her normal libidinous instincts have been powerfully inhibited, like those of Goodman Brown, by her parents and by a Victorian middle-class society even more repressive than the Puritan. She is admittedly infatuated with the children's uncle ("a gentleman, a bachelor in the prime of life, such a figure as had never risen, save in a dream or an old novel, before a fluttered, anxious girl out of a Hampshire vicarage"), and it is dressed in the uncle's clothing that the red-headed Peter Quint first appears. Not only this, but Quint—whose very name is a metonymy of his libidinous function—makes his first appearance on the tower, a phallic symbol, just as Miss Jessel first appears beside the lake, a female symbol. Wilson lends further support to his case by pointing out the pieces of wood with which little Flora is playing under the fascinated gaze of the governess at the time of Miss Jessel's initial appearance; the child is attempting to insert the mast of a toy ship (a concave vessel) into its appropriate hole. To sum up the Freudian case in Wilson's words:

> When we look back in the light of these hints, we are inclined to conclude from analogy that the story is primarily intended as a characterization of the governess: her somber and guilty visions and the way she behaves about them seem to present, from the moment we examine them from the obverse side of her narrative, an accurate and distressing picture of the poor country parson's daughter, with her English middle-class class-consciousness, her inability to admit to herself her natural sexual impulses and the relentless English "authority" which enables her to put over on inferiors even purposes which are totally deluded and not at all in the other people's best interests. . . . We find now that [this story] is a variation of one of [James's] familiar themes: the thwarted Anglo-Saxon spinster. . . . [p. 95]

E. Death-Wish in Poe's Fiction

Aside from Ernest Jones's *Hamlet and Oedipus* and Edmund Wilson's essay on *The Turn of the Screw*, one of the most widely known psychoanalytic studies of literature is Marie Bonaparte's *Life and Works of Edgar Allan Poe* (London: Imago, 1949). A pupil of Sigmund Freud, Bonaparte is, like Jones, one of those rare critics who has combined a thorough professional knowledge of psychoanalysis with a comparable grasp of her literary subject. For the uninitiated her book is as fantastic as it is fascinating. Her main thesis is that Poe's life and works are informed throughout by the Oedipal complex: hatred of father and psychopathic love of mother. The rejection of authority forms the core of Poe's critical writings; the mother fixation (the death wish or longing to return to the womb, manifested, for example, in his obsession with premature burial) is the matrix for Poe's poetry and fiction. Even his fatal weakness for drink is explained as a form of escape that enabled him to remain faithful to his dead mother, through a rigidly enforced chastity that was further ensured by alcoholic over-indulgence. As Bonaparte writes,

> Ever since he was three, in fact, Poe had been doomed by fate to live in constant mourning. A fixation of a dead mother was to bar him forever from earthly love, and make him shun health and vitality in his loved ones. Forever faithful to the grave, his imagination had but two ways open before it: the heavens or the tomb according to whether he followed the "soul" or body of his lost one. . . .
>
> Thus, through his eternal fidelity to the dead mother, Poe, to all intents, became necrophilist. . . . Had [his necrophilia] been unrepressed, Poe would no doubt have been a criminal. [p.83]

Using such psychoanalytic theories as her foundation, Bonaparte proceeds to analyze work after work with a logical consistency that is as disturbing as it is monotonous. "The Cask of Amontillado" and "The Tell-Tale Heart" are seen as tales of revenge against the father. The wine vault in the former story is a symbol of the "interior of the woman's body . . . where the coveted, supreme intoxication dwells, [and] thus becomes the instrument of retribution . . . ." The victim in "The Tell-Tale Heart" is likewise interpreted as a symbol of Poe's hated foster father, John Allan, and his horrible blind eye is a token of retributive castration. "The Fall of the House of Usher" is a psychoanalytic model of the Oedipal guilt complex. Madeline Usher, the vault in which she is prematurely interred, the house itself are all, according to Freudian symbology, mother images. The weird tale of Ethelred, read to Roderick by the narrator and climaxed by the slaying of the dragon, is a reenactment of the slaying of the father to gain the mother-treasure.

F. Love and Death in Blake's "The Sick Rose"

Though few writers lend themselves so readily as Poe to the psychoanalytic approach, a great deal of serious literature, if we accept Marie Bonaparte's premises, can be interpreted along those same basic lines established by Freud. The Romantic poets especially are susceptible of Freudian interpretations, because, as F. L. Lucas has asserted, Romanticism is related to the unconscious—as opposed to Classicism, which, with its emphasis on restraint and order, is oriented toward the conscious, particularly the ego and superego.

A richly symbolic poem like William Blake's "The Sick Rose" is exemplary:

> O Rose, thou art sick!
> The invisible worm,
> That flies in the night,
> In the howling storm,
> Has found out thy bed
> Of crimson joy;
> And his dark secret love
> Does thy life destroy.

From the Freudian perspective the sexual implications of Blake's imagery are readily discernible. The rose is a classic symbol of feminine beauty. But this beauty is being despoiled by some agent of masculine sexuality: the worm, symbol of death, of decay, and also of the phallus (worm= serpent=sexual instinct). Again, as in Poe's "Ulalume," we encounter flying as a symbol of the sex act. Images of night, darkness, and howling storm suggest attributes of the unconscious or the id, as in the forest of "Young Goodman Brown." The second stanza sets forth in rather explicit

147

images the idea of sensual destruction. In short, Blake's poem is a vaguely disturbing parable of the death instinct, which psychoanalysts affirm is so closely conjoined with sexual passion. The sharp juxtaposition of "crimson joy" and "destroy" (coupled with "bed" and "his dark secret love") suggests that Eros, unmitigated by higher spiritual love, is the agent of evil as well as of mortality.

G. Sexual Imagery in "To His Coy Mistress"

We see a similar juxtaposition in Andrew Marvell's "To His Coy Mistress," one of the most celebrated erotic poems in English literature. The speaker begins his propositon of love by stating an impossible condition: "Had we but world enough, and time,/This coyness, Lady, were no crime." Flattering his prospective mistress as "Lady" (a condition as improbable as those following, if we accept the cynical realism of the narrator), he proceeds to outline the "ideal" relationship of the two lovers:

> We would sit down and think which way
> To walk and pass our long love's day.
>
> . . .
>
> For, Lady, you deserve this state,
> Nor would I love at lower rate.

The speaker's argument in this first stanza achieves a fine sublimation. He has managed to refine his seductive motive of all its grossness yet, ever so subtly, has not swerved from his main purpose. His objective, despite the contradictory deceptiveness of "vegetable love" (a passion whose burning is so slow as to be imperceptible), is nevertheless the same: The woman must, ultimately at some distant time, capitulate to his blandishments. It is only a matter of time.

But this "only" makes all the difference in the world, as he demonstrates in his second stanza, shifting dramatically from the "soft sell" of the first stanza to the "hard sell":

> But at my back I always hear
> Time's wingèd chariot hurrying near;

> And yonder all before us lie
> Deserts of vast eternity.

The flying chariot of Time (again we find the subtle implication of sexual union in the image of flying) is juxtaposed against an eternity of oblivion, just as the slow but sure fecundity of a vegetable love growing to the vastness of empires is contrasted with the barren deserts of death. After setting forth this prospect, the speaker dares to reveal precisely what all this means in terms of love:

> Thy beauty shall no more be found,
> Nor, in thy marble vault, shall sound
> My echoing song; then worms shall try
> That long preserved virginity,
> And your quaint honor turn to dust,
> And into ashes all my lust.

This statement, in even sharper contrast with the gentle cajolery of the first stanza, is brutal in its explicitness. The "marble vault" is a thinly disguised vaginal metaphor suggesting both rigor mortis and the fleshless pelvis of the skeleton. "My echoing song" and the sensual meanings of the lines following are extremely coarse (cf. "quaint" and James's "Quint" as yonic puns). From the eternal burning of a vegetable passion, in the face of reality, we see that all love must at last end in ashes—just as all chastity must end, the same as sexual profligacy, in dust. The speaker concludes his "hard sell" with a couplet unrivaled in our literature for devastating anticlimax:

> The grave's a fine and private place,
> But none, I think, do there embrace.

In the final stanza the speaker relaxes his harsh irony and appeals passionately to his reluctant sweetheart to seize the moment. Again, in contrast with both the vegetable metaphor of the first stanza and the frightening directness of the second stanza, he achieves a sublimation of sensual statement through the bold sincerity of his passion and through the brilliance of his imagery:

Now therefore, while the youthful hue
Sits on thy skin like morning dew,
And while thy willing soul transpires
At every pore with instant fires,
Now let us sport us while we may,
And now, like amorous birds of prey,
Rather at once our time devour
Than languish in his slow-chapped power.
Let us roll all our strength and all
Our sweetness up into one ball,
And tear our pleasures with rough strife
Thorough* the iron gates of life:
Thus, though we cannot make our sun
Stand still, yet we will make him run.

Here too the sexual imagery is overt. The fire image, which smolders in stanza one and turns to ashes in stanza two, explodes into passion in this concluding stanza. ("Fire, in the unconscious," says Marie Bonaparte, "is the classic symbol of urethral eroticism.") Furthermore, in contrast to the tone of Blake's "Sick Rose," here love-as-destruction is set forth rapturously. The poet conveys, instead of sinister corruption, a sense of desperate ecstasy. The eating-biting metaphor (oral eroticism in its primal form) is fused with the flying symbol in "amorous birds of prey" and set with metaphysical brilliance against the alternative of a slow, cannibalistic dissolution within the horrible maw of Time. In his last four lines the lover drives his message home with an orgastic force through the use of harshly rhythmic spondees ("Thus, though" and "Stand still") and strongly suggestive puns ("make our sun" and "make him run").

To read Marvell's great poem as nothing more than a glorification of sexual activity is, of course, a gross oversimplification. "To His Coy Mistress" is much more than this, as we have indicated in the preceding chapters and will elaborate in the following chapters. We agree with the

---

* Thorough: through

formalistic critic that literature is autonomous, but we must also concur with critic Wayne Shumaker that it is "continuous with nonaesthetic life." As Simon Lesser has said, "Among stories whose artistic authenticity cannot be questioned we give the highest place precisely to those works which ignore no aspect of man's nature, which confront the most disagreeable aspects of life deliberately and unflinchingly...." Great literature has always dealt not merely with those aspects of the human mind that are pleasant and conscious but with the total human psyche, many facets of which are both unpleasant and unconscious. The enduring appeal of Marvell's poem, like that of the other works we have examined, derives from this kind of artistic and honest confrontation.

III. Some Concluding Remarks: Other Possibilities and Limitations of the Approach

This brings us to a final recapitulation and a few words of defense as well as of caution about the Freudian approach. First, in defense: incredibly farfetched as some psychoanalytic interpretations seem to many readers, such interpretations, handled by qualified critics, are not unsubstantiated in fact; they are based upon psychological insights often derived from and supported by actual case histories, and they are set forth in such works as those of Ernest Jones and Marie Bonaparte with remarkable consistency. They are—if we accept the basic premises of psychoanalysis—very difficult to refute. Furthermore, regardless of their factual validity, such theories have had a tremendous impact upon modern writing (in the works of such creative artists as James Joyce, Eugene O'Neill, Tennessee Williams, and Philip Roth, to mention only a few) and upon modern literary criticism (for example, in the essays of such major critics as Edmund Wilson, Lionel Trilling, F. L. Lucas, and Frederick Hoffman). It is therefore important that the serious student of literature be acquainted with psychoanalytic theory.

The danger is that the serious student may become theory-ridden, forgetting that Freud's is not the only approach to literary analysis. To see a great work of fiction or a great poem primarily as a psychological case study is often to miss its wider significance and perhaps even the essential aesthetic experience it should provide. A number of great works, despite the claims of the more zealous Freudians, do not lend themselves readily, if at all, to the psychoanalytic approach and even those that do cannot be studied exclusively from the psychological perspective. Literary interpretation and psychoanalysis are two distinct fields, and though they may be closely associated, they can in no sense be regarded as parts of one discipline. The literary critic who views the masterpiece solely through the lens of Freud is liable to see art through a glass darkly. However, the reader who rejects psychoanalysis as neurotic nonsense deprives himself of a valuable tool in understanding not only literature but human nature and himself as well.

CHAPTER 4

MYTHOLOGICAL AND ARCHETYPAL APPROACHES

I. DEFINITIONS AND MISCONCEPTIONS

In *The Masks of God: Primitive Mythology* (New York: Viking Press, 1959), Joseph Campbell recounts a curious phenomenon of animal behavior. Newly hatched chickens, bits of eggshells still clinging to their tails, will dart for cover when a hawk flies overhead; yet they remain unaffected by other birds. Furthermore, a wooden model of a hawk, drawn forward along a wire above their coop, will send them scurrying (if the model is pulled backward, however, there is no response). "Whence," Campbell asks, "this abrupt seizure by an image to which there is no counterpart in the chicken's world? Living gulls and ducks, herons and pigeons, leave it cold; but *the work of art strikes some very deep chord!*" (p. 31, our italics).

Campbell's hinted analogy, though only roughly approximate, will serve nonetheless as an instructive introduction to the mythological approach. For it is with the relationship of literary art to "some very deep chord" in human nature that mythological criticism deals. The myth critic is concerned to seek out those mysterious elements that inform certain literary works, and that elicit, with almost uncanny force, dramatic and universal human reactions. He wishes to discover how it is that certain works of literature, usually those that have become, or promise to become, "classics," image a kind of reality to which readers give perennial response—while other works, seemingly as well constructed, and even some forms of reality, leave us cold. Speaking figuratively, the myth critic studies in depth the "wooden hawks" of great literature: the so-called archetypes or archetypal patterns that the writer has drawn forward along the tensed structural wires of his masterpiece and that vibrate in such a way that a sympathetic resonance is started deep within the reader.

An obviously close connection exists between mythological criticism and the psychological approach discussed in Chapter 3: Both are concerned with the motives underlying human behavior. The differences between the two approaches are those of degree and of affinities. Psychology tends to be experimental and diagnostic; it is closely related to biological science. Mythology tends to be speculative and philosophic; its affinities are with religion, anthropology, and cultural history. Such generalizations, of course, risk oversimplification; for instance, a great psychologist like Sigmund Freud ranged far beyond experimental and clinical study into the realms of myth, and his distinguished sometime protégé, Carl Jung, became one of the foremost mythologists of our time. Even so, the two approaches are distinct, and mythology is wider in its scope. For example, what psychoanalysis attempts to disclose about the individual personality, the study of myths reveals about the mind and character of a people. And just as dreams reflect the unconscious desires and anxieties of the individual, so myths are the symbolic projections of a people's hopes, values, fears, and aspirations.

According to the common misconception and misuse of the term, myths are merely primitive fictions, illusions, or opinions based upon false reasoning. Actually, mythology encompasses more than grade school stories about the Greek and Roman deities or clever fables invented for the amusement of children (or the harassment of students in college literature courses). It may be true that myths do not meet our current standards of factual reality, but then neither does any great literature. Instead, they both reflect a more profound reality. As Mark Schorer has said in *William Blake: The Politics of Vision* (New York: Holt, Rinehart and and Winston, 1946), "Myth is fundamental, the dramatic representation of our deepest instinctual life, of a primary awareness of man in the universe, capable of many configurations, upon which all particular opinions and attitudes depend" (p. 29). According to Alan W. Watts in *Myth and Ritual in Christianity* (New York: Vanguard Press, 1954), "Myth is to be defined as a complex of stories—some no doubt fact, and some fantasy—which, for various reasons, human beings regard as demonstrations of the inner meaning of the universe and of human life" (p.7). George Whalley asserts in *Poetic Process* (London: Routledge and Kegan Paul, 1953) that myth

> is a direct metaphysical statement beyond science. It embodies in an articulated structure of symbol or narrative a vision of reality. It is a condensed account of man's Being and attempts to represent reality with structural fidelity, to indicate at a single stroke the salient and fundamental relations which for a man constitute reality. . . . Myth is not an obscure, oblique, or elaborate way of expressing reality— it is the *only* way.

Myths are, by nature, collective and communal; they bind a tribe or a nation together in that people's common psychological and spiritual activities. In *The Language of Poetry*, edited by Allen Tate (New York: Russell and Russell, 1960), Philip Wheelwright explains, "Myth is the expression of a profound sense of togetherness—a togetherness not merely upon the plane of the intellect . . . but a togetherness of feeling and of action and of wholeness of living" (p. 11). Moreover, like Melville's famous white whale (itself an archetypal image), myth is ubiquitous in time as well as place. It is a dynamic factor everywhere in human society; it transcends time, uniting the past (traditional modes of belief) with the present (current values) and reaching toward the future (spiritual and cultural aspirations).

II. SOME EXAMPLES OF ARCHETYPES

Having established the significance of myth, we need to examine its relationship to archetypes and archetypal patterns. Although every people has its own distinctive mythology that may be reflected in legend, folklore, and ideology (although, in other words, myths take their specific shapes from the cultural environments in which they grow) myth is, in the general sense, universal. Furthermore, similar motifs or themes may be found among many different mythologies, and certain images that recur in the myths of peoples widely separated in time and place tend to have a common meaning or, more accurately, tend to elicit comparable psychological responses and to serve similar cultural functions. Such motifs and images are called archetypes. Stated simply, archetypes are universal symbols. As Wheelwright explains in *Metaphor and Reality* (Bloomington: Indiana University Press, 1962), such symbols are

> those which carry the same or very similar meanings for a large portion, if not all, of mankind. It is a discoverable fact that certain symbols, such as the sky father and earth mother, light, blood, up-down, the axis of a wheel, and others, recur again and again in cultures so remote from one another in space and time that there is no likelihood of any historical influence and causal connection among them. [p. 111]

Examples of these archetypes and the symbolic meanings with which they tend to be widely associated follow (it should be noted in preface that these meanings may vary significantly from one context to another):

A. Images
1. Water: the mystery of creation; birth-death-resurrection; purification and redemption; fertility and growth.

157

According to Carl Jung, water is also the commonest symbol for the unconscious.

    a. The sea: the mother of all life; spiritual mystery and infinity; death and rebirth; timelessness and eternity; the unconscious.

    b. Rivers: death and rebirth (baptism); the flowing of time into eternity; transitional phases of the life cycle; incarnations of deities.

2. Sun (fire and sky are closely related): creative energy; law in nature; consciousness (thinking, enlightenment, wisdom, spiritual vision); father principle (moon and earth tend to be associated with female or mother principle); passage of time and life.

    a. Rising sun: birth; creation; enlightenment.

    b. Setting sun: death.

3. Colors:

    a. Red: blood, sacrifice, violent passion; disorder.

    b. Green: growth; sensation; hope; fertility; in negative context may be associated with death and decay.

    c. Blue: usually highly positive, associated with truth, religious feeling, security, spiritual purity.

    d. Black (darkness): chaos, mystery, the unknown; death; primal wisdom; the unconscious; evil; melancholy.

    e. White: highly multivalent, signifying, in its positive aspects, light, purity, innocence, and timelessness; in its negative aspects, death, terror, the supernatural, and the blinding truth of an inscrutable cosmic mystery (see, for instance, Herman Melville's chapter on "The Whiteness of the Whale" in *Moby-Dick*).

4. Circle (sphere): wholeness, unity.

    a. Mandala (a geometric figure based upon the squaring of a circle around a unifying center; see the following illustration of the classic Shri-Yantra mandala): the desire for spiritual unity and pyschic integration. Note that in its classic oriental forms the mandala features the juxtaposition of the triangle, the square, and the circle with their numerical equivalents of *three*, *four*, and *seven*.

b. Egg (oval): the mystery of life and the forces of generation.

c. Yang-Yin: a Chinese symbol representing the union of the opposite forces of the Yang (masculine principle, light, activity, the conscious mind) and the Yin (female principle, darkness, passivity, the unconscious).

d. Ouroboros: the ancient symbol of the snake biting

its own tail, signifying the eternal cycle of life, primordial unconsciousness, the unity of opposing forces (cf. Yang-Yin).

5. Serpent (snake, worm): symbol of energy and pure force (cf. libido); evil, corruption, sensuality; destruction; mystery; wisdom; the unconscious.

6. Numbers:
   a. Three: light; spiritual awareness and unity (cf. the Holy Trinity); the male principle.
   b. Four: associated with the circle, life cycle, four seasons; female principle, earth, nature; four elements (earth, air, fire, water).
   c. Seven: the most potent of all symbolic numbers—signifying the union of *three* and *four*, the completion of a cycle, perfect order.

7. The archetypal woman (Great Mother—the mysteries of life, death, transformation):
   a. The Good Mother (positive aspects of the Earth Mother): associated with the life principle, birth, warmth, nourishment, protection, fertility, growth, abundance (for example, Demeter, Ceres).
   b. The Terrible Mother (including the negative aspects of the Earth Mother): the witch, sorceress, siren, whore, femme fatale—associated with sensuality, sexual orgies, fear, danger, darkness, dismemberment, emasculation, death; the unconscious in its terrifying aspects.
   c. The Soul Mate: the Sophia figure, Holy Mother, the princess or "beautiful lady"—incarnation of inspiration and spiritual fulfillment (cf. the Jungian *anima*).

8. The Wise Old Man (savior, redeemer, guru): personification of the spiritual principle, representing "knowledge, reflection, insight, wisdom, cleverness, and intuition on the one hand, and on the other, moral qualities such as goodwill and readiness to help, which make his 'spiritual' character sufficiently plain.... Apart from his cleverness, wisdom, and insight, the old man ... is

also notable for his moral qualities; what is more, he even tests the moral qualities of others and makes gifts dependent on this test. . . . The old man always appears when the hero is in a hopeless and desperate situation from which only profound reflection or a lucky idea . . . can extricate him. But since, for internal and external reasons, the hero cannot accomplish this himself, the knowledge needed to compensate the deficiency comes in the form of a personified thought, i.e., in the shape of this sagacious and helpful old man" (C. G. Jung, *The Archetypes and the Collective Unconscious*, trans. R. F. C. Hull, 2d ed. [Princeton, N.J.: Princeton University Press, 1968], pp. 217 ff.).

9. Garden: paradise; innocence; unspoiled beauty (especially feminine); fertility.
10. Tree: "In its most general sense, the symbolism of the tree denotes life of the cosmos: its consistence, growth, proliferation, generative and regenerative processes. It stands for inexhaustible life, and is therefore equivalent to a symbol of immortality" (J. E. Cirlot, *A Dictionary of Symbols*, trans. Jack Sage [New York: Philosophical Library, 1962], p. 328; cf. the depiction of the Cross of Redemption as the Tree of Life in Christian iconography).
11. Desert: spiritual aridity; death; nihilism, hoplessness.

These examples are by no means exhaustive, but represent some of the more common archetypal images that the reader is likely to encounter in literature. The images we have listed do not necessarily function as archetypes every time they appear in a literary work. The discreet critic interprets them as such only if the total context of the work logically supports an archetypal reading.

B. Archetypal Motifs or Patterns

1. Creation: perhaps the most fundamental of all archetypal motifs—virtually every mythology is built on some account of how the Cosmos, Nature, and Man

were brought into existence by some supernatural Being or Beings.

2. Immortality: another fundamental archetype, generally taking one of two basic narrative forms:

   a. Escape from time: "Return to Paradise," the state of perfect, timeless bliss enjoyed by man before his tragic Fall into corruption and mortality.

   b. Mystical submersion into cyclical time: the theme of endless death and regeneration—man achieves a kind of immortality by submitting to the vast, mysterious rhythm of Nature's eternal cycle, particularly the cycle of the seasons.

3. Hero archetypes (archetypes of transformation and redemption):

   a. The quest: the hero (savior, deliverer) undertakes some long journey during which he must perform impossible tasks, battle with monsters, solve unanswerable riddles, and overcome insurmountable obstacles in order to save the kingdom and perhaps marry the princess.

   b. Initiation: the hero undergoes a series of excruciating ordeals in passing from ignorance and immaturity to social and spiritual adulthood, that is, in achieving maturity and becoming a full-fledged member of his social group. The initiation most commonly consists of three distinct phases: (1) separation, (2) transformation, and (3) return. Like the quest, this is a variation of the death-and-rebirth archetype.

   c. The sacrificial scapegoat: the hero, with whom the welfare of the tribe or nation is identified, must die to atone for the people's sins and restore the land to fruitfulness.

In *The Myth of the Birth of the Hero* (New York: Random House [Vintage Books], 1959; first published in 1914) Otto Rank, in studying some seventy different heroes (including Moses, Hercules, Oedipus, Siegfried, and Jesus), presents the following basic components of what he terms the "standard saga":

[1] The hero is the child of most distinguished parents, usually the son of a king. [2] His origin is preceded by difficulties, such as continence, or prolonged barrenness, or secret intercourse of the parents due to external prohibition or obstacles. [3] During or before the pregnancy, there is a prophecy, in the form of a dream or oracle, cautioning against his birth, and usually threatening danger to the father (or his representative). [4] As a rule, he is surrendered to the water, in a box. [5] He is then saved by animals, or by lowly people (shepherds), and is suckled by a female animal or by a humble woman. [6] After he has grown up, he finds his distinguished parents, in a highly versatile fashion. [7] He takes revenge on his father, on the one hand, and is acknowledged, on the other. [8] Finally he achieves rank and honors. [p.65]

C. Archetypes as Genres

Finally, in addition to appearing as images and motifs, archetypes may be found in even more complex combinations as genres or types of literature that conform with the major phases of the seasonal cycle. Northrop Frye, in his *Anatomy of Criticism* (Princeton, N.J.: Princeton University Press, 1957), indicates the correspondent genres for the four seasons as follows:

1. The mythos of spring: comedy
2. The mythos of summer: romance
3. The mythos of fall: tragedy
4. The mythos of winter: irony

With brilliant audacity Frye identifies myth with literature, asserting that myth is a "structural organizing principle of literary form" (p. 341) and that an archetype is essentially an "element of one's literary experience" (p. 365). And in *The Stubborn Structure* (Ithaca, N.Y.: Cornell University Press, 1970) he claims that "mythology as a whole provides a kind of diagram or blueprint of what literature as a whole is all about, an imaginative survey of the human situation from the beginning to the end, from the height to the depth, of what is imaginatively conceivable" (p. 102).

III. Myth Criticism in Practice

Frye's contribution leads us directly into the mythological approach to literary analysis. As our discussion of mythology has shown, the task of the myth critic is a special one. Unlike the traditional critic, who relies heavily on history and the biography of the writer, the myth critic is interested more in prehistory and the biographies of the gods. Unlike the formalistic critic, who concentrates on the shape and symmetry of the work itself, the myth critic probes for the inner spirit which gives that form its vitality and its enduring appeal. And, unlike the Freudian critic, who is prone to look on the artifact as the product of some sexual neurosis, the myth critic sees the work holistically, as the manifestation of vitalizing, integrative forces arising from the depths of mankind's collective psyche.

Despite the special importance of the myth critic's contribution, this approach is, for several reasons, poorly understood. In the first place, only during the present century have the proper interpretive tools become available through the development of such disciplines as anthropology, psychology, and cultural history. Second, many scholars and teachers of literature have remained skeptical of myth criticism because of its tendencies toward the cult and the occult. Finally, there has been a discouraging confusion over concepts and definitions among the myth "initiates" themselves, the sound and fury of which has caused many would-be myth critics to turn their energies to more clearly defined approaches such as the traditional or formalistic. In carefully picking our way through this maze, we can discover at least three separate though not necessarily exclusive disciplines, each of which has figured prominently in the development of myth criticism. We examine these in roughly chronological order, noting how each may be applied to critical analysis.

A. Anthropology and Its Uses

The rapid advancement of modern anthropology since the end of the nineteenth century has been the most important single influence on the growth of myth criticism. Shortly after the turn of the century this influence was revealed in a series of important studies published by the Cambridge Hellenists, a group of British scholars who applied recent anthropological discoveries to the understanding of Greek classics in terms of mythic and ritualistic origins. Noteworthy contributions by members of this group include *Anthropology and the Classics* (New York: Oxford University Press, 1908), a symposium edited by R. R. Marett; Jane Harrison's *Themis* (London: Cambridge University Press 1912); Gilbert Murray's *Euripides and His Age* (New York: Holt, Rinehart and Winston, 1913); and F. M. Cornford's *Origin of Attic Comedy* (London: Arnold, 1914). But by far the most significant member of the British school was Sir James G. Frazer, whose monumental *The Golden Bough* has exerted an enormous influence on twentieth-century literature, not merely on the critics but also on such creative writers as James Joyce, Thomas Mann, and T. S. Eliot. Frazer's work, a comparative study of the primitive origins of religion in magic, ritual, and myth, was first published in two volumes in 1890, later expanded to twelve volumes, and then published in a one-volume abridged edition in 1922. Frazer's main contribution was to demonstrate the "essential similarity of man's chief wants everywhere and at all times," particularly as these wants were reflected throughout ancient mythologies; he explains, for example, in the abridged edition (New York: Macmillan, 1922), that

> Under the names of Osiris, Tammuz, Adonis, and Attis, the peoples of Egypt and Western Asia represented the yearly decay and revival of life, especially vegetable life, which they personified as a god who annually died and rose again from the dead. In name and detail the rites varied from place to place: in substance they were the same. [p. 325]

The central motif with which Frazer deals is the archetype of crucifixion and resurrection, specifically the myths describing the "Killing of the Divine King." Among many primitive peoples it was believed that the ruler was a divine or semidivine being whose life was identified with the life cycle in nature and in human existence. Because of this identification, the safety of the people and even of the world was felt to depend upon the life of the god-king. A vigorous, healthy ruler would ensure natural and human productivity; on the other hand, a sick or maimed king would bring blight and disease to the land and its people. Frazer points out that if

> the course of nature is dependent on the man-god's life, what catastrophes may not be expected from the gradual enfeeble-ment of his powers and their final extinction in death? There is only one way of averting these dangers. The man-god must be killed as soon as he shows symptoms that his powers are beginning to fail, and his soul must be transferred to a vigorous successor before it has been seriously impaired by threatened decay. [p. 265]

Among some peoples the kings were put to death at regular intervals to ensure the welfare of the tribe; later, however, substitute figures were killed in place of the kings them-selves, or the sacrifices became purely symbolic rather than literal.

Corollary to the rite of sacrifice was the "scapegoat" archetype. This motif centered in the belief that, by trans-ferring the corruptions of the tribe to a sacred animal or man, then by killing (and in some instances eating) this scapegoat, the tribe could achieve the cleansing and atone-ment thought necessary for natural and spiritual rebirth. Pointing out that food and children are the primary needs for human survival, Frazer emphasizes that the rites of blood sacrifice and purification were considered by an-cient peoples as a magical guarantee of rejuvenation, an insurance of life, both vegetable and human. If such customs strike us as incredibly primitive, we need only to recognize their vestiges in our own civilized world—for example, the irrational satisfaction that some people gain by the persecution of such minority groups as blacks and Jews as scapegoats, or the more wholesome feelings of renewal derived from our New Year's festivities and resolutions, the homely tradition of spring-cleaning, our celebration of Easter, and even the Eucharist. Modern writers themselves have employed the scapegoat motif with striking relevance (for example, Shirley Jackson in "The Lottery," Robert Heinlein in *Stranger in a Strange Land* and Tom Tryon in *Harvest Home*).

The insights given us by Frazer and the Cambridge Hellenists have been extremely helpful in myth criticism, especially in the mythological approach to drama. Many scholars theorize that tragedy originated from the primitive rites we have been describing. The tragedies of Sophocles and Aeschylus, for example, were written to be played during the Festival of Dionysos, annual vegetation ceremonies during which the ancient Greeks celebrated the deaths of the winter-kings and the rebirths of the gods of spring and renewed life.

Sophocles' *Oedipus* is an excellent example of the fusion of myth and literature. Sophocles produced a great play, but the plot of *Oedipus* was not his invention. It was a well-known mythic narrative long before he immortalized it as tragic drama. Both the myth and the play contain a number of familiar archetypes, as a brief summary of the plot indicates. The king and queen of ancient Thebes, Laius and Jocasta, are told in a prophecy that their newborn son, after he has grown up, will murder his father and marry his mother. To prevent this catastrophe, the king orders one of his men to pierce the infant's heels and abandon him to die in the wilderness. But the child is saved by a shepherd and taken to Corinth, where he is reared as the son of King Polybus and Queen Merope, who lead the boy to believe that they are his real parents. After reaching maturity and hearing of a prophecy that he is destined to commit patricide and incest, Oedipus flees from Corinth to Thebes. On his journey he meets an old

167

man and his servants, quarrels with and kills them. Before entering Thebes he encounters the Sphinx (who holds the city under a spell), solves her riddle, and frees the city; his reward is the hand of the widowed Queen Jocasta. He then rules a prosperous Thebes for many years, fathering four children by Jocasta. At last, hoewever, a blight falls upon his kingdom because Laius's slayer has gone unpunished. Oedipus starts an intensive investigation to find the culprit—only to discover ultimately that he himself is the guilty one, that the old man whom he had killed on his journey to Thebes was Laius, his real father. Overwhelmed by this revelation, Oedipus blinds himself with a brooch taken from his dead mother-wife, who has hanged herself, and goes into exile. Following his sacrificial punishment, Thebes is restored to health and abundance.

Even in this bare summary we may discern at least two archetypal motifs: (1) In the quest motif, Oedipus, as the hero, undertakes a journey during which he encounters the Sphinx, a supernatural monster with the body of a lion and the head of a woman; by answering her riddle, he delivers the kingdom and marries the queen. (2) In the king-as-sacrificial-scapegoat motif, the welfare of the state, both human and natural (Thebes is stricken by both plague and drought), is bound up with the personal fate of the ruler; only after Oedipus has offered himself up as a scapegoat is the land redeemed.

Considering that Sophocles wrote his tragedy expressly for a ritual occasion, we are hardly surprised that *Oedipus* reflects certain facets of the fertility myths described by Frazer. More remarkable, and more instructive for the student interested in myth criticism, is the revelation of similar facets in the great tragedy written by Shakespeare 2000 years later.

1. THE SACRIFICIAL HERO: HAMLET

One of the first modern scholars to point out these similarities was Gilbert Murray. In his "Hamlet and Orestes," delivered as a lecture in 1914 and subsequently published in *The Classical Tradition in Poetry* (Cambridge, Mass.: Harvard University Press, 1927), Murray indicated a number of parallels between the mythic elements of Shakespeare's play and those in *Oedipus* and the *Agamemnon* of Aeschylus. The heroes of all three works derive from the Golden Bough Kings; they are all haunted, sacrificial figures. Furthermore, as with the Greek tragedies, the story of Hamlet was not the playwrights's invention but was drawn from legend. As literary historians tell us, the old Scandinavian story of Amlehtus or Amlet, Prince of Jutland, was recorded as early as the twelfth century by Saxo Grammaticus in his *History of the Danes*. Murray cites an even earlier passing reference to the prototypal Hamlet in a Scandinavian poem composed about 980 A.D. Giorgio de Santillana and Hertha von Dechend in *Hamlet's Mill* (Boston: Gambit, 1969) have traced this archetypal character back through the legendary Icelandic Amlodhi to Oriental mythology. It is therefore evident that the core of Shakespeare's play is mythic. In Murray's words,

> The things that thrill and amaze us in Hamlet ... are not any historical particulars about mediaeval Elsinore ... but things belonging to the old stories and the old magic rites, which stirred and thrilled our forefathers five and six thousand years ago; set them dancing all night on the hills, tearing beasts and men in pieces, and giving up their own bodies to a ghastly death, in hope thereby to keep the green world from dying and to be the saviours of their own people. [p.236]

By the time Sophocles and Aeschylus were producing their tragedies for Athenian audiences, such sacrifices were no longer performed literally but were acted out symbolically on stage; yet their mythic significance was the same. Indeed, their significance was very similar in the case of Shakespeare's audiences. The Elizabethans were a myth-minded and symbol-receptive people. There was no need for Shakespeare to interpret for his audience: They *felt* the mythic content of his plays. And though myth may smolder only feebly in the present-day audience, we still respond, despite our intellectual sophistication, to the archetypes in *Hamlet*.

Such critics as Murray and, more recently, Francis Fergusson have provided us with clues to many of Hamlet's archetypal mysteries. In *The Idea of a Theater* (Princeton, N. J.: Princeton University Press, 1949), Fergusson discloses point by point how the scenes in Shakespeare's play follow the same ritual pattern as those in Greek tragedy, specifically in *Oedipus*; he indicates that

> in both plays a royal sufferer is associated with pollution, in its very sources, of an entire social order. Both plays open with an invocation for the well-being of the endangered body politic. In both, the destiny of the individual and of society are closely intertwined; and in both the suffering of the royal victim seems to be necessary before purgation and renewal can be achieved. [p. 118]

To appreciate how closely the moral norms in Shakespeare's play are related to those of ancient vegetation myths, we need only to note how often images of disease and corruption are used to symbolize the evil that has blighted Hamlet's Denmark. The following statement from Philip Wheelwright's *The Burning Fountain* (Bloomington: Indiana University Press, 1954), explaining the organic source of good and evil, is directly relevant to the moral vision in *Hamlet*, particularly to the implications of Claudius's crime and its disastrous consequences. From the natural or organic standpoint,

> Good is life, vitality, propagation, health; evil is death, impotence, disease. Of these several terms *health* and *disease* are the most important and comprehensive. Death is but an interim evil; it occurs periodically, but there is the assurance of new life ever springing up to take its place. The normal cycle of life and death is a healthy cycle, and the purpose of the major seasonal festivals [for example, the Festival of Dionysos] was at least as much to celebrate joyfully the

turning wheel of great creative Nature as to achieve magical effects. Disease and blight, however, interrupt the cycle; they are the real destroyers; and health is the good most highly to be prized. [p.197]

Wheelwright continues by pointing out that because murder (not to be confused with ritual sacrifice) does violence to both the natural cycle of life and the social organism, the murderer is symbolically diseased. Furthermore, when the victim is a member of the murderer's own family, an even more compact organism than the tribe or the political state, the disease is especially virulent.

We should mention one other myth that relates closely to the meaning of *Hamlet,* the myth of "divine appointment." This was the belief, strongly fostered by such Tudor monarchs as Henry VII, Henry VIII, and Elizabeth I, that not only had the Tudors been divinely appointed to bring order and happiness out of civil strife but also any attempt to break this divine ordinance (for example, by insurrection or assassination) would result in social, political, and natural chaos. We see this Tudor myth reflected in several of Shakespeare's plays (for example, in *Richard III, Macbeth,* and *King Lear*) where interference with the order of divine succession or appointment results in both political and natural chaos, and where a deformed, corrupt, or weak monarch epitomizes a diseased political state. This national myth is, quite obviously, central in *Hamlet.*

The relevance of myth to *Hamlet* should now be apparent. The play's thematic heart is the ancient, archetypal mystery of the life cycle itself. Its pulse is the same tragic rhythm that moved Sophocles' audience at the Festival of Dionysos and moves us today through forces that transcend our conscious processes. Through the insights provided us by the anthropological scholars, however, we may perceive the essential archetypal pattern of Shakespeare's tragedy. Hamlet's Denmark is a diseased and rotten state because Claudius's "foul and most unnatural murder" of his king-brother has subverted the divinely ordained laws of nature and of kingly succession. The disruption is intensified by the blood kinship between victim and murderer. Claudius, whom the ghost identifies as "The Serpent," bears the primal blood curse of Cain. And because the state is identified with its ruler, Denmark shares and suffers also from his blood guilt. Its natural cycle interrupted, the nation is threatened by chaos: civil strife within and war without. As Hamlet exclaims, "The time is out of joint; O cursed spite,/That ever I was born to set it right!"

Hamlet's role in the drama is that of the prince-hero who, to deliver his nation from the blight that has fallen upon it, must not only avenge his father's murder but also offer himself up as a royal scapegoat. As a member of the royal family, Hamlet is infected with the regicidal virus even though he is personally innocent. We might say, using another metaphor from pathology, that Claudius's murderous cancer has metastasized so that the royal court and even the nation itself is threatened with fatal deterioration. Hamlet's task is to seek out the source of this malady and to eliminate it. Only after a thorough purgation can Denmark be restored to a state of wholesome balance. Hamlet's reluctance to accept the role of cathartic agent is a principal reason for his procrastination in killing Claudius, an act that may well involve his self-destruction. He is a reluctant but dutiful scapegoat, and he realizes ultimately that there can be no substitute victim in this sacrificial rite—hence his decision to accept Laertes's challenge to a dueling match that he suspects has been fixed by Claudius. The bloody climax of the tragedy is therefore not merely spectacular melodrama but an essential element in the archetypal pattern of sacrifice-atonement-catharsis. Not only must all those die who have been infected by the evil contagion (Claudius, Gertrude, Polonius, Rosencrantz and Guildenstern—even Ophelia and Laertes), but the prince-hero himself must suffer "crucifixion" before Denmark can be purged and reborn under the healthy new regime of Fortinbras.

Enhancing the motif of the sacrificial scapegoat is Hamlet's long and difficult spiritual journey—his initiation, as it were—from innocent, carefree youth (he has been a university student) through a series of painful ordeals to sadder, but wiser, maturity. His is a long night journey of the soul, and Shakespeare employs archetypal imagery to convey this thematic motif: *Hamlet* is an autumnal, night-time play dominated by images of darkness and blood, and the hero appropriately wears black, the archetypal color of melancholy. The superficial object of his dark quest is to solve the riddle of his father's death. On a deeper level, his quest leads him down the labyrinthine ways of the human mystery, the mystery of man's life and destiny. (Observe how consistently his soliloquies turn toward the puzzles of life and of self.) As with the riddle of the Sphinx, the enigmatic answer is "man," the clue to which is given in Polonius's glib admonition, "To thine own self be true." In this sense, then, Hamlet's quest is the quest undertaken by all of us who would gain that rare and elusive philosopher's stone, self-knowledge.

2. ARCHETYPES OF TIME AND IMMORTALITY— "TO HIS COY MISTRESS"

Even though the mythological approach lends itself more readily to the interpretation of drama and the novel than to shorter literary forms such as the lyric poem, it is not uncommon to find elements of myth in these shorter works. In fact, mythopoeic poets like William Blake, William Butler Yeats, and T. S. Eliot carefully structured many of their works on myth. Even those poets who are not self-appointed mythmakers often employ images and motifs that, intentionally or not, function as archetypes. Andrew Marvell's "To His Coy Mistress" seems to fit into this latter category.

Because of its strongly suggestive (and suggested) sensuality and its apparently cynical theme, "To His Coy Mistress" is sometimes dismissed as an immature if not immoral love poem. But to see the poem as little more than a clever "proposition" is to miss its greatness. No literary classic survives because it is merely "clever," or merely well written. It must partake somehow of the universal and, in doing so, may contain elements of the archetypal. Let us examine "To His Coy Mistress" with an eye to its archetypal content.

Superficially a love poem, "To His Coy Mistress" is, in a deeper sense, a poem about time. As such, it is concerned with immortality, a fundamental motif in myth. In the first two stanzas we encounter an inversion or rejection of traditional conceptions of human immortality. Stanza 1 is an ironic presentation of the "escape from time" to some paradisal state in which lovers may dally for an eternity. But such a state of perfect, eternal bliss is a foolish delusion, as the speaker suggests in his subjunctive "Had we . . ." and in his description of love as some kind of monstrous vegetable growing slowly to an infinite size in the archetypal garden. Stanza 2 presents, in dramatic contrast, the desert archetype in terms of another kind of time, naturalistic time. This is the time governed by the inexorable laws of nature (note the sun archetype imaged in "Time's wingèd chariot"), the laws of decay, death, and physical extinction. Stanza 2 is as extreme in its philosophical realism as the first stanza is in its impracticable idealization.

The concluding stanza, radically altered in tone, presents a third kind of time, an escape into cyclical time and thereby a chance for immortality. Again we encounter the sun archetype, but this is the sun of "soul" and of "instant fires"—images not of death but of life and creative energy, which are fused with the sphere ("Let us roll all our strength and all/Our sweetness up into one ball"), the archetype of primal wholeness and fulfillment. In *Myth and Reality* (New York: Harper & Row, 1963), Mircea Eliade indicates that one of the most widespread motifs in immortality myths is the *regressus ad uterum* (a "return to the origin" of creation or to the symbolic womb of life) and that this return is considered to be symbolically feasible by some philosophers (for example, the Chinese Taoists) through alchemical fire:

During the fusion of metals the Taoist alchemist tries to bring about in his own body the union of the two cosmological principles, Heaven and Earth, in order to reproduce the primordial chaotic situation that existed before the Creation. This primordial situation . . . corresponds both to the egg [that is, the archetypal sphere] or the embryo and to the paradisal and innocent state of the uncreated World. [pp. 83-84]

We are not suggesting that Marvell was familiar with Taoist philosophy or that he was consciously aware of immortality archetypes. However, in representing the age-old dilemma of time and immortality, Marvell employed a cluster of images charged with mythic significance. His poet-lover seems to offer the alchemy of love as a way of defeating the laws of naturalistic time; love is a means of participating in, even intensifying, the mysterious rhythms of nature's eternal cycle. If life is to be judged, as some philosophers have suggested, not by duration but by intensity, then Marvell's lovers, at least during the act of love, will achieve a kind of immortality by "devouring" time or by transcending the laws of clock time ("Time's wingèd chariot"). And if this alchemical transmutation requires a fire hot enough to melt them into one primordial ball, then it is perhaps also hot enough to melt the sun itself and "make him run." Thus we see that the overt sexuality of Marvell's poem is, in a mythic sense, suggestive of a profound metaphysical insight, an insight that continues to fascinate those philosophers and scientists who would penetrate the mysteries of time and eternity.

B. Jungian Psychology and Its Archetypal Insights

The second major influence on mythological criticism is the work of Carl Jung, the great psychologist-philosopher and one-time student of Freud who broke with the master because of what he regarded as a too narrow approach to psychoanalysis. Jung believed libido (psychic energy) to be more than sexual; also, he considered Freudian theories too negative because of Freud's emphasis on the neurotic rather than the healthy aspects of the psyche.

Jung's primary contribution to myth criticism is his theory of racial memory and archetypes. In developing this concept, Jung expanded Freud's theories of the personal unconscious, asserting that beneath this is a primeval, collective unconscious shared in the psychic inheritance of all members of the human family. As Jung himself explains in *The Structure and Dynamics of the Psyche* (*Collected Works*, vol. VIII [Princeton, N. J.: Princeton University Press, 1960]):

> If it were possible to personify the unconscious, we might think of it as a collective human being combining the characteristics of both sexes, transcending youth and age, birth and death, and, from having at its command a human experience of one or two million years, practically immortal. If such a being existed, it would be exalted over all temporal change; the present would mean neither more nor less to it than any year in the hundredth millennium before Christ; it would be a dreamer of age-old dreams and, owing to its immeasurable experience, an incomparable prognosticator. It would have lived countless times over again the life of the individual, the family, the tribe, and the nation, and it would possess a living sense of the rhythm of growth, flowering, and decay. [pp. 349-350]

Just as certain instincts are inherited by the lower animals (for example, the instinct of the baby chicken to run from a hawk's shadow), so more complex psychic predispositions (that is, a "racial memory") are inherited by human beings. Jung believed, contrary to eighteenth-century Lockean psychology, that "Mind is not born as a *tabula rasa* [a clean slate]. Like the body, it has its pre-established individual definiteness; namely, forms of behaviour. They become manifest in the ever-recurring patterns of psychic functioning" (*Psyche and Symbol* [Garden City, N.Y.: Doubleday, 1958], p. xv). Therefore what Jung called "myth-forming" structural elements are ever present in the unconscious psyche; he refers to the manifestations of these elements as "motifs," "primordial images," or "archetypes."

Jung was also careful to explain that archetypes are not inherited ideas or patterns of thought, but rather that they are predispositons to respond in similar ways to certain stimuli: "In reality they belong to the realm of activities of the instincts and in that sense they represent inherited forms of psychic behaviour" (p. xvi). In *Psychological Reflections* (New York: Harper & Row, 1961), he maintained that these psychic instincts "are older than historical man . . . have been ingrained in him from earliest times, and, eternally living, outlasting all generations, still make up the groundwork of the human psyche. It is only possible to live the fullest life when we are in harmony with these symbols; wisdom is a return to them" (p. 42).

In stressing that archetypes are actually "inherited forms," Jung also went further than most of the anthropologists, who tended to see these forms as social phenomena passed down from one generation to the next through various sacred rites rather than through the structure of the psyche itself. Furthermore, in *The Archetypes and the Collective Unconscious* (New York: Pantheon Books, 1959), he theorized that myths do not derive from external factors such as the seasonal or solar cycle but are, in truth, the projections of innate psychic phenomena.

> All the mythologized processes of nature, such as summer and winter, the phases of the moon, the rainy seasons, and so forth, are in no sense allegories of these objective occurrences; rather they are symbolic expressions of the inner, unconscious drama of the psyche which becomes accessible to man's consciousness by way of projection—that is, mirrored in the events of nature. [p. 6]

In other words, myths are the means by which archetypes, essentially unconscious forms, become manifest and articulate to the conscious mind. Jung indicated further that archetypes reveal themselves in the dreams of individuals, so that we might say that dreams are "personalized myths" and myths are "depersonalized dreams."

Jung detected an intimate relationship between dreams,

myths, and art in that all three serve as media through which archetypes become accessible to consciousness. The great artist, as Jung observes in *Modern Man in Search of a Soul* (New York: Harcourt Brace Jovanovich, n.d.; first published in 1933), is the man who possesses the "primordial vision," a special sensitivity to archetypal patterns and a gift for speaking in primordial images that enable him to transmit experiences of the "inner world" to the "outer world" through his art form. Considering the nature of his raw materials, Jung suggests it is only logical that the artist "will resort to mythology in order to give his experience its most fitting expression." This is not to say that the artist gets his materials secondhand: "The primordial experience is the source of his creativeness; it cannot be fathomed, and therefore requires mythological imagery to give it form" (p. 164). By asserting that the artist is "man" in a higher sense—"collective man"—and that the "work of the poet comes to meet the spiritual need of the society in which he lives" (p. 171), Jung restores him to the same exalted role to which Emerson, Whitman, and other Romantic critics had assigned the poet in the nineteenth century.

Although Jung himself wrote relatively little that could be called literary criticism, what he did write leaves no doubt that he believed literature, and art in general, to be a vital ingredient in human civilization. Most important, his theories have expanded the horizons of literary interpretation for those critics concerned to use the tools of the mythological approach and for psychological critics who have felt too tightly constricted by Freudian theory.

1. SOME SPECIAL ARCHETYPES—SHADOW, PERSONA, AND ANIMA

In *The Archetypes and the Collective Unconscious* (New York: Pantheon Books, 1959), Jung discusses at length many of the archetypal patterns that we have already examined (for example, water, colors, rebirth). In this way, though his emphasis is psychological rather than anthropological, a good deal of his work overlaps that of Frazer and the others. But, as we have already indicated, Jung is not merely a derivative or secondary figure; he is a major influence in the growth of myth criticism. For one thing, he provided some of the favorite terminology now current among myth critics. The term "archetype" itself, though not coined by Jung, enjoys its present widespread usage among the myth critics primarily because of his influence. Also, like Freud, he was a pioneer whose brilliant flashes of insight have helped to light our way in exploring the darker recesses of the human mind.

One major contribution is Jung's theory of *individuation* as related to those archetypes designated as the *shadow*, the *persona*, and the *anima*. Individuation is a psychological "growing up," the process of discovering those aspects of one's self that make one an individual different from other members of his species. It is essentially a process of recognition—that is, as he matures, the individual must consciously recognize the various aspects, unfavorable as well as favorable, of his total self. This self-recognition requires extraordinary courage and honesty but is absolutely essential if one is to become a well-balanced individual. Jung theorizes that neuroses are the results of the person's failure to confront and to accept some archetypal component of his unconscious. Instead of assimilating this unconscious element to his consciousness, the neurotic individual persists in projecting it upon some other person or object. In Jung's words, projection is an "unconscious, automatic process whereby a content that is unconscious to the subject transfers itself to an object, so that it seems to belong to that object. The projection ceases the moment it becomes conscious, that is to say when it is seen as belonging to the subject" (*Archetypes and the Collective Unconscious*, p. 60). In layman's terms, the habit of projection is reflected in the attitude that "Everybody is out of step but me" or "I'm the only honest person in the crowd." It is a commonplace that we can project our own unconscious faults and weaknesses on others much more easily than accept them as part of our own nature.

The shadow, persona, and anima are structural components of the psyche that man has inherited, just as the chicken has inherited his built-in response to the hawk. We encounter the symbolic projections of these archetypes throughout the myths and the literatures of mankind. In melodrama, such as the television or Hollywood western, the persona, the anima, and shadow are projected respectively in the characters of the hero, the heroine, and the villain. The shadow is the darker side of our unconscious self, the inferior and less pleasing aspects of the personality, which we wish to suppress. "Taking it in its deepest sense," writes Jung in *Psychological Reflections*, "the shadow is the invisible saurian [reptilian] tail that man still drags behind him" (p. 217). The most common variant of this archetype, when projected, is the Devil, who, in Jung's words in *Two Essays on Analytical Psychology* (New York: Pantheon Books, 1953), represents the "dangerous aspect of the unrecognized dark half of the personality" (p. 94). In literature we see symbolic representations of this archetype in such figures as Shakespeare's Iago, Milton's Satan, Goethe's Mephistopheles, and Conrad's Kurtz.

The anima is perhaps the most complex of Jung's archetypes. It is the "soul-image," the spirit of man's *élan vital*, his life force or vital energy. In the sense of "soul," says Jung, anima is the "living thing in man, that which lives of itself and causes life. . . . Were it not for the leaping and twinkling of the soul, man would rot away in his greatest passion, idleness" (*Archtypes and the Collective Unconscious*, pp. 26-27). Jung gives the anima a feminine designation in the male psyche, pointing out that the "anima-image is usually projected upon women" (in the female psyche this archetype is called the *animus*). In this sense, anima is the contrasexual part of man's psyche, the image of the opposite sex that he carries in both his personal and his collective unconscious. As an old German proverb puts it, "Every man has his own Eve within him"—in other words, the human psyche is bisexual, though the psychological characteristics of the opposite sex in each of us are generally unconscious, revealing themselves only in dreams or in projections on someone in our environment. The phenomenon of love, especially love at first sight, may be explained at least in part by Jung's theory of the anima: We tend to be attracted to members of the opposite sex who mirror the characteristics of our own inner selves. In literature, Jung regards such figures as Helen of Troy, Dante's Beatrice, Milton's Eve, and H. Rider Haggard's She as personifications of the anima. Following his theory, we might say that any female figure who is invested with unusual significance or power is likely to be a symbol of the anima. One other function of the anima is noteworthy here. The anima is a kind of mediator between the ego (the conscious will or thinking self) and the unconscious or inner world of the individual. This function will be somewhat clearer if we compare the anima with the persona.

The persona is the obverse of the anima in that it mediates between our ego and the external world. Speaking metaphorically, let us say that the ego is a coin. The image on one side is the anima; on the other side, the persona. The persona is the actor's mask that we show to the world—it is our social personality, a personality that is sometimes quite different from our true self. Jung, in discussing this social mask, explains that, to achieve psychological maturity, the individual must have a flexible, viable persona that can be brought into harmonious relation with the other components of his psychic makeup. He states, furthermore, that a persona that is too artificial or rigid results in such symptoms of neurotic disturbance as irritability and melancholy.

2. "YOUNG GOODMAN BROWN"— A FAILURE OF INDIVIDUATION

The literary relevance of Jung's theory of shadow, anima, and persona may be seen in our analysis of Hawthorne's story "Young Goodman Brown." In the first place, Brown's persona is both false and inflexible. It is the social mask of a God-fearing, prayerful, self-righteous Puritan— the persona of a "good man" with all the pietistic connotations. Brown considers himself both the good Christian and the good husband married to a "blessed angel on earth." In truth, however, he is much less the good man than the bad boy. His behavior from start to finish is that of the adolescent male. His desertion of his wife, for example, is motivated by his juvenile compulsion to have "one last fling" as a moral Peeping Tom. His failure to recognize himself (and his own base motives) when he confronts Satan—his shadow—is merely another indication of his spiritual immaturity.

Just as his persona has proved inadequate in mediating between Brown's ego and the external world, so his anima fails in relating to his inner world. It is only fitting that his "soul-image" or anima should be named Faith. His trouble is that he sees Faith not as a true wifely companion but as a mother (Jung points out that, during childhhood, anima is usually projected on the mother), as is revealed when he thinks that he will "cling to her skirts and follow her to heaven." In other words, if a young man's Faith has the qualities of the Good Mother, then he might expect to be occasionally indulged in his juvenile escapades. But mature faith, like marriage, is a covenant that binds both parties mutually to uphold its sacred vows. If one party breaks this covenant, as Goodman Brown does, he must face the unpleasant consequences: at worst, separation and divorce; at best, suspicion (perhaps Faith herself has been unfaithful), loss of harmony, trust, and peace of mind. It is the latter consequences that Brown has to face. Even then, he still behaves like a child. Instead of admitting to his error and working maturely for a reconciliation, he sulks.

In clinical terms, young Goodman Brown suffers from a failure of personality integration. He has been stunted in his psychological growth (individuation) because he is unable to confront his shadow, recognize it as a part of his own psyche, and assimilate it to his consciousness. He persists, instead, in projecting the shadow image: first, in the form of the Devil; then on the members of his community (Goody Cloyse, Deacon Gookin, and others); and, finally upon Faith herself (his anima), so that ultimately, in his eyes, the whole world is one of shadow, or gloom. As Jung explains in *Psyche and Symbol* (Garden City N. Y.: Doubleday, 1958), the results of such projections are often disastrous for the individual:

> The effect of projection is to isolate the subject from his environment, since instead of a real relation to it there is now only an illusory one. Projections change the world into the replica of one's own unknown face. . . . The resultant [malaise is in] turn explained by projection as the malevolence of the environment, and by means of this vicious circle the isolation is intensified. The more projections interpose themselves between the subject and the environment, the harder it becomes for the ego to see through its illusions. [Note Goodman Brown's inability to distinguish between reality and his illusory dream in the forest.]
>
> It is often tragic to see how blatantly a man bungles his own life and the lives of others yet remains totally incapable of seeing how much the whole tragedy originates in himself, and how he continually feeds it and keeps it going. Not *consciously*, of course—for consciously he is engaged in bewailing and cursing a *faithless* [our italics] world that recedes further and further into the distance. Rather, it is an unconscious factor which spins the illusions that veil his world. And what is being spun is a cocoon, which in the end will completely envelop him. [p. 8]

Jung could hardly have diagnosed Goodman Brown's malady more accurately had he been directing these comments squarely at Hawthorne's story. That he was generalizing adds impact to his theory as well as to Hawthorne's moral insight.

3. SYNTHESES OF JUNG AND ANTHROPOLOGY

As we can see from our interpretation of "Young Goodman Brown," the application of Jungian theory to literary analysis is likely to be closer to the psychological than to the mythological approach. We should therefore realize that most of the myth critics who use Jung's insights also use the materials of anthropology. A classic example of this kind of mythological eclecticism is Maud Bodkin's *Archetypal Patterns in Poetry*, first published in 1934 and now recognized as the pioneer work of archetypal criticism. Bodkin acknowledges her debt to Gilbert Murray and the anthropological scholars, as well as to Jung. She then proceeds to trace several major archetypal patterns through the great literature of Western civilization (for example, rebirth in Coleridge's *Rime of the Ancient Mariner*; heaven-hell in Coleridge's "Kubla Khan," Dante's *Divine Comedy*, and Milton's *Paradise Lost*; the image of woman as reflected in Homer's Thetis, Euripides' Phaedra, and Milton's Eve). The same kind of critical synthesis may be found in more recent mythological studies like Northrop Frye's *Anatomy of Criticism*, in which literary criticism, with the support of insights provided by anthropology and Jungian psychology, promises to become a new "social science."

One of the best of these recent myth studies is James Baird's *Ishmael: A Study of the Symbolic Mode in Primitivism* (New York: Harper, 1960). Baird's approach derives not only from Jung and the anthropologists but also from such philosophers as Susanne Langer and Mircea Eliade. Though he ranges far beyond the works of Herman Melville, Baird's primary objective is to find an archetypal key to the multilayered meanings of *Moby-Dick* (which, incidentally, Jung considered "the greatest American novel"). He finds this key in primitive mythology, specifically in the myths of Polynesia that young Melville had been exposed to during his two years of sea duty in the South Pacific. (Melville's early success as a writer was largely due to his notoriety as the man who had lived for a month among the cannibals of Taipi.) Melville's literary primitivism is authentic, unlike the sentimental primitivism of such writers as Rousseau, says Baird, because he had absorbed certain Oriental archetypes or "life symbols" and then transformed these creatively into "autotypes" (that is, individualized personal symbols).

The most instructive illustration of this creative fusion of archetype and autotype is Moby-Dick, Melville's infamous white whale. Baird points out that, throughout Oriental mythology, the "great fish" recurs as a symbol of divine creation and life; in Hinduism, for example, the whale is an avatar (divine incarnation) of Vishnu, the "Preserver contained in the all being of Brahma." (We might also note the designation of Christ as a "fisherman" in Christian tradition.) Furthermore, Baird explains that *whiteness* is the archetype of the all-encompassing, inscrutable deity, the "white sign of the God of all being who has borne such Oriental names as Bhagavat, Brahma—the God of endless contradiction." Melville combined these two archetypes, the great fish or whale and whiteness, in fashioning his own unique symbol (autotype), Moby-Dick. Baird's reading of this symbol is substantiated by Melville's remarks about the contrarieties of the color white (terror, mystery, purity) in his chapter on "The Whiteness of the Whale," as well as by the mysterious elusiveness and awesome power with which he invests Moby-Dick. Moby-Dick is therefore, in Baird's words, a "nonambiguous ambiguity." Ahab, the monster of intellect, destroys himself and his crew because he would "strike through the mask" in his insane compulsion to understand the eternal and unfathomable mystery of creation. Ishmael alone is saved because, through the wholesome influence of Queequeg, a Polynesian prince, he has acquired the primitive mode of accepting this divine mystery without question or hostility.

C. Myth Criticism and the American Dream

In addition to anthropology and Jungian psychology, a third influence has been prominent in recent myth criticism, especially in the interpretation of American literature. This influence, deriving not only from those already mentioned but also from a new historical focus upon the informing myths of our culture, has shown itself in a growing interest in that cluster of indigenous myths called "The American Dream" and, subsequently, in an intensified effort by literary scholars to analyze those elements that constitute the peculiar "Americanness" of our literature. The results of such analysis indicate that the major works produced by American writers possess a certain uniqueness and that this uniqueness can largely be attributed to the influence, both positive and negative, of the American Dream.

The central facet of this myth cluster is the Myth of Edenic Possibilities, which reflects the hope of creating a second Paradise, not in the next world and not outside time, but in the bright New World of the American continent. From the time of its first settlement America was seen from European eyes as a land of boundless opportunity, a place where man, after centuries of poverty, misery, and corruption, could have a second chance to fulfill, in reality, his mythic yearnings for a return to Paradise. As early as 1654 Captain Edward Johnson announced to the Old-World-weary people of England that America was "the place":

> All you the people of Christ that are here Oppressed, Imprisoned and scurrilously derided, gather yourselves together, your Wifes and little ones, and answer to your several Names as you shall be shipped for His service, in the Westerne World, and more especially for planting the united Colonies of new England.... Know this is the place where the Lord will create a new Heaven, and a new Earth in new Churches, and a new Commonwealth together.

Frederic I. Carpenter, in *American Literature and the Dream* (New York: Philosophical Library, 1955), has pointed out that, although the Edenic Dream itself was "as old as the mind of man," the idea that "this is the place" was uniquely American:

> Earlier versions had placed it in Eden or in Heaven, in Atlantis or in Utopis; but always in some country of the imagination. Then the discovery of the new world gave substance to the old myth, and suggested the realization of it

on actual earth. America became "the place" where the religious prophecies of Isaiah and the Republican ideals of Plato [and even the mythic longings of primitive man, we might add] might be realized. [p. 6]

The themes of moral regeneration and bright expectations, which derive from this Edenic myth, form a major thread in the fabric of American literature, from Crèvecoeur's *Letters from an American Farmer* through the works of Emerson, Thoreau, and Whitman to such modern writers as Hart Crane and Thomas Wolfe.

Closely related to the Myth of Edenic Possibilities is the concept of the American Adam, the mythic New World hero. In *The American Adam* (Chicago: University of Chicago Press, 1955), R. W. B. Lewis describes the type: "a radically new personality, the hero of the new adventure: an individual emancipated from history, happily bereft of ancestry, untouched and undefiled by the usual inheritances of family and race; an individual standing alone, self-reliant and self-propelling, ready to confront whatever awaited him with the aid of his own unique and inherent resources" (p. 5). One of the early literary characterizations of this Adamic hero is James Fenimore Cooper's Natty Bumppo, the central figure of the Leatherstocking saga. With his moral purity and social innocence, Natty is an explicit version of Adam before the Fall. He is a child of the wilderness, forever in flight before the corrupting influences of civilization—and from the moral compromises of Eve. (Cooper never allows his hero to marry.) He is also, as we might guess, the literary great-grandfather of the Western hero. Like the hero of Owen Wister's *The Virginian* and, more recently, Matt Dillon of TV's *Gunsmoke*, he is clean living, straight shooting, and celibate. (In his civilized version, the American Adam is the central figure of another corollary myth of the American Dream: the Dream of Success. The hero here is that popular figure epitomized in Horatio Alger's stories and subsequently treated in the novels of Howells, London, Dreiser and

Fitzgerald: the self-made man who, through luck, pluck, and all the Ben Franklin virtues, rises from rags to riches, or from log cabin to White House.)

More complex, and therefore more interesting, than this uncorrupted Adam is the American hero during and after the Fall. It is with this aspect of the dream rather than with the adamant innocence of a Leatherstocking that our best writers have most often concerned themselves. The symbolic loss of Edenic innocence and the painful initiation into an awareness of evil constitutes a second major pattern in American literature from the works of Hawthorne and Melville through Mark Twain and Henry James to Hemingway and Faulkner. This is the darker thread in our literary fabric, which, contrasting as it does with the myth of bright expectancy, lends depth and richness to the overall design; it also reminds us of the disturbing proximity of dream and nightmare. From this standpoint, then, we may recall Hawthorne's young Goodman Brown as a representative figure—the prototypal American hero haunted by the obsession with guilt and original sin that is a somber but essential part of America's Puritan heritage.

The English novelist D. H. Lawrence was first among the modern critics to perceive the "dark suspense" latent in the American Dream. As early as 1923 he pointed out the essential paradox of the American character in his *Studies in Classic American Literature* (New York: Viking Press 1964; a reissue), a book whose cantankerous brilliance has only lately come to be fully appreciated by literary scholars. "America has never been easy," he wrote, "and is not easy today. Americans have always been at a certain tension. Their liberty is a thing of sheer will, sheer tension: a liberty of THOU SHALT NOT. And it has been so from the first. The land of THOU SHALT NOT" (p. 5). Lawrence saw Americans as a people frantically determined to slough off the old skin of European tradition and evil, but constricted even more tightly by their New World heritage of Puritan conscience and inhibition. He pointed out the evidence of this "certain tension" in the writings of such classic American authors as Cooper, Poe, Hawthorne, and Melville. Though Lawrence is certainly not the only source of such insights, much of the recent myth criticism of American literature—notably such work as that by Leslie Fiedler in *An End to Innocence* (Boston: Beacon Press, 1955), *Love and Death in the American Novel* (New York: Criterion, 1960), and *No! in Thunder* (Boston: Beacon Press, 1960)—reflects his brilliantly provocative influence.

1. HUCKLEBERRY FINN AS THE AMERICAN ADAM

Adventures of Huckleberry Finn is one of the half dozen most significant works in American literature. Many critics rank it among the masterpieces of world literature, and not a few consider it to be the Great American Novel. The reasons for this high esteem may be traced directly to the mythological implications of Twain's book: More than any other novel in our literature, *Huckleberry Finn* embodies myth that is both universal and national. The extent of its mythic content is such that we cannot hope to grasp it all in this chapter; we can, however, indicate a few of those elements that have helped to give the novel its enduring appeal.

First, *Huckleberry Finn* is informed by several archetypal patterns encountered throughout world literature:

1. *The Quest:* Like Don Quixote, Huck is a wanderer, separated from his culture, idealistically in search of a reality more substantial than that embraced by the materialistic society he has rejected.

2. *Water Symbolism:* The great Mississippi River, like the Nile and the Ganges, is invested with sacred attributes. As T. S. Eliot has written, the river is a "strong brown god"; it is an archetypal symbol of the mystery of life and creation—birth, the flowing of time into eternity, and rebirth. (Note, for example, Huck's several symbolic deaths, his various disguises and new identities as he returns to the shore from the river; also note the mystical lyricism with which he describes the river's majestic beauty.) The river is also a kind of Paradise, the "Great Good

Place," as opposed to the shore, where Huck encounters hellish corruption and cruelty. It is, finally, an agent of purification and of divine justice.

3. *Shadow Archetype:* Huck's pap, with his sinister repulsiveness, is a classic representation of the devil figure designated by Jung as the shadow.

4. *Wise Old Man:* In contrast to pap, the Terrible Father, Jim exemplifies the Jungian concept of the wise old man who provides spiritual guidance and moral wisdom for the young hero.

5. *Archetypal Women:*

   a. The Good Mother: the Widow Douglas, Mrs. Loftus, Aunt Sally Phelps.
   b. The Terrible Mother: Miss Watson, who becomes the Good Mother at the end of the novel.
   c. The Soul-Mate: Sophia Grangerford, Mary Jane Wilks.

6. *Initiation:* Huck undergoes a series of painful experiences in passing from ignorance and innocence into spiritual maturity; he comes of age—is morally reborn—when he decides to go to hell rather than turn Jim in to the authorities.

In addition to these universal archetypes, *Huckleberry Finn* contains a mythology that is distinctively American. Huck himself is the symbolic American hero; he epitomizes conglomerate paradoxes that make up the American character. He has all the glibness and practical acuity that we admire in our businessmen and politicians; he is truly a self-made youth, free from the materialism and morality-by-formula of the Horatio Alger hero. He possesses the simple modesty, the quickness, the daring and the "guts," the stamina and the physical skill that we idolize in our athletes. He is both ingenious and ingenuous. He is mentally "sharp," but not intellectual. He also displays the ingratiating capacity for buffoonery that we so dearly love in our public entertainers. Yet, with all these extraverted virtues, Huck is also a sensitive, conscience-burdened "loner" troubled by man's inhumanity to man and by his own occasional callousness to Jim's feelings. Notwithstanding his generally realistic outlook and his practical bent, he is a moral idealist, far ahead of his age in his sense of human decency, and at times, a mystic and a daydreamer (or, more accurately, a night dreamer) who is uncommonly sensitive to the presence of a divine beauty in nature. He is, finally, the good Bad Boy whom Americans have always idolized in one form or another. And, though he is exposed to as much evil in human nature as young Goodman Brown had seen, Huck is saved from Brown's pessimistic gloom by his sense of humor and, what is more crucial, by his sense of humanity.

IV. Limitations of Myth Criticism

It should be apparent from the foregoing illustrations that myth criticism offers some unusual opportunities for the enhancement of our literary appreciation and understanding. No other critical approach possesses quite the same combined breadth and depth. As we have seen, an application of myth criticism takes us far beyond the historical and aesthetic realms of literary study—back to the beginnings of mankind's oldest rituals and beliefs and deep into our own individual hearts of darkness. Because of the vastness and the complexity of mythology, a field of study whose mysteries the anthropologists and psychologists are still working to penetrate, our brief introduction can give the reader only a superficial and fragmentary overview. But we hope the interested student has received a glimpse of new vistas and that he will be encouraged to explore the dark continent of myth of his own.

We should point out some of the inherent limitations of the mythological approach. As with the psychological approach, the reader must take care that his enthusiasm for a new-found interpretive key does not tempt him to discard other valuable critical instruments or to try to open all literary doors with this single key. Just as the Freudian critic sometimes loses sight of a great work's aesthetic values in his passion for sexual symbolism, so the myth critic tends to forget that literature is more than a vehicle for archetypes and ritual patterns. In other words, he runs the risk of being distracted from the aesthetic experience of the work itself. He forgets that literature is, above all else, art. As we have indicated before, the discreet critic will apply such extrinsic perspectives as the mythological and psychological only as far as they enhance the experience of the art form, and only as far as the structure and potential meaning of the work consistently support such approaches.

THE EXPONENTIAL APPROACH

1. Traps and the Motif of Love
2. Traps and the Motif of Reason, Madness, and Brutishness
3. Traps and the Motif of Thought and Action
4. Traps and the Dilemmas of Religion and Culture

I. THE PRINCIPLES OF THE APPROACH

A. Definition

Regardless of which critical approach a reader may favor, he will always be concerned with the themes of a literary work and the ways in which he can follow those themes. The thematic "statements" made in literature are frequently more implicit than explicit, if only because they are often made by the communicative and evocative power of symbols and images rather than by expository language. One of the basic steps in the full appreciation of a work, then, is the recognition of such images and symbols.

But recognition alone is not enough. A more important step is to consider the artistic weaving of those instances into meaningful patterns, including ideational and verbal patterns of cognates, antonyms, and associated connotations that are not necesssarily dependent on images (but may coexist with them). Such a method compares with what we developed in the formalist approach but lays significantly greater stress on the experience and meanings of the patterns. In this chapter we consider how to follow

195

these patterns by learning to follow their *exponents*, that is, those words, objects, people that represent or symbolize— or even constitute—the patterns. In the process of studying patterns we shall be doing as readers what August Strindberg, the important Swedish novelist and playwright, says he did as author in his drama *Miss Julie*. In the preface to the play, Strindberg said that he "let people's minds work irregularly, as they do in real life." As a consequence, "The dialogue wanders, gathering in the opening scenes material which is later picked up, worked over, repeated, expounded and developed like the theme in a musical composition."

Tracing such thematic patterns in a literary composition assumes that significant literature does attempt to communicate, or at least to embody, meaningful experience in an aesthetically appealing form. This is not to say that literature merely sugarcoats a beneficial pill. It is to say that in the creation of any given work, a literary artist has an idea, or an actual experience, or an imagined experience that he wishes to communicate or to embody. Consciously or otherwise, he then chooses a means of doing it. He must select, or his unconscious mind must present, specific devices, and he must arrange them so that he can embody or communicate that experience. Once the author has created for us such a work, we readers must re-create the experience, in part by carefully tracing the motifs used to communicate it. If Strindberg has given us "material" in *Miss Julie* that he later picked up, worked over, and developed "like the theme in a musical composition," then our role is to seek out the signs or exponents of the theme. Bit by bit, as we notice instances of a pattern, we work our way into the experience of the story, poem, or play. As we follow the hints of thematic statement, recognize similar but new images, or identify related symbols, we gradually come to live the experience inherent in the work. The evocative power of steadily repeated images and symbols makes the experience a part of our own consciousness and sensibility. Thus the image satisfies our senses, the pattern our instinctive desire for order, and the thematic statement our intellect and our moral sensibility.

Unlike the convenient terms that we can use in the first four chapters of this handbook—such as the biographical, the formalist, or the mythic approach—there is no clearly established term for what we wish to exemplify in this chapter (though there is some similarity to methods surveyed in Chapters 2 and 6, such as the phenomenological approach). Some well-established terms serve our needs occasionally in our exemplifications, but not in all. Patterns such as we are discussing, for example, are sometimes called *motives* or *motifs*. In the following pages, we shall use the latter spelling to avoid confusion with motivations in characters, for there is no necessary relationship between motifs as we use the term and motives for behavior. But there is a relationship between the literary use of motifs and the use of leitmotifs (subjects or themes) in music—the comparison drawn by Strindberg being particularly apt. Sometimes what we are here calling the exponential approach might as well be called the symbolic approach. In this chapter we will talk of symbols, as when we speak of those images that are charged with meaning beyond their usual denotations. Sometimes these symbols are also archetypal images, as we have seen in the mythological approach; in this sense archetypes are much the same as exponents of experience. However, rather than multiply terms and definitions and rather than use an awkward phrase like "motival approach," we designate this method as the exponential approach because the inclusiveness of that term suggests at once the several meanings of motif, image, symbol, and archetype.

B. Related Scholarly and Critical Studies

The pursuit of the image has provided literary scholarship with some outstanding contributions. Caroline Spurgeon, for example, catalogued Shakespeare's imagery in an effort to understand Shakespeare himself and his plays. Significantly for our present concern, her study was entitled *Shakespeare's Imagery and What It Tells Us* (Boston: Beacon Press, 1958; first published in 1935). Early in her book she says:

> The greater and richer the work the more valuable and suggestive become the images, so that in the case of Shakespeare I believe one can scarcely overrate the possibilities of what may be discovered through a systematic examination of them. It was my conviction of this which led me to assemble and classify all his images, so as to have in orderly and easily accessible form the material upon which to base my deductions and conclusions. [p. 5]

In this chapter we are not concerned with the biographical aspects that Spurgeon sought in Shakespeare's imagery, but we are concerned with seeing how imagery can tell us much.

Although the books of Kenneth Burke are more difficult for the beginning student of literature, he too has shown us how to follow patterns of imagery and symbols. In *Counter-Statement* (Los Altos, Calif.: Hermes, 1953) his definition of symbol as the "verbal parallel to a pattern of experience" (p. 152) is much like our definition of exponent. Just as we emphasize the role of exponents as guides, he talked of "cues" and "clues" that lead us to "clusters" of imagery and on to "symbolic meaning." As Stanley Hyman pointed out in *The Armed Vision* (New York: Random House [Vintage Books], 1955, p. 344), this technique is analogous to those of Spurgeon and Edward A. Armstrong, whose book *Shakespeare's Imagination* (Drummond, 1946) extended Spurgeon's insights.

A particularly well-known classic of scholarship that has traced motifs or patterns of imagery, though for a somewhat different purpose, is John Livingston Lowes's *The Road to Xanadu: A Study in the Ways of the Imagination* (Boston: Houghton Mifflin, 1927). Lowes found that the mind of Samuel Taylor Coleridge was a "chaos" of stored information and images, a kind of "deep well" within which these many details were in a constantly shifting solution. Thus when Coleridge thought of one "hooked atom," it quite likely suggested another, so that when he pulled the first to the surface of his conscious mind it pulled a second, "hooks and eyes" fashion. Together, the hooked atoms could be woven into a "pattern" of intricate relationships, the "magical synthesis" being provided by the "shaping spirit of the imagination." Lowes studied only *The Rime of the Ancient Mariner* and "Kubla Khan"; later his method was extended by Arthur H. Nethercot to *Christabel* in *The Road to Tryermaine: A Study of the History, Background, and Purposes of Coleridge's "Christabel"* (New York: Russell & Russell, 1962; first published in 1939).

Although Lowes and Nethercot pursued images and motifs in an effort to trace the sources of the three works they studied, their books (Lowes's in particular) laid great stress on the relationships of these images, as we are doing with exponents. Such a stress on elements of the poems is interesting for another reason: Coleridge himself defined "poem" in such a way that he emphasized equally the "gratification from each component *part*" and the "delight from the *whole*" (*Biographia Literaria, Chap. 14*). The tracing of exponents (the parts within the whole) generates a pleasure, an anticipated surprise, in the discovery or the recognition of ideas and feelings. This seems consonant with Coleridge's use of words like "gratification" and "delight," and this joy of fulfillment and discovery seems to be at the heart of much artistic response. In *Biographia Literaria* (chap. 14), Coleridge wrote of the "power of exciting the sympathy of the reader by a faithful adherence to the truth of nature, and the power of giving the interest of novelty by the modifying colors of imagination." Here Coleridge suggested the double principle of recognition and surprise, a principle often evident, for example, in his *Rime of the Ancient Mariner*. Extending this double principle to the study of motifs, we see that the recurrence of thematic statement, image, or symbol comes to be a pleasure whenever we find a new instance of a motif.

Conversely, when we recognize the motif in a *different* manifestation, our pleasurable recognition is augmented by the pleasurable perception of difference. Nor is this all, for the perception of sameness and of difference is more than mere pleasurable stimulus, a play of the mind. It opens out to the richness and truth of a given experience by gradually revealing its essence to the reader. Coleridge himself, while stressing that the immediate purpose of poetry was pleasure, also said that its ultimate purpose was truth. Furthermore, the perception of sameness within difference is typical of the functioning of the mature mind, a mind capable of appreciating the complexities of reality.

C. Some Brief Examples

Thus far we have been discussing the exponential approach in a theoretical way and have been examining scholarly and critical works that have something in common with this approach. Let us now turn to some practical illustrations of exponential patterns in literary works, after which we will be able to apply these principles more fully to the four particular works we are studying. These preliminary illustrations emphasize (1) imagery, both when one sense is appealed to and when clusters of images are used; (2) ideas that form themselves into patterns; and (3) plot incidents whose relationships suggest a theme.

The first of these, imagery, can be as varied as the human senses—not just the appeals to the classic five senses, but to others and to variations and refinements of them. Miss Spurgeon, for example, would include as an image "any and every imaginative picture or other experience, drawn in every kind of way, which may have come to the poet, not only through any of his senses, but through his mind and emotions as well, and which he uses, in the forms of simile and metaphor in their widest sense, for purposes of analogy" (p. 5). Conventional enough are the consistent appeals to a dominant image, such as sound in Poe's "The Bells," or sight, especially colors, in Poe's "The Masque of the Red Death." Less conventional is Keats's

"The Eve of St. Agnes," which has not only classic appeals to the visual imagination, but some effective thermal and gustatory images. For example, Keats opposes heat and cold in "Full on this casement shone the wintry moon,/ And threw warm gules on Madeline's fair breast"; and he stresses taste when he describes

> . . . a heap
> Of candied apple, quince, and plum, and gourd;
> With jellies soother than the creamy curd,
> And lucent syrups, tinct with cinnamon.

Hemingway's "The Short, Happy Life of Francis Macomber" has a striking appeal to the kinetic sense when the speeding hunters pursue the buffalo. A notable use of both the kinesthetic and the kinetic in the metrics of poetry is the sound of horses' hooves in Browning's "How They Brought the Good News from Ghent to Aix":

> I sprang to the stirrup, and Joris, and he;
> I galloped, Dirck galloped, we galloped all three.

Besides varying the sensuous appeals within a motif, the author can vary whole patterns. He can make one image pattern interact with another. He can let them run parallel or on intersecting lines. He can complement or contrast one with another. He can intrigue, stimulate, or even startle us. In turn, we can discover one image, only to be led gradually into another. We can see first the cracked exterior of Roderick Usher's home, and later watch the man's very mind cracking, and we can read with deeper understanding "The Haunted Palace" within the story. We can follow the brute animal imagery of "The Death of the Ball-Turret Gunner" and then realize that the same images also are images of maternal and familial love. We can follow thirteen lines of Sidney's "Come Sleep! O Sleep," only to find in the fourteenth that we have read a love sonnet, not a poem on sleep. We can sense the thermal images in "The Eve of St. Agnes" and then realize that we are reading, in part, about warm life and cold death.

Regularly we can see that what we are discovering in the image pattern is the repeated but contrasting use of the same "ideo-feeling."

Two of Shakespeare's sonnets are especially illustrative of these points. "That Time of Year" (Sonnet 73) employs three specific patterns in three successive quatrains. The first takes as its core the nearly bare tree in autumn, the second the nearly set sun as night approaches, the third the nearly extinguished fire. Thus there are three separate images, or sets of images; but obviously they all share the quality of "almost," and not so obviously they are variations on the themes of heat and cold, death and decay. Each quatrain, though different from the other two, intensifies the other two by its similarities. Even more varied in its sameness is Shakespeare's "Like as the waves make towards the pebbled shore" (Sonnet 60). Again the three quatrains share a common theme—the effect of time—but the subject matter of each is at first glance unrelated to that of the other two. The first quatrain takes its pictures from the seashore, where each wave contends with the next in making its way toward the pebbled shore. The second uses more than imagery. It is also a synopsis of a person's growth, for "Nativity . . . /Crawls to maturity," only to be eclipsed when time later takes away what once it gave. The third quatrain takes its imagery from vegetation and farming ("flourish," "delves the parallels," "feeds on the rarities," "stands," "scythe," and "mow"). Seashore, growth, farming, three seemingly unrelated patterns, are all united as exponents of the central theme of time and its effects.

Variations within a pattern need not be limited to imagery, as we have already seen in the growth synopsis of Shakespeare's sonnet. Thus the central theme of honor in *Henry IV, Part One* is evident in explicit statements by a melodramatic Hotspur (I, iii; V, iv) and by a no-nonsense, pragmatic Falstaff (V, i; V, iii); in the regal demeanor and haughty tone of King Henry; and in the "grinning honor [which] Sir Walter hath" as he lies dead. Some of this is imagistic (the dead Blunt, Hotspur's metaphorical language), but some of it is direct statement (as in III, ii). In addition, the theme of the play—the conflict between the wronged honor of one family and the wronged honor of another—is so pervasive that it is difficult to say where the motif does *not* appear. In *Moby-Dick* the mysteries of the universe are suggested repeatedly by the passages on the white whale himself, sometimes at length as in the chapter on the whiteness of the whale. But to these we must add the sea as an "image of the ungraspable phantom of life" (chap. 1); the puzzling painting of a ship in a storm (chap. 3); the several allusions to destiny or necessity, chance, and free will; the spirit spout (chap. 51); and the "monstrous" pictures of whales (chap. 55). There are many passages on mysteries and riddles, such as that about the maststander who is so lulled "by the blending cadence of waves with thoughts, that at last he loses his identity; takes the mystic ocean at his feet for the visible image of that deep, blue, bottomless soul, pervading mankind and nature . . ." (chap. 35).

Related plot incidents can provide another type of exponential pattern. For example, in *The Return of the Native*, accidental occurrences follow so quickly upon one another that the theme of chance is developed largely from incidents in the plot sequence: an error in a marriage license; the timing of the return of the native; the coincidence as Mrs. Yeobright approaches her son's cottage, and Eustacia's failure to open the door for her; the snakebite; the consequent yet chance revelations of the circumstances of her death; the deaths of Eustacia and Damon. This sequence of plot incidents invites a formalistic approach, but what we are suggesting here is that the theme of chance is not solely an element of plot structure or form. Once set forth, the theme is an idea unto itself, though plot gives rise to it.

In summary, then, motifs or exponents can be diverse images, diverse actions or episodes, and different personalities; they can be mixtures of pictures, meditations, and symbols. We may begin with a seemingly minor detail, but can be led by it almost inexorably to more details, to richer patterns, and to shifting relationships. But always the disparate items fuse or synthesize, and our realization of the synethesis becomes the joy of discovering what we already have dimly perceived. We are stimulated, in Coleridge's phrase, to see a "unity, that blends, and (as it were) fuses, each into each, by that synthetic and magical power to which we have exclusively appropriated the name of imagination." Such are the principles of the exponential approach and some of the critical, scholarly, and psychological background of this basic tool of the close reader. With these principles in mind, we may now look more closely at the four particular works we are stressing to see in detail how the principles can be used.

II. THE EXPONENTIAL APPROACH IN PRACTICE

A. Exponents in "To His Coy Mistress": From Verbal Pattern to Philosophic Concerns

The opening line of "To His Coy Mistress" ("Had we but world enough and time") introduces a theme that runs throughout the poem: the space-time continuum. Rich in possibilities of verbal patterns, the motif is much more, for the structure of the poem depends on the subjunctive concept, the condition contrary to fact, which gives the whole poem its meaning: "Had we," the speaker says, knowing they do not. From that point on, the hyperbole, the playfulness, the grim fear of annihilation are all based on the feeling of the speaker that he *is* bound by the dimensions of space and time. Clearly, this poem is a proposition made by the eternal male to the eternal female. Just as clearly, and in a wholly different realm, the motif of space and time shows this poem to be a philosophical consideration of time, of eternity; of man's present pleasure (hedonism) and of salvation in an afterlife (traditional Christianity). In this way, Marvell includes in one short poem the range between man's lust and man's philosophy.

On the other hand, we find that the words used to suggest this range tend to be suggestive, to shift their meanings in such fashion as to demand that they be read at different levels at the same time. Let us begin with those exponents that represent the space motif. We have already seen how motifs can shift from one type of manifestation to another. In the same way the space motif of the present poem appears not just in obvious but in veiled allusions. Instances of the space motif in the first section of the poem include "world," "sit down," "which way/To walk," the suggested distance between "Indian Ganges" and the Humber, the distance implicit in the allusions to the Flood and to the widespread Jews of the Diaspora, "vaster than empires," the sense of spatial movement as the speaker's eyes move over the girl's body, and the hint of spatial relationship in "lower rate." The word "long" (line 4) refers to time, but has spatial meaning, too. Several other words ("before," "till," "go," "last") also have overlapping qualities, but perhaps we strain too far to consider them.

Space and time are clearly related in the magnificent image of the opening lines of the second stanza: "But at my back I always hear/Time's wingèd chariot hurrying near." The next couplet provides "yonder," "before," "deserts," and, again, a phrase that suggests both space and time: "vast eternity." In the third stanza the word "sits" echoes the earlier use of the word, and several words suggest movement or action in space: "transpires," "sport," "birds of prey," "devour," "languish in slow-chapped power," "roll," "tear . . . / Thorough." The space motif climaxes in an image that again incorporates the time motif: the sun, by which man measures time, and which will not stand still in space, will be forced to run.

The time motif also appears in its own right, and not only by means of imagery. The word itself appears once in each stanza: near the beginning of stanzas 1 and 2 (lines 1, 22), and in the third as a central part of the lover's proposition (39). Clustering around this basic exponent are these phrases and allusions from the first stanza: the "long love's day" already mentioned; the specific time spans spent in adoring the girl's body and the vaster if less specific "before the Flood" and "Till the conversion of the Jews"; the slow growth of "vegetable love" and the two uses of "age" (lines 17, 18). At the beginning of the second stanza the powerful image of time's winged chariot as it moves across a desert includes the words "always" and "eternity." Other time words are "no more" and "long-preserved." There is also the sense of elapsed time in the allusions to the future decomposition of the lovers' bodies. The third stanza, although it delays the use of the word "time," has for its first syllable the forceful, imperative "now." The word appears twice more in the stanza (lines 37, 38). It is strengthened by "instant," "at once," and "languish in [Time's] slow-chapped power." The phrase "thorough the iron gates of life," though it has more important meanings, also may suggest the passing from temporal life into the not so certain eternity mentioned earlier. The concluding couplet of the poem, as already shown, combines space and time. Further, it may extend time backward to suggest Old Testament days and classic mythology: Joshua stopped the sun so that the Israelites could win a battle, and, even more pertinently, Zeus lengthened the night he spent with Amphitryon's wife.

For the poem is also a love poem, both in its traditional context of the courtly love complaint and in the simple fact of its subject matter: fearing that the afterlife may be a vast space without time, the speaker looks for a means of enjoying whatever he can. This *carpe diem* theme is not uncommon, nor is the theme of seduction. What gives the poem unusual power, however, is the overbearing sense of a cold, calculated drive to use the pleasures of sex to counterbalance the threats of empty eternity. Thus a second major motif used to present the theme, after the space-time relationship, is the sexual. Now let us see what exponents help us to follow this theme.

The title itself immediately sets up the situation. In the

second line, the word "coyness" leads us into the poem itself; even the word "crime" suggests the unconventional (though crime and conventional morality are reversed in the context of the lover's address). The motif gradually emerges, romantically at first, but more frankly, even brutally, as the speaker continues. In the first stanza the distant Ganges and the redness of rubies are romantic enough; the word "complain," in the sense of the courtly lover's song, echoes the whole courtly tradition. The word "love" appears twice before the courtly catalogue of the lady's beautiful body. The catalogue in turn builds to a climax with the increasing time spans and the veiled suggestiveness of "rest" and "part."

The second stanza, though it continues to be somewhat veiled, is less romantic, and it becomes gruesome even while insisting upon sexual love. The lady's beauty will disappear in the marble vault, we are told, and we may associate the word "marble" with the texture and loveliness of the living girl's skin. Now, however, the lover stresses the time when that loveliness will be transferred to stone. In the same type of transference the lover's song, which finds no echoes in that vault, is a veiled image of unrealized sexual union in life. Worms will corrupt the girl in a way that the lover could not. "Quaint honor" is an ironic play on words to suggest the pudendum ("quaint" as in Middle English "queynte"; see Chaucer's "Miller's Tale"). The fires of lust will become ashes (with an implicit comparison to the coldness of marble), and the stanza closes with puns on "private" and "embrace."

The third stanza resumes the romantic imagery of the first ("youthful hue," "morning dew"), but it continues the bolder imagery of the second section. "Pore" is a somewhat unromantic allusion to the girl's body, and "instant fires" recalls the lust and ashes of the preceding stanza. "Sport" takes still a different tack, though it reminds us of the playfulness of the first stanza. After this line, the grimness of the second stanza is even more in evidence. The amorous birds are not turtledoves, but birds of prey, devouring time—and each other. Although the romantic or sentimental is present in the speaker's suggestion that they "roll all our strength and all / Our sweetness up into one ball," the emphasis on the rough and violent continues in the paradoxical "tear our pleasures with rough strife." Once the coy lady's virginity is torn away, the lover will have passed not through the pearly gates of eternity, but through the iron gates of life. Thus the lover's affirmation of life, compounded of despair and defiance, is made by his suggestion that the birth canal of life and procreation is preferable to the empty vault and to the deserts of vast eternity. On the one hand, the exponents of the sexual motif point to a degeneration from romantic convention in the first section to scarcely veiled explicitness in the last. But on the other hand, the speaker has proceeded from a question about the nature of eternity and the meaning of the space-time relationship in this world to an affirmation of what he suspects is one of the few realities left him. The very concreteness, the physicality of the sexual motif provides an answer to the philosophic speculation about space, time, and eternity. Obviously different, the motifs just as obviously fuse to embody the theme of the poem.

There are other, lesser motifs that we could trace had we ourselves space enough and time, such as wings and birds, roundness, and minerals and other things of earth (rubies, marble, iron, ashes, and dust). Each of these serves as an exponent for greater insights into the poem.

A completely different type of motif, much less dependent on specific imagery, is the interplay of sardonic humor and hyperbole, on the one hand, with the brutal and gruesome, on the other. Much of this has already been suggested insofar as these contrasting tones relate to the idealized love-sexual love contrast. The present point is that tones as such can also run through a literary work. Here the pleasant exaggerations of the first section are answered in ironic echo by the sardonic understatement of "The grave's a fine and private place, / But none, I think, do there embrace." Both tones contrast with the matter-of-fact tones of the second and third stanzas. The apparently factual last couplet of the first stanza is actually the most hyperbolical of all. Also, the apparent flatness of the final couplet of the poem masks a boldly impossible statement at the literal level (though it is metaphorically possible). Even the verbs of the poem can serve as exponents for this interplay. The subjunctive nature of the first stanza is evident in "had we," "were," "shouldst," the four uses of "would," and the four uses of "should"—a total of eleven times in twenty lines. This mood changes to the simple expectancy of the indicatives in the second stanza. In turn, these two stanzas lead into the imperatives of the third, where the two uses of "let us" are the key verbs of that section, excepting only the matter-of-fact indicative of the final couplet. Thus, tone, as well as images and symbols, functions as a motif in literature and can manifest itself even in the grammar of verbs.

B. Exponents in "Young Goodman Brown": From Symbolic Object to Theological Complexity

Perhaps the most obviously recurrent symbol in "Young Goodman Brown" is the set of pink ribbons worn by Goodman Brown's wife, Faith. Whatever she is, the pink ribbons are her emblem as much as the scarlet letter is Hester Prynne's. They are mentioned three times in the first page or so of the story. Near the center of the story, a pink ribbon falls, or seems to fall, from a cloud that Goodman Brown sees, or thinks he sees, overhead. At the end of the story, when Faith eagerly greets her returning husband, she still wears her ribbons. Clearly Hawthorne meant them to be suggestive, an exponent of one or of several of the themes of his tale. But of what? Are they emblematic of love, of innocence, of good? Conversely, do they suggest evil, or hypocrisy, or the ambiguous and puzzling blend of good and evil? Are they symbolic of sex and femininity, or of Christian faith? Should we even attempt to limit the meaning to one possibility? Would we be wise—or slovenly—to let the ribbons mean more than one thing during the story? Of this we can be sure: to follow the motif as it guides us to related symbols is to probe the complex interweaving of ideas within the story. Specifically, in the interpretation that follows we suggest that the mysterious pink ribbons are (at least among other things) an exponent of the mysteries of theology. To see that relationship let us first consider the theological matrix of the story.

Because the Puritan setting of "Young Goodman Brown" is basic to the story, we can expect that some of its thematic patterns derive from traditional Christian concepts. For example, readers generally assume that Goodman Brown loses his faith—in Christ, human beings, or both. Thomas E. Connolly (*American Literature*, 28 [1956], 370-375) has argued, however, that the story is an attack on Calvinism, and that Faith (that is, faith) is not lost in the story. On the contrary, he says, Goodman Brown is confirmed in his faith, made aware of "its full and terrible significance." Either way—loss of faith or still firmer belief—we see the story in a theological context. Although we do not have to accept either of these views, we do not have to deny them either. Instead, let us accept this theological matrix. As a matter of fact, let us pursue this theological view by following the exponents of faith, hope, and love, and their opposed vices. We shall examine them in a twofold context: first, Christian revelation and dogma; and, second, a demonic liturgy raised up as a defiant travesty of traditional Christianity.

1. THE THREE THEOLOGICAL VIRTUES AND OTHER BIBLICAL ECHOES

We can assume that Hawthorne was familiar with some of the numerous passages from the Bible that bear upon the present interpretation. Twice in the first epistle to the Thessalonians, St. Paul mentions the need for faith, hope, and love (1:3 and 5:8). In I Corinthians 13, after extolling love as the most abiding of the virtues, Paul concludes his eloquent description with this statement: "So there abide faith, hope, and love, these three; but the greatest of these is love." St. Peter wrote in his first epistle, "But above all things have a constant mutual love among yourselves; for love covers a multitude of sins" (4:8). To these may be added the telling passages on love of God and neighbor (Matthew 22:36-40, Romans 13:9-10) and related passages on love (such as Colossians 3:14 and I Timothy 1:5). Faith, hope, and love, we should note, have traditionally been called the theological virtues because they have God (*theos*) for their immediate object.

Quite possibly Hawthorne had some of these passages in mind, for it appears that he wove into the cloth of "Young Goodman Brown" a pattern of steady attention to these virtues. Surely he provided a clue for us when he chose "Faith" as a name for Goodman Brown's wife. By so naming her, Hawthorne gave faith first place in the story, not necessarily because faith is the story's dominant theme (contrary to what many critics believe, love may well be the dominant theme), but because faith is important in Puritan theology and because it is traditionally listed as the first of these three virtues. Allusions to faith could be made explicit in so many passages in the story and implicit in so many others that they would provide an exponential pattern to suggest clearly the other two virtues. (Similarly, the epithet "goodman" could take on symbolic qualities and function almost as Brown's given name, not simply as something comparable to modern "mister.")

An analysis of these passages, for example, shows not only explicit mentions of faith but also implicit allusions to the virtues of faith, hope, and love; and to their opposed vices, doubt, despair, and hatred. The first scene includes these: "And Faith, as the wife was aptly named"; "My love and my Faith"; "dost thou doubt me already...?"; "he looked back and saw the head of Faith still peeping after him with a melancholy air"; "Poor little Faith!"; and "I'll cling to her skirts and follow her to heaven." Both Goodman Brown and the man he meets in the forest make similar allusions in the second scene, where we read:

211

"Faith kept me back a while"; "We have been a race of honest men and good Christians"; "We are a people of prayer, and good works to boot" (a hint of the theological debate on faith and good works); "Well, then, to end the matter at once, there is my wife, Faith"; "that Faith should come to any harm"; and "why I should quit my dear Faith and go after [Goody Cloyse]." In the episode after the older man leaves Goodman Brown, we have these passages: "so purely and sweetly now, in the arms of Faith!"; "He looked up to the sky, doubting whether there really was a heaven above him"; "With heaven above and Faith below, I will yet stand firm against the devil!"; "a cloud," "confused and doubtful sound of voices," "he doubted"; " 'Faith!' shouted Goodman Brown, in a voice of agony and desperation"; and "My Faith is gone! ... Come, devil .... And, maddened with despair ...." The last scenes, the forest conclave and young Goodman Brown's return home, offer these: " 'But where is Faith?' thought Goodman Brown; and, as hope came"; "the wretched man beheld his Faith ... before that unhallowed altar"; " 'Faith! Faith!' cried the husband, 'look up to heaven ...' "; "the head of Faith ... gazing anxiously"; "a distrustful, if not a desperate man"; "he shrank from the bosom of Faith ... and turned away"; and "no hopeful verse ... , for his dying hour was gloom."

With these passages in mind, let us recall that there may be both symbolical and allegorical uses of the word "faith." Such an ambivalent use can complicate a reading of the story. If the tale is allegorical, for example, it may be that Goodman Brown gained his faith (that is, the belief that he is one of the elect) only three months before the action of the story, since he and Faith have been married three months. The fall of the pink ribbon may be a sin or a fall, just as Adam's fall was the original sin, a lapse from grace. The allegory may further suggest that Goodman Brown shortly loses his new faith, for "he shrank from the bosom of Faith." But allegory is difficult to maintain, often requiring a rigid one-to-one equivalence between the surface meaning and a "higher" meaning. Thus if Faith is faith, and Goodman Brown loses the latter, how do we explain the fact that Faith remains with him and even outlives him? Strict allegory would require that she disappear, perhaps vanish in that dark cloud from which the pink ribbon apparently falls. On the other hand, a pattern of symbolism centering on Faith is easier to handle, and may even be more rewarding by offering us more pervasive, more subtly interweaving ideas that, through their very ambiguity, suggest the difficulties of the theological questions in the story. Such a symbolic view also frees the story from a strict adherence to the Calvinistic concept of election and conviction in the faith, so that the story becomes more universally concerned with Goodman Brown as Everyman Brown.

Whether we emphasize symbol or allegory, however, Goodman Brown must remain a character in his own right, one who progressively loses faith in his ultimate salvation, in his forebears as members of the elect or at least as "good" people, and in his wife and fellow townspeople as holy Christians. At a literal level, he does not lose Faith, for she greets him when he returns from the forest, she stills wears her pink ribbons, she follows his corpse to the grave. Furthermore, she keeps her pledge to him, for it is he who shrinks from her. In other words, Brown has not completely lost Faith; rather he has lost faith, a theological key to heaven.

But when faith is lost, not all is lost, though it may very nearly be. That total loss comes later and gradually as Brown commits other sins. We can follow this emerging pattern when we recall that the loss of faith is closely allied to the loss of hope. We find that, in the story, despair (the vice opposed to hope) can be easily associated with doubt (the vice opposed to faith). For example, the two vices are nearly allied when Goodman Brown recognizes the pink ribbon: " 'My Faith is gone!' cried he, after one stupefied moment. 'There is no good on earth; and sin is but a name. Come, devil; for to thee is this world given.'

And, maddened with *despair*, so that he laughed loud and long, did Goodman Brown grasp his staff and set forth again . . . " (our emphasis).

Doubt, although surely opposed to belief, here leads to despair as much as to infidelity. Similarly, many passages that point to faith also point to hope. When Goodman Brown says, "I'll follow her to heaven," he expresses hope as well as belief. When he says, "With heaven above and Faith below," he hopes to "stand firm against the devil." When he cries, "Faith, look up to heaven," he utters what may be his last hope for salvation. Once again we see how motifs function: It is easy to touch the web at any one point and make it vibrate elsewhere.

Thus we must emphasize that Brown's hope is eroded by increasing doubt, the opposite of faith. We recall that the passages already quoted include the words "desperate," "despair," and "no hopeful verse." When Goodman Brown reenters the town, he has gone far toward a complete failure to trust in God. His thoughts and his actions when he sees the child talking to Goody Cloyse border on the desperate, both in the sense of despair and in the sense of frenzy. Later, we know that he has fully despaired, "for his dying hour was gloom."

"But the greatest of these is love," and "love covers a multitude of sins," the Scriptures insist. Goodman Brown sins against this virtue too, and as we follow these exponents we may well conclude that Hawthorne considered this sin the greatest sin in Brown's life. Sins against love of neighbor are important in other Hawthorne stories. It is a sin against love that Ethan Brand and Roger Chillingworth commit. It is a sin against love of which Rappaccini's daughter accuses Guasconti: "Farewell, Giovanni! Thy words of hatred are like lead within my heart; but they, too, will fall away as I ascend. Oh, was there not, from the first, more poison in thy nature than in mine?" In *The House of the Seven Gables,* it is love that finally overcomes the hate-engendered curse of seven generations.

In "Young Goodman Brown," perhaps the motif of love-hate is first suggested in the opening scene, when Goodman Brown refuses his wife's request that he remain: "My love and my Faith," replied young Goodman Brown, "of all nights in the year, this one night must I tarry away from thee . . . . What, my sweet, pretty wife, dost thou doubt me already, and we but three months married?" Significantly, the words "love" and "Faith" are used almost as synonyms. When the pink ribbons are mentioned in the next paragraph almost as an epithet ("Faith, with the pink ribbons"), they are emblematic of one virtue as much as the other. Later, Goodman Brown's love of others is diminished when he learns that he is of a family that has hated enough to lash the "Quaker woman so smartly through the streets of Salem" and "to set fire to an Indian village." Instead of being concerned for his own neighbor, he turns against Goody Cloyse, resigning her to the powers of darkness: "What if a wretched old woman do choose to go to the devil . . . ?" He turns against Faith and against God Himself when, after the pink ribbon has fallen from the cloud, he says, "Come, devil; for to thee is this world given." To be sure, he still loves Faith enough at the forest conclave to call upon her yet to look to heaven; but next morning when she almost kisses her husband in front of the whole village, "Goodman Brown looked sternly and sadly into her face, and passed on without a greeting." By this time he is becoming guilty of the specific sin called rash judgment, for he rashly makes successive judgments on his neighbors. He shrinks from the blessing of "the good old minister," he disparages the prayers of old Deacon Gookin, he snatches a child away from the catechizing of "Goody Cloyse, that excellent old Christian." Thenceforth he stubbornly isolates himself from his fellow men and from his own wife. On the Sabbath day he questions their hymns and their sermons, at midnight he shrinks from his wife, at morning or eventide he scowls at family prayers. Having given his allegiance to the devil, he cannot fulfill the injunction of the second great commandment any more than he can fulfill that of the first. Unable to love himself,

215

to love himself, he is unable to love his neighbor.

"Faith, hope, and love: these three" he has lost, replacing them with their opposed vices, and the pink ribbons serve as exponents for them all and lead to a double pattern of virtues and vices. Now we can explore further, for the two counterrunning patterns from theology exist in a context of additional religiously oriented motifs—the symbolic patterns associated with the Garden of Eden and with the Mass, communion, and baptism. Thus, apart from the motif of virtues and their opposing vices, we have motifs both from Old Testament tradition and from New Testament liturgy. Let us look first at the echoes of the Old Testament.

The forest into which Goodman Brown ventures, dark and forbidding as it is, equates generally with temptation and sin. Clearly he is uneasy about venturing upon this temptation, about leaving Faith behind him. But as any sinner might think, he seems to say, "Just this once, and then .... " Specifically, however, the forest equates with the Garden of Eden, where grew the Tree of Knowledge of Good and Evil. Thus it is not surprising that the "good man" meets there the Puritan dark man, that is, an embodiment of the dark forces that Eve had encountered in the serpent. To be sure, this time the avatar is a man "in grave and decent attire" and he has an "indescribable air of one who knew the world and who would not have felt abashed at the governor's table or in King William's court .... " But he is soon identified with specific evil actions in the past, and when Goody Cloyse meets him, she screams, "The devil!" Though he appears as a man this time, not as the serpent of Genesis, he carries a staff that writhes like a snake; and we recall not only the snake of the Garden of Eden, but Aaron's staff that, when thrown down before Pharaoh, turned into a snake (Exodus 7:9–12). Should we miss the motif in its early instance, Hawthorne soon draws the explicit comparison of the staff to the "rods which its owner had formerly lent to the Egyptian Magi." When Goodman Brown approaches the central temptation in the forest congregation of devotees, he, like Adam, like

Everyman, is initiated into the knowledge of his race. At this time we should recall a maxim in *The New England Primer:* "In Adam's fall, we sinned all."

Still following these echoes of the Old Testament story, we can now extend our exponential pattern to include the Calvinist setting of early New England. Hawthorne and Goodman Brown, we must note here, are not necessarily thinking in identical ways. Instead, Hawthorne permits Brown's speeches and those of the dark man to carry forward the theological implications of man's depraved nature. It is Goodman Brown who sees evil in all he sees, including himself and Faith. As he and Faith, like Adam and Eve before them, stand at the place of temptation (where not two but four trees mark the place of sin), it is the dark man who insists upon their identity with their race, their knowledge of evil:

> Welcome, my children, to the communion of your race. Ye have found thus young your nature and your destiny.
>
> . . .
>
> Yet here are they all in my worshipping assembly.
>
> . . .
>
> By the sympathy of your human hearts for sin . . .
>
> . . .
>
> It shall be yours to penetrate, in every bosom, the deep mystery of sin . . .
>
> . . .
>
> Evil is the nature of mankind. Evil must be your only happiness. Welcome again, my children, to the communion of your race.

Thus when Goodman Brown calls upon Faith to "look up to heaven," he cannot forget that the pink ribbon has already fallen from heaven. For the Calvinist Brown, original sin is a reality. His cry to Faith is quite literally "after the Fall" (postlapsarian), and the Fall cannot be wished away.

But whether Hawthorne or his reader is Calvinist or not, whether the fall is dream or not, the damage is done to

Goodman Brown. On this Hawthorne and the reader can agree, for faith, hope, and love come near to vanishing along with the forest conclave when it dissolves into ambiguous shadow. In this way, Hawthorne need not commit himself to Calvinism or, conversely, to an attack upon it. As with the dream, "be it so if you will." The effect on Goodman Brown remains: Whether because of his own fault or because of the depraved nature that is a consequence of Adam's fall, Goodman Brown has lost faith, and hope, and love. He has lost them in a context derived from the Old Testament story of original sin.

2. LITURGICAL PARALLELS

The perversion of these three virtues, especially the travesty of the cardinal injunction to love God and neighbor, has a counterpart in still another pattern of images and symbols. If we perceive the exponents of the story of Genesis—garden, trees, devil, snake, and staff—we must be aware too of New Testament motifs, based in part on the same objective items. For example, the forest ritual is a perversion of the Mass. Instead of being a demonstration of God's love for man, it is the devil's mass or the witches' Sabbath described by Cotton Mather in his "Hortatory and Necessary Address," a section of his *Wonders of the Invisible World:* "These Witches . . . have met in Hellish Rendezvouzes, wherein the Confessors do say, they have had their diabolical Sacraments, imitating the *Baptism* and the *Supper* of our Lord." Just as the orthodox Mass is a ritual involving congregation and priest, the forest conclave has a congregation presided over by a kind of minister. "Converts" or "proselytes" await admission to the group. Before the group rises a "rock, bearing some rude, natural resemblance either to an altar or a pulpit, and surrounded by four blazing pines, their tops aflame, their stems untouched, like candles. . . ." In the rock is something akin to a baptismal font, "a basin . . . hollowed, naturally, in the rock." It may contain water, "reddened by the lurid light," or liquid flame, "or was it blood?" If it is the latter, it incorporates not only baptismal imagery but also hints of the Holy Grail, the vessel that, according to widespread legend, contained the blood of Christ at the Last Supper and after his sacrificial crucifixion. There are several allusions to communion, once during the forest walk, when the dark man says that he has drunk the communion wine with many deacons, and twice in his address to the conclave. During that conclave both the idea and the word are stressed. Although the vision vanishes before Goodman Brown and Faith partake of the sacramental sign of baptism, which through the hint of blood is both baptism and communion, the "sable form" twice urges upon them the "communion of your race" and develops the concept of their bond, their "sympathy" (thus communion) with other evil persons. Finally, if Goodman Brown is the equivalent of the Old Testament Adam, he is the ironic contrast to the New Testament Adam, a travesty of the loving Christ, whose sacrificial blood—if it is in the font—is there only for desecration at a devil's mass.

In orthodox Christianity the principles of theology are presented both explicitly and implicitly in the Scriptures; in turn, Christian liturgy is derived from those Scriptures. In "Young Goodman Brown" the motifs of faith, hope, and love, summed up in the pink ribbons, blend each into each in a context that derives from both the Old and New Testaments and that is informed by a parody of Christian liturgy. If the blend sometimes confuses us, like the alternating light and dark of the forest conclave, and more particularly like the mystery of the pink ribbons, it is perhaps no less than Hawthorne intended when he used motifs to suggest Goodman Brown's knowledge of good and evil, a knowledge that rapidly becomes confusion. For Goodman Brown it is a knowledge by which he seems to turn the very names and epithets of Goodman, Goody, and Gookin into variant spellings of "evil," just as he transmutes faith, hope, and love into their opposed vices.

C. Exponents in *Adventures of Huckleberry Finn:* From Image Cluster to Sociopolitical Commentary

As we turn our attention to the novel, we find that the use of motifs is not different from the use made in the genres we have already considered. But there is an amplitude in the novel that goes beyond that of the poem and the short story. Hence the novel may more easily develop or suggest many things at many levels. *Adventures of Huckleberry Finn* unquestionably does so. What we can observe in this chapter is how one pattern can suggest a means of entry into the rich stores of such a novel; we do not exhaust the book.

As a matter of fact, the motifs that run through *Huckleberry Finn* are so numerous and so diverse that only recently have critics begun to probe the depths of the book, showing in study after study the many threads that run through the novel. Among them are the questions of religion, of conscience, and of good and evil; the nature of aristocracy, of kingship; the criticism of slavery, of caste, of "civilization"; Huck's maturation and his initiation into adult life; the search for a father; the prevalence of cruelty and violence; escape, the death wish, and the womb image; humor, in an abundance of forms; and the river, as a god and as a means of rebirth.

But this fullness need not frighten the reader from tracing these themes, for each of them has its exponents. Each provides clues that enable the reader to delve deeper and deeper into a given theme and to see the relationship between one theme and another. No matter how widely any one of these themes may range, it is an idea that must be founded on the details of Twain's book, on the words that present this idea. For example, one of the most encompassing ideas in the novel is that of civilization. Thus it is not only interesting but important for the full appreciation of the book that we note Huck's attitude toward civilization. In Chapter 1 he says, "The Widow Douglas she took me for her son, and allowed she would sivilize me . . . ." With this we may compare the last two sentences of the novel: "But I reckon I got to light out for the territory ahead of the rest, because Aunt Sally she's going to adopt me and sivilize me, and I can't stand it. I been there before." Huck also says in the sixth chapter: "This [possible return to the Widow] shook me up considerable, because I didn't want to go back to the widow's any more and be so cramped up and sivilized, as they called it." Of course the questions of what civilization is and who is civilized appear in many forms throughout the novel. The point here is that at beginning and end Twain uses the very word to remind us of the idea; he uses an exponent to represent the pattern.

Keeping in mind this emphasis on specific words on one side and wide dimensions on the other, let us now look at just one aspect of civilization, the novel's direct references to kings and related matters. On the one side, we find that the words "king," "duke," "dauphin," and "royalty" and the names of kings occur so often that they etch themselves into our minds. On the other side, these words and allusions are exponents for the entire complex of aristocracy, feudal lordship, serfdom, and slavery. The resulting image cluster (cf. Spurgeon's and Kenneth Burke's terminology) is an unusually rich blend of ideas, images, allusions, and related words. From this complex we may easily move still deeper into an appreciation of Twain's sociological criticism, his views on political and religious tyranny, and his attack on the romanticism that causes Americans to this day to respond to the trappings associated with royalty—ranging from the New Orleans Mardi Gras to national beauty queens and some television programs. The sociological and political pattern—so large in itself—is closely entwined, then, with the equally large theme of Romanticism. But by restricting ourselves to the motif of kingship we can deal specifically with one approach to a theme about which full-length books and numerous articles have been written. Now let us see how such a study might begin.

1. EXPLICIT ALLUSIONS TO KINGSHIP AND ROYALTY

With the exception of Tom's passing reference to an "emperor's daughter" near the end of Chapter 3, the first mention of kings is in Chapter 14, "Was Solomon Wise?" Significantly for Twain's treatment of monarchy, the commonsense answer that Jim offers is that Solomon's proverbial wisdom amounted only to "de dad-fetchedes' ways I ever see." After Jim fairly well establishes the foolishness of Solomon, Huck goes on to talk about other kings:

> So I went to talking about other kings, and let Solomon slide. I told about Louis Sixteenth that got his head cut off in France long time ago; and about his little boy the dolphin, that would 'a' been a king, but they took and shut him up in jail, and some say he died there.
> "Po' little chap."
> "But some says he got out and got away, and come to America."
> "Dat's good! But he'll be pooty lonesome—dey ain' no kings here, is dey, Huck?"
> "No."
> "Den he cain't git no situation. What he gwyne to do?"

The chapter containing this passage is not the only one that alludes to kings in its title. Others are "The Duke and the Dauphin Come Aboard," "What Royalty Did to Parkville," "The Orneriness of Kings," "The King Turns Parson," "I Steal the King's Plunder," and "The Pitiful Ending of Royalty." In short, seven of the forty-three chapter titles allude to royalty in an American frontier setting—incongruous in one way, but consistent with the folly of Solomon's "wisdom."

These last six chapter titles result from Huck's having aided two renegades, the younger of whom soon announces, "By rights, I am a duke!" Of course it is not long before the older one counters with a claim to be "the late Dauphin," the very person about whom Huck has told Jim. From this time forth, references to "the Duke" and "the King" and epithets like "Your Grace" and "Your Majesty" sprinkle the pages. The two scoundrels even invent some new titles for each other, as when the Duke says, "But the histrionic muse is the darling. Have you ever trod the boards, Royalty?" The King answers no, and then the Duke says, "You shall, then, before you're three days older, Fallen Grandeur." But perhaps the King already has gotten the better of the Duke with his mispronunciation of the Duke's assumed name of Bridgewater as Bilgewater. At any rate, the Duke and the King appear under their titles on almost every page of the middle third of the novel: Royalty now floats on the Mississippi.

In addition, the presence of the two "frauds" (one of Huck's favorite words for them) is the effective means of introducing a number of allusions to kings, especially those who appear in drama. (The fact that drama is a form of make-believe may be a commentary in itself.) For example, the Duke tries to teach the King a garbled soliloquy from *Hamlet,* a play about kings and a prince, and he confusedly echoes *Macbeth,* another play about kings. There are allusions to plays about Richard III and King Lear. But not only do the frauds echo the pseudoreality of drama, they themselves produce a "drama." In at least six separate instances (chaps. 22, 24, 28, 31 [twice], and 33) we are reminded of the very name of their spectacle, "The Royal Nonesuch." By it Twain seems to suggest that just as there are nonreal kings on the Mississippi who talk of make-believe dramas, there are "no such" things as royalty—anywhere—for any claim to royalty is a fraud. The "orneriness" of kings is demonstrated in a different way by Huck's confused but hilarious lecture to Jim on the villainous royalty he knows of from history. In the brilliant catalogue he includes Henry VIII, Charles II, Louis XIV, Louis XV, James II, Edward II, Richard III, "them Saxon heptarchies," and "forty more." Then he sums up: "All I say is, kings is kings, and you got to make allowances. Take them all around, they're a mighty ornery lot. It's the way they're raised." One more king is mentioned in this section. This time Huck has less disparaging, if somewhat manufactured and irrelevant, things to say about William IV, whom Huck claims to have seen regularly at church. When he is caught in the lie by one of the Wilks girls, he simply creates one more incongruous picture, that of King William taking sea baths in an inland city.

Even after royalty meets its pitiful end in tar and feathers, Huck is still not free from kings and their baleful influence, for now Tom Sawyer reenters the story, bringing with him his highly romantic—and therefore equally fraudulent—concept of kings, ladies of the courts, and coats of arms. Tom's lecture on royal, or at least aristocratic, escapes compares with Huck's on the orneriness of kings; like Huck he catalogues aristocrats mentioning specifically Baron Trenck, Casanova, Benvenuto Cellini, and Henri IV, and alludes to the romantic old areas of Languedoc and Navarre. Later, after Huck makes one more ludicrous error about royalty (he has William the Conqueror on the *Mayflower*), Tom adds another list: "Look at Lady Jane Gray," he says; "look at Gilford Dudley; look at old Northumberland. . . . Jim's got to do his inscription and coat of arms. They all do." Tom then describes the projected coat of arms, mixing some traditional terms and colors of heraldry with his own symbols and interpretations. Having criticized kings, Twain now seems to say that the proposed heraldic emblem is just as fraudulent—or as legitimate—as any coat of arms ever was. Near the end of the book we find still more allusions, two to Louis XIV and two to Louis XVI. Twain's choice of these seems consistent with the idea of fraud and its reward: Louis XIV was known as the Sun King; Louis XVI was beheaded during the Reign of Terror.

Such are the kings and dukes and aristocratic ladies and gentlemen who people Huck's world and Tom's reading. They are "nonesuch" and pitiful rascals; they are unwise and ornery; they are imprisoned and executed. They are frauds all, whether Huck and Jim know them to be such or Tom unwittingly shows them to be so. From the words clustering around the concept of kingship, we can move steadily to such indictments.

2. IMPLIED REFERENCES TO SOUTHERN ARISTOCRATS

But how much further does the motif lead us? Surely it is an indictment of royalty and aristocracy in ages past and in distant lands. But it is more than that. It is an indictment of the American counterpart on the frontier and in the South. In other words, although the words "king" and "duke" are exponents of a pattern, a set of themes, the pattern itself is an exponent of one of America's sorriest chapters in history—the preservation of the feudal concept of over-lords and vassals in the American system of planters and slaves. To illustrate this point, let us look again at Tom's suggested coat of arms: "On the scutcheon we'll have a bend *or* in the dexter base, a saltire *murrey* in the fess, with a dog, couchant, for common charge, and under his foot a chain embattled, for slavery . . . ; crest, a runaway nigger, *sable*, with his bundle over his shoulder on a bar sinister. . . ." Of course Tom is naively unaware of the moral significance of slavery and of the cruelty he inflicts upon the compliant Jim. (Tom, we must remember, is shaped by "civilization" and has not had the instructive experiences Huck has had.) Even so, Tom unwittingly brings in the indictment: His coat of arms includes the imagery of the dog and the chain and the theme of domination suggested by the reclining dog. He himself uses the word "slavery," and there are possible puns in the words "common charge" and "bar sinister." Above these details stands the whole ironic paradox of a coat of arms for a "runaway nigger, *sable*." Just as Twain has already asked who is royal and who is fraud, he now asks who is noble and who is slave.

The coat of arms is a clear and specific exponent of the motif of kingship. But earlier in the novel we have met a less clear variation of the pattern, one that is more perva-sive but no less real—the variation in the chapters in which the Grangerfords and the Shepherdsons appear. As with many episodes in the novel, there are several motifs: We can immediately recognize the antiromanticism seen elsewhere in the book; the attack on pseudoculture, bad poetry, and tasteless interior decoration; and possibly even the conflicts between grange (farm) workers and shep-herds (with further echoes of Cain and Abel, Romeo and

Juliet). But we are here concerned specifically with how the two families fit the pattern of royalty and aristocracy. If we remember that the word "gentleman" was once reserved only to the aristocracy, we can see the significance of Huck's description of Colonel Grangerford: "Colonel Grangerford was a gentleman, you see. He was a gentleman all over; and so was his family. He was well born, as the saying is, and that's worth as much in a man as it is in a horse, so the Widow Douglas said, and nobody ever denied that she was of the first aristocracy in our town . . . ." Shortly after this passage Huck describes the ritualistic toast the Grangerford children drink to their parents: There is ceremonious bowing, and the children stand until the elders are seated.

Such are the pseudoroyalty on the banks of the Mississippi. And they are not alone, for the Shepherdsons are "another clan of aristocracy around there." By now, however, the point is obvious, and we know what will soon happen to them all. In spite of their veneer of culture, their decorous formality within the family, these people are not better than Huck's Henry VIII, who "used to marry a new wife every day, and chop off her head next morning." Their feud is no better—and no worse—than the butchery of Richard III or Henry VIII or the French Revolution, nor any more or less sensible in its result than the tarring and feathering of another set of aristocratic personages in this novel. One can only oppose to it the un-Solomon-like wisdom of Sophia Grangerford (her first name means "wisdom"), who runs away from the entire foolishness.

As we said earlier, a novel has ample space for many themes and for exponents to guide the reader to them, and it can develop these themes at many levels at once. Certainly this is true of *Huckleberry Finn*. We have traced just one of these motifs, that of kingship as it recurs in words, in the names of kings and aristocratic persons, and other exponents. In turn the motif raises questions about what kingship is, where it can be found, what types of tyranny and foolishness it thrives on, what effects it has, what slavery it imposes. Additionally, this motif impinges on the themes of morality and romanticism. Finally, it raises these questions in the context of some of the richest humor in American literature, humor that stands both as indictment of and cure for human folly.

To paraphrase Huck, this is what comes of handling words.

D. Exponents in *Hamlet:* From Recurrent Symbol to "Felt Life"

Like Twain's *Huckleberry Finn,* Shakespeare's *The Tragedy of Hamlet, Prince of Denmark* is a highly complex masterpiece: It has so many levels that scholars continue to find great rewards in studying it. Again, however, we need not panic as we approach a work that challenges experts. The tools we have used are still available. In considering *Huckleberry Finn* we used numerous exponents of kingship as guides to a much larger theme, a commentary on society. In discussing *Hamlet* we will start with one specific symbol, but that symbol will enable us to go at least as far as we did in *Huckleberry Finn,* for it reaches at least to four thematic levels. First, that specific symbol: the trap.

Several times in the play, but in varying images, we find allusions to different kinds of entanglement. Polonius injudiciously uses the metaphor to warn Ophelia away from Hamlet's "holy vows of heaven," vows that he says, are "springes to catch woodcocks" (I, iii). More significant is Hamlet's deliberate misnaming of "The Murder of Gonzago"; he calls it "The Mousetrap" (III, ii), because it is, as he says elsewhere, "the thing / Wherein I'll catch the conscience of the King" (II, ii). Claudius feels that he is trapped: "O limed soul, that, struggling to be free, / Art more engag'd" (III, iii). Hamlet, in the hands of plotters, finds himself "thus be-netted round with villainies" and one for whom Claudius has "Thrown out his angle [fishhook] for my proper life" (V, ii). The dying Laertes echoes his father's metaphor when he tells Osric that he is "as a woodcock to mine own springe" (V, ii). Thus we begin our study with traps—springes, lime, nets, mousetraps, and angles or hooks. Now these are normally for animals, and surely animals are here—the woodcocks, the mice. But we are talking of human beings, persons who are trapped like animals. Perhaps they are animals. Perhaps their dilemmas are traps. With these larger questions now raised, we can proceed.

Of several major motifs orchestrated in the play, we consider four at length: (1) the various kinds of love; (2) the relationship of reason, madness, and brutishness; (3) the conflict between thought and action; and (4) the influence of religion and culture. These four motifs share at least one major characteristic: the persons of the drama are *trapped* in the complexities of all four themes. The motif of revenge is of course at the heart of this tragedy of blood, and much has been said of it. We confine ourselves to a consideration of revenge only as it appears within the contexts of the four motifs mentioned. As we have seen in other works considered earlier in this chapter, we shall see again that interlocking patterns, comparisons, and contrasts abound. For example, we could begin with love and move from that to madness (as Polonius thinks Hamlet has done) and thus see irrational man as an animal; then we could come full circle to the motif of love in the crude sensualism of Gertrude and Claudius. Similarly, we could note repeated allusions to fate and to memory and the patterns of symbolism that involve not only animals and traps but also rottenness and decay and gardens, for these exponents also lead us into the themes of the play. The point is that there is no one place to begin; we simply must begin someplace.

1. TRAPS AND THE MOTIF OF LOVE

Let us first consider love. This basic theme ranges in the play from the purest form of friendship through varieties of familial and romantic love down to lust (remembered by Polonius and realized between Gertrude and Claudius) and even incest (as seen by the ghost and Hamlet in Gertrude's new marriage; see chapter 1, II, B, 3).

Immediately we see how one motif absorbs another. As we know from historical criticism, this revenge tragedy is like a number of lesser plays written in the same era. The obvious and conventional motivation of the drama is Hamlet's desire for revenge against his murderous uncle. But Shakespeare takes this traditional theme and fuses it with the larger pattern of love. In this way he greatly complicates Hamlet's dilemma, his sense of being "be-netted." First, Hamlet's hatred of his uncle is paradoxically motivated by his love of his father. Second, his disappointment with his mother ("Frailty, thy name is woman") derives partly from his disillusionment with her for her forsaking the memory of "Hyperion" for a "satyr," partly from the jolt given to his youthful concepts of romantic love, partly from his reaction to a marriage he considers incestuous. But perhaps the greatest element in this disappointment, at least for many modern interpreters of the play, is the emotional turmoil brought on by the Oedipus complex: Hamlet's feelings for his mother are not only those of a cast-off son, but those of a rejected and jealous lover. Third, Hamlet's notions of romantic love, which his mother helps to shatter, are centered in Ophelia. This romantic love steadily complicates Hamlet's own turmoil—and further orchestrates the entire theme. Polonius, without Hamlet's knowledge, forbids Ophelia to see the prince; the ghost's demand for revenge makes it impractical for Hamlet to think of courtship; reasons of state may necessitate his marrying elsewhere (I, iii); Ophelia's lie about her father's whereabouts convinces Hamlet of her disaffection and duplicity (III, i). The combination of these elements prompts Hamlet's violent reaction against Ophelia—and against "woman," including his mother: "if thou wilt needs marry, marry a fool; for wise men know well enough what monsters you make of them" (III, i).

Though less important than the emotions centering on romantic love, Hamlet's friendship for Horatio deserves special mention as what is possibly the purest form of love in the play. Certainly for Elizabethan audiences, friendship was one of the highest virtues. Friendship between man and man was looked upon not through modern eyes that tend to see homosexual implications but through Elizabethan eyes that saw Platonic idealism. Thus Hamlet is able to say to Horatio:

> Nay, do not think I flatter
> For what advancement may I hope from thee
> That no revenue hast but thy good spirits
> To feed and clothe thee? . . .

And he adds:

> Since my dear soul was mistress of my choice
> And could of men distinguish, her election
> Hath seal'd thee for herself. . . .
>   Give me that man
> That is not passion's slave, and I will wear him
> In my heart's core, ay, in my heart of heart,
> As I do thee. [III, ii]

Hamlet's varied emotional attachments have counterparts in the Polonius family at two levels: (1) There is a series of individual foil relationships; (2) the lesser family is a group symbolic of the royal family. Realizing this, we must broaden the orchestration—almost double the instruments; and in doing so we better appreciate the web or net of human emotions. We should remember that minor characters frequently are used as foils to help us understand the protagonists, and that a minor plot may be used to balance and clarify the main action. Of the first sort we have Hamlet-Laertes, the ghost-Polonius, and Gertrude-Ophelia; of the second, we find that the minor plot reaches its catastrophe (the deaths of Polonius and Ophelia) earlier than the fifth act and that it has themes similar to those of the main action. The familial pattern is obvious early in the play when Laertes bids farewell to his father and his sister. His sense of filial duty, even to a doddering old man, and Ophelia's simple, obedient "I shall obey, my lord," are shortly echoed in Hamlet's cry to the ghost,

> Remember thee!
> Ay, thou poor ghost, while memory holds a seat
> In this distracted globe. [I, v]

Ophelia's love for her father appears poignantly (and echoes Hamlet's cry) when, after her beloved has slain her father, she sings her songs in the mad scene of Act IV and says, "There's rosemary, that's for remembrance. Pray you, love, remember . . ." (IV, v). The two familial patterns interlock in Acts IV and V, when Laertes works for revenge for Polonius's death at Hamlet's hands and struggles with Hamlet over Ophelia's body. Thus in the Polonius family the entire pattern of active duty and filial obedience, combined with sincere love, contrasts with Halmet's own dormant obligation to achieve revenge, although he loves sincerely. Nor is the similarity lost on Hamlet, who says of Laertes: "For by the image of my cause, I see / The portraiture of his" (V, ii).

Hamlet's love of his parents and Ophelia, his friendship for Horatio, the affections within the Polonius family—all are either noble or conventionally acceptable. Other exponents suggest, however, the lust between Gertrude and Claudius, a brutish love to which even they at least implicitly admit. Although their marriage is apparently legal (Henry VIII had a dispensation for a similar marriage), Hamlet and the ghost both call it incestuous, and its lustful, animal nature is a motif projected through images and symbols throughout the play. For example, the ghost calls Claudius "that incestuous, that adulterate beast" who lies in a "couch for luxury and damned incest" [I, v]. With similar imagery Claudius admits that he murdered to win the queen as well as the crown; his fratricide is "rank, it smells to heaven . . ." (III, iii). When the queen admits her guilt to Hamlet, she looks into her soul and sees there "such black and grained spots / As will not leave their tinct." Hamlet remonstrates with her for living

> In the rank sweat of an enseamed bed,
> Stew'd in corruption, honeying and making love
> Over the nasty sty! ... [III, iv]

When Hamlet kills Claudius he says, "Here, thou incestuous, murderous, damned Dane" (V, ii). In short, their love is much like the lust defined in Shakespeare's Sonnet 129: "Th' expense of spirit in a waste of shame / Is lust in action. ..." Even if we grant that there is something nobler than lust in Gertrude's love for Claudius (witness her behavior when Laertes confronts them in Act IV), the Gertrude-Claudius sexual entrapment contrasts with the purer involvements among the other characters.

2. TRAPS AND THE MOTIF OF REASON, MADNESS, AND BRUTISHNESS

The animal imagery of the play (and of Sonnet 129) leads us to explore further the contrast between man's brutish and man's higher natures, for the contrast is not merely a matter of lust and ideal love. Hamlet makes the contrast for us in a passage filled with words that serve us as exponents:

> What is a man,
> If his chief good and market of his time
> Be but to sleep and feed? A beast, no more.
> Sure, He that made us with such large discourse,
> Looking before and after, gave us not
> That capability and god-like reason
> To fust in us unus'd. Now, whether it be
> Bestial oblivion, or some craven scruple
> Of thinking too precisely on th' event,—
> A thought which, quarter'd, hath but one part wisdom
> And ever three parts coward,—I do not know
> Why yet I live to say, "This thing's to do ...." [IV, iv]

Claudius later talks of the loss of judgment, "Without the

which we are pictures, or mere beasts" (IV, v). And yet it is this same Claudius whose irrational lusts detract from his humanity and whose drinking spurs Hamlet's thoughts on men and their vices (I, iv). Irrationality in the form of mental illness, when the "god-like reason" ceases to function, appears in three different ways in the play. Ophelia is completely insane in Act IV: Having lost both father and lover, she is reduced to singing plaintive, even bawdy songs. Polonius, though not insane, is possibly senile; ironically, it is he who tries to find the cause of Hamlet's lunacy, and the degeneration he traces is comparable to the toll the years have taken of him. Hamlet is not, of course, insane. His own explanations of his strategy and actions attest to his sanity and his pretended insanity (I, v; III, ii; III, iv). But his pretense and his emotional intensity are further indices of the themes of sanity and insanity, reason and unreason, the human and the animal. Ophelia's lament about him shows this interplay:

> O, what a noble mind is here o'erthrown!
> The courtier's, soldier's, scholar's, eye, tongue, sword;
> The expectancy and rose of the fair state,
> The glass of fashion and the mould of form,
> The observ'd of all observers, quite quite down!
> And I, of ladies most deject and wretched,
> That suck'd the honey of his music vows.
> Now see that noble and most sovereign reason,
> Like sweet bells jangled, out of tune and harsh;
> That unmatch'd form and feature of blown youth
> Blasted with ecstasy. [III, i]

It is a lovely but only partially accurate description; it gains its full relevance in the next act, when Ophelia herself is "blasted with ecstasy."

These three levels of mental aberration—true insanity, pretended insanity, and senility—are in a sense negative exponents of the question "What is man?" In the motifs of aberrant love and aberrant rationality we can see the theme of men being trapped, ensnared by folly or by their lesser nature. It is to the higher aspects of man's nature that Hamlet addresses himself when he exclaims: "What a piece of work is a man!" The motifs that we have just followed, the very ones Ophelia thinks of, are here too:

> What a piece of work is a man! How noble in reason! How infinite in faculty! In form and moving how express and admirable! In action how like an angel! In apprehension how like a god! The beauty of the world! The paragon of animals! And yet, to me, what is this quintessence of dust? [II,ii]

Implicit here is that man is an animal endowed with a deep ability to love ("infinite in faculty"); hence we recall the motif of the kinds of love. Explicit here is that man is also noble in reason; hence we recall the contrast between reason and insanity. Furthermore, man can "move" and "act" and "apprehend," and this combination becomes our next major concern.

3. TRAPS AND THE MOTIF OF THOUGHT AND ACTION

Another motif that stretches through the whole play might call the tension between thought and action, because Hamlet is a man of both. It is evident in the most famous speech of all, the "To be or not to be" soliloquy, when Hamlet says,

> Thus conscience [reflection] does make cowards of us all;
> And thus the native hue of resolution
> Is sicklied o'er with the pale cast of thought,
> And enterprises of great pith and moment
> With this regard their currents turn awry,
> And lose the name of action. [III, i]

In two other soliloquies Hamlet is concerned with the relationship between thought and his own failure to act: "Now I am alone" (II, ii) and "How all occasions" (IV, iv). Late in the play he reminds Laertes of his (Hamlet's) mixture of action and inaction: "though I am not splenitive and rash,/Yet have I something in me dangerous . . . " (V, i). Another clear statement of this motif is that by Claudius (who regularly deserves careful comparison with Hamlet):

> That we would do,
> We should do when we would; for this "would" changes,
> And hath abatements and delays as many
> As there are tongues, are hands, are accidents . . . . [IV, vii]

However much he is aware of his internal struggle between reflection and action, Hamlet does act. He keeps the secret of the ghost; he arranges for the play within the play; he kills Polonius (taking him for Claudius); he foils the emissaries escorting him to England and later deals with the pirates; he bests Laertes and kills Claudius. He also praises impetuous action:

> Rashly,—
> And prais'd be rashness for it: let us know
> Our indiscretion sometime serves us well
> When our deep plots do pall . . . . [V, ii]

On other occasions, however, he is the thinker, as in his five soliloquies, his talks with Horatio and with Rosencrantz and Guildenstern, his fears that the ghost might be a devil, his decision not to kill Claudius in Act III. This contrast between Hamlet the man of thought and Hamlet the man of action keeps both character and play in constant tension. Sometimes like Horatio, the man of thought, sometimes like Laertes and Fortinbras, the men of action, Hamlet veers toward one side, then the other, and does not kill Claudius until he, Hamlet, is about to die. Having killed Claudius, he dies in the arms of the scholar Horatio, but his eulogy is pronounced by the soldier Fortinbras. Like the limed bird, struggling to be free, Hamlet is only more engaged, till death frees him.

4. TRAPS AND THE DILEMMAS OF RELIGION AND CULTURE

Much of this tension in Hamlet is the result of two conflicting ethics. The vengeance desired by both Hamlet and the ghost derives generally from the tradition of the blood feud, perhaps from the ancient culture of the Danes.

Conceivably, the spirit of the *comitatus*—the loyalty between chieftain and followers—is still present: The king
has been killed, the blood feud requires that he be
avenged, filial duty demands that Hamlet perform the rite.
Possibly the Germanic concept of *Wyrd* (fate) is also
reflected in Hamlet's several allusions to fate (I, iv; V, i; V,
ii). But Hamlet's Germanic culture notwithstanding, the
Everlasting has fixed His canon against suicide (I, ii) and
against murder and revenge. For Hamlet is not only Teu-
tonic but Christian. The highest ethic of the Christian is to
love. To murder is to violate this principle, as even Claudius well knows. His offense "hath the primal eldest curse
upon 't, / A brother's murder." Surely Claudius's thoughts
about Cain and Abel find an echo in Hamlet's hesitancy to
murder his uncle. Even the ghost, while urging revenge,
says that the "best" of murders is "most foul." Hamlet's
knowledge of Christianity serves him ironically well at the
turning point of the play when he deliberately postpones
murdering Claudius. He realizes that possibly Claudius
has achieved perfect contrition; if such is the case, then
Claudius will go to the Christian's heaven, and the pagan's
revenge will be incomplete. Thus Hamlet must wait for a
time when Claudius's soul is in greater jeopardy. When he
mistakes Polonius for Claudius, he kills the old man in the
queen's bedchamber, where Claudius's lust may have
damned his soul anew. When he kills Claudius it is after
Claudius has plotted murder. So does the Christian injunction to love one's enemies clash with the ancient injunction
to avenge one's king and father. So do thought and action
resolve themselves.

But if they resolve themselves, the resolution comes only
in the deaths of the principals. They have struggled with
themselves and with each other; they have been caught up
in springes and lime and nets. In that quandary called life,
they have come to feel what they cannot quite understand.
Their very emotions and thoughts, some base, some noble,
their actions and inactions, and their codes of behavior
have all compounded to hold them in a trap. They have

felt life and, finally, have met death. By participating in the drama, the reader (or viewer) also experiences what that quandary of life is, and how limited is the release from that quandary. Perhaps this is the meaning of Hamlet's last line, when, released from springes and nets, from struggle and tension, he says, "The rest is silence."

Besides the four motifs we have followed, other threads of thematic imagery and statement have their place in the tapestry that is *Hamlet*, each thread working out its pattern to present the richness of the experience. But these four suffice to show that the rich experience of Shakespeare's most famous work can begin with a perception of some of the exponents of the play's finely wrought motifs.

What we have seen in *Hamlet* is what we have seen throughout this chapter. Like the threads of a tapestry, like the notes and chords and melodies of music, the images, the statements, the themes of literature rise and fall, meet and join or clash. Any one of these can be an exponent of the entire pattern, a clue to the full experience. Once we understand how these exponents help us, we gain much insight into the nature of literary art and communication. As in life, we may not at first perceive all the relationships inherent in a situation, but as we gradually become aware of them they project to us the richness and complexity of the art object. In reaching toward the meaning of literature, we enjoy and we profit from the discovery of the unknown and the recognition of what was once only dimly perceived.

OTHER APPROACHES

At any given moment in mature interpretation of a piece of literature the reader may be responding from one particular orientation—perhaps a biographical, historical, formalistic, or psychological approach. Ideally, however, the ultimate response should be multiple and eclectic. This is so because a work of literary art is the embodiment of a potential human experience; and because human experience is multidimensional, the reader needs a variety of ways to approach and realize ("make real") that experience.

In this chapter we therefore offer further indications of contemporary approaches to literature, either because they are different from those in the preceding chapters or because they place different emphases upon some of the aspects of those chapters. In addition, we depart in this chapter from the established pattern in that we do not offer explications of the four works common to each of the first five chapters. Rather, we suggest a number of approaches that may profitably be studied further.

In offering varied approaches, this chapter is a logical development from the first five, with Chapter 5 something of a bridge between this one and the first four. The first four are demonstrations of particular approaches and well-established methodologies. In Chapter 5 some of the insights of the preceding four come together because the technique of close reading stressed by the formalists combines with other approaches; these other approaches thus take the reader not only into the work, as the formalists do, but into other domains as well—into questions of value, religion, and social concern and of philosophy beyond the aesthetics stressed by formalism. By emphasizing the tracing of exponents (the recurrent symbols, words, devices, or other motifs that open out to the fullness of the work and its experience), Chapter 5 is itself eclectic: It combines the methodology of close reading with the methodology of traditional approaches and psychological insights. In addition, it demonstrates that the richness of literary experience is, like life itself, the composite of many elements, any one of which may lead to another. In the present chapter we suggest other approaches the reader may pursue for himself and may apply on any given occasion to seek that richness.

Besides the eclectic stress of this chapter, there are several other characteristics that we may note. First, after the great and salutary success of the New Critics in teaching us to return to the printed text and to see it as artifact, it is not surprising—indeed, it was to be expected—that a reaction should take us somewhat away from formalism. A number of "schools" or approaches have suggested that in emphasizing the artifact the formalists neglected the humanness of the experience of literature, neglected the social milieu of literature, or falsified the vision of a true eclectic (for example, by being male-dominated). Consequently, several of the approaches we survey here reflect this swing away from the allegedly objective approach of the New Critics. Second, some of the approaches in this chapter have European origins. The great movement of the New Critics was centered in America, with some ties to or even some origins in England. But more recent movements—structuralism, the new stylistics, the phenomenological approach—have predominantly Continental origins, and are exerting significant influence upon American criticism. Third, a number of the approaches in this chapter are in some respects quite traditional and are partly suggested in Chapter 1. However, not all approaches could be discussed in the context of Chapter 1, and some have new dimensions. Consequently, although their roots are traditional enough, their contemporary manifestations may seem quite different. We have in mind, for example, the neo-Aristotelians, the rhetorical approach, the genres approach, the history of ideas, and source and influence studies (including some aspects of "genetic" criticism).

Still another characteristic of this chapter is its special kind of utility. As already indicated, the following sections do not offer readings of *Adventures of Huckleberry Finn*, *Hamlet*, "Young Goodman Brown," or "To His Coy Mistress." Rather, the eleven sections are as many stepping-stones to that eclectic reading we have stressed, whatever work the reader is interested in. Each of the sections provides some orientation to the approach under discussion, perhaps something of its history, sometimes an indication of how it overlaps with other approaches, frequently the names of critics and their works associated with the approach, and occasionally some very brief examples of the approach in practice. There is usually a range within a section, so that, on the one hand, the neophyte may at the very least may become aware of the existence of the approach and, on the other, the more advanced reader can see where he might go to learn more. It is for this last reason that the sections are consciously allusive and sometimes resemble annotated bibliographies. Not all the books and articles cited are explicitly on the approach under consideration, but they are germane or at least suggestive and frequently contain annotations and bibliographies of their own that will lead the reader to additional materials.

In sum, this chapter of "other approaches" continues the

notion that has informed this handbook throughout: because literature is the verbal artistic expression of man *qua* man, with all the richness, depth, and complexity that concept suggests, literary criticism is necessarily the composite of many ways of reaching to that experience. It is necessarily eclectic because no one way of reading a piece of literature can capture all that is there, just as no simplistic notion can embody all that the human being is. For that we need many approaches; in brief form, we now offer eleven more, in alphabetical order so as not to impose any seeming hierarchy.

I. ARISTOTELIAN CRITICISM (INCLUDING THE "CHICAGO SCHOOL")

Few works of literary criticism can hope to wear so well, or so long, as Aristotle's *Poetics* (4th century B.C.). Our theories of drama and of the epic, the recognition of genres as a way of studying a piece of literature, and our methodology of studying a work or group of works and then inducing theory from practice can all find beginning points in the *Poetics*. More specifically, from the *Poetics* we have such basic notions as catharsis, the characteristics of the tragic hero (the noble figure; tragic pride, or *hubris*; the tragic flaw), the formative elements of drama (action or plot, character, thought, diction, melody, and spectacle), the necessary unity of plot, and perhaps most significantly, the basic concept of *mimesis*, or imitation, the idea that works of literature are imitations of actions, the differences among them coming by means, by objects, and by manner.

In practice, any reader may be "Aristotelian" when he distinguishes one genre from another, when he questions whether Arthur Miller's Willy Loman can be tragic or argues that Melville's Ahab is, when he stresses plot rather than character or diction, or when he stresses the mimetic role of literature. In formal criticism the reader will do well to study Matthew Arnold's 1853 preface to his poems as a notable example of Aristotelian criticism in the nineteenth century. In this century one critic has said that the "ideal critic" will be neo-Aristotelian if he "scrupulously [induces] from practice" (Stanley Edgar Hyman, *The Armed Vision* [New York: Random House (Vintage Books), 1955], p. 387).

The most concerted use in this century of Aristotelian principles (and the reason for placing Aristotelianism in this chapter rather than in Chapter 1 as a traditional approach, though the principles are operative there) is that associated with a group of critics who were colleagues at the University of Chicago during the 1940s. Though stressing their humanistic concern and their pervading hope for a broadly based literary criticism, the members of the "Chicago School" were in part reacting against what seemed to them to be an inadequacy in the work of the New Critics: for Ronald S. Crane, "bankruptcy" and "critical monism." Consequently, they called for an openness to critical perspectives, a "plurality" of methods, and they advocated the use of Aristotle's principles as being comprehensive and systematic enough to be developed beyond what Aristotle himself had set down.

That call was made by Crane, in his introduction to *Critics and Criticism: Ancient and Modern* (Chicago: University of Chicago, 1952, p. 18); in that book Crane and his colleagues gathered papers that they had published as early as 1936. Besides Crane, the contributors were W. R. Keast, Richard McKeon, Norman Maclean, Elder Olson, and Bernard Weinberg. Arranged in three sections, the essays deal with "representative critics of the present day," "figures and episodes in the history of criticism from the Greeks through the eighteenth century," and "theoretical questions relating to the criticism of criticism and of poetic forms" (p. 1). Not all the essays are explicitly "Aristotelian," though Crane makes it clear that a "major concern of the essays . . . is with the capacities for modern development and use of . . . the poetic method of Aristotle" (p. 12). (Given the humanistic and traditional background, the rhetorical bent of some of the essays is understandable and points up the necessity of our understanding that labeling any approach to literature should not mislead us into thinking that critical approaches are mutually exclusive. Compare for example, both the rhetorical and the generic approaches below.)

Another work of importance produced by this movement is Crane's *The Languages of Criticism and the Structure of Poetry* (Toronto: University of Toronto, 1953). But although this book and *Critics and Criticism* are frequently alluded to by other critics, the impact of the Chicago neo-Aristotelians has been less than that of the New Critics against whom they took arms. Ten years after *The Languages of Criticism,* for example, Walter Sutton wrote:

> The neo-Aristotelian position developed by Crane and his colleagues is valuable for its emphasis upon theory, historical perspective, and scholarly discipline. It has, however, stimulated very little practical criticism. The active movement that the leaders hoped for never developed, although their work undoubtedly encouraged a renewal of interest in genre criticism, shared by critics like Kenneth Burke and Northrop Frye in modified forms and by many other scholar critics within the universities. (*Modern American Criticism* [Englewood Cliffs, N.J.: Prentice-Hall, 1963], p. 173)

The reader will find Sutton's chapter on the neo-Aristotelians helpful because it provides not only interpretive summaries of some of their work but also commentary on possible deficiencies of the neo-Aristotelians and on relationships to other schools of criticism.

Although Sutton may have been correct in saying that the neo-Aristotelian efforts of the Chicago School "stimulated very little practical criticism," renewed efforts in rhetorical criticism, and possibly in genre criticism, and in some of the later stresses on fiction as a serial form may be more recent mutations of Aristotelian criticism. This seems to be the thought of Donald Pizer when he writes that neo-Aristotelianism can be seen today in "new and influential forms." Pizer cites as examples two books: Charles C. Walcutt, *Man's Changing Mask* (Minneapolis: University of Minnesota Press, 1966); and Robert Scholes and Robert Kellogg, *The Nature of Narrative* (New York: Oxford University Press, 1966). These books, according to Pizer, deal with the similarities between "all serial art" and fiction, which is seen as "a late example of . . . permanent elements" of narrative and characterization. Because of these similarities, the books by Walcutt and by Scholes and Kellogg, among others, "reflect what can be called an Aristotelian temper" ("A Primer of Fictional Aesthetics," *College English*, 30 [April 1969], 574).

II. FEMINIST CRITICISM

Whether a new consciousness was indeed rising in America in the 1960s perhaps only later historians will be able to say. Although the interrelatedness of the various protest movements of the 1960s and 1970s is beyond the scope of a handbook of critical approaches to literature, certain movements seem to have some aspects in common: the protest against the Vietnam War, the campus revolts because of various other matters (curriculum revision, the "free speech" movement), the various efforts of the black liberation movement, the gay liberation movement (for literary aspects, see the special issue of *College English*, 36 [November 1974]), and the women's liberation movement. For our purposes, the particular aspect of concern is the shared belief that something in American consciousness has not been right and that a reorienting of what is said to be white, middle-American, male thinking is necessary to correct it.

A part of this general movement, and perhaps the most important from a literary point of view, is what has come to be called feminist literary criticism. Although the traditional view may be that good literary criticism is sexless, the feminist critic argues that if it is to be valid at all, a literary criticism that claims universality must include the feminine consciousness. Usually the feminist critic claims that earlier criticism has been male-dominated and must be redone to include the feminine consciousness, even, if necessary, to the extent of reshaping systems of values. Some argue that feminist criticism must be primarily political and social in its orientation. Some say that to be good, both criticism and literature itself must move beyond both sexes into an androgynous point of view. Although these several views are not necessarily shared by all feminist critics, they seem to agree in attacking the shapers of earlier criticism. Against those who would argue that the "good" literary criticism of the past is still good regardless of the sex of the author, against those who would argue that criticism must be "objective" to be valid, the feminists would argue one or more of the theses just reviewed.

The increasing number of voices in this movement and the increasing volume of their work certainly is evidence of their vitality, and if their work is not yet in the mainstream of American literary criticism, their claim that it ought to be and in time will be must be recognized. A brief guide to recent work will help orient the reader in the movement as it develops further.

Some works that have a place in the writings of feminist critics date from the 1960s and one particularly important name is from considerably earlier: Virginia Woolf (especially A Room of One's Own [1929]). However, the clear rise of the feminist critical movement begins in the early 1970s, possibly aided by the formation in 1969 of the Modern Language Association's Commission on the Status of Women. For example, we may note the subtitle of the bibliography done by Carol Fairbanks Myers, Women in Literature: Criticism of the Seventies (Metuchen, N.J.: Scarecrow Press, 1976). This bibliography, which covers the period from January of 1970 to the spring of 1975, includes both new feminist criticism and traditional critical approaches that deal with women characters in various relationships. A bibliographical survey of the movement done by Cheri Register also generally cites works since 1970, and it is she who cites the formation of the MLA Commission as the "beginning of an organized critical

effort" ("American Feminist Literary Criticism: A Bibliographical Introduction," in *Feminist Literary Criticism:
Explorations in Theory*, ed. Josephine Donovan [Lexing-
ton: University Press of Kentucky, 1975], pp. 1–28). The
emphasis on the 1970s is also evident in the citations
provided by Annis V. Pratt, "The New Feminist Criticisms:
Exploring the History of the New Space" (in *Beyond
Intellectual Sexism: A New Woman, A New Reality*, ed.
Joan I. Roberts [New York: David McKay, 1976]. pp. 175–
195). The two essays by Register and Pratt are more than
mere bibliographical lists, for they provide something of
the thinking of the feminist literary critics as well. Recent
critical works (in contrast to primarily bibliographical ones)
are Sydney Janet Kaplan, *Feminine Consciousness in the
Modern British Novel* (Urbana: University of Illinois
Press, 1975); Judith Fryer, *The Faces of Eve: Women in the
Nineteenth Century American Novel* (New York: Oxford
University Press, 1976); Ellen Moers, *Literary Women*
(Garden City, N.Y.: Doubleday, 1976); Arlyn Diamond and
Lee Edwards, *The Authority of Experience: Essays in
Feminist Criticism* (Amherst: University of Massachusetts
Press, 1977); and Elaine Showalter, *A Literature of Their
Own: British Women Novelists from Bronte to Lessing*
(Princeton, N.J.: Princeton University Press, 1977). This last
has been called an "outstanding contribution to literary
history" (Mary McBride, *Library Journal*, January 15,
1977).

Cheri Register, in the bibliographical article already
cited, identifies three subdivisions of feminist criticism,
only the first two of which are "well defined": "(1) the
analysis of the 'image of women,' nearly always as it
appears in work by male authors, and (2) the examination
of existing criticism of female authors" (p. 2). The third
type, Register believes, needs further formulation but may
become the most important subdivision: It is "prescrip-
tive," because it sets standards "for literature that is 'good'
from a feminist viewpoint." This kind of criticism, she says,
"is best defined in terms of the ways in which literature

can serve the cause of liberation" (p. 18). In this stance Register reflects what a number of feminist critics argue: (1) that literary criticism has a social context, and feminist criticism has a sociopolitical purpose in that context, and conversely, (2) that the claims to objectivity made by formalist critics (such as the New Critics) are specious and inadequate whenever they fail to pay heed to the social context. Similarly, certain psychological interpretations are held to be deficient because of their failure to understand feminine consciousness, with consequent errors in literary evaluations and interpretations. The archetypal approach of Carl Jung is an example of this deficiency. Annis Pratt, in the article cited earlier, argues that although she trained herself as an archetypal critic and continues to use the approach, archetypal criticism is defective in understanding the roles of the female: "Jung himself, toward the end of his life, admitted that one of the chief problems he and his followers had was a tendency to locate women 'just where man's shadow falls. So that he is only too liable to confuse her with his own shadow. Then, when he wishes to repair this misunderstanding, he tends to overvalue the woman and believe in her desiderata.' " Pratt can nonetheless make use of Jungian insights; for example, she writes that she can deal with the "psyche of the female hero in literature" by adapting "Jung's descriptions of the quest of the young hero for adulthood and of the older hero for rebirth and full individuation. As a feminist critic, however, I had to postulate woman as human; to Jung, she had not quite made the grade" (p. 179).

The notion that the new movement in feminist criticism will develop ultimately not a new feminine vision (alone) but an androgynous vision may be one of the helpful correctives to come out of the movement. In its simplest form, the call for androgyny (not to be confused with homosexuality) is found in comments like that of Josephine Donovan, when she states that a "feminine aesthetic will provide for the integration into the critical process of the experiences denoted as 'feminine' in our culture" ("After-

word: Critical Re-Vision" in *Feminist Literary Criticism,*
p. 79). In context, because her assumption is that our
culture heretofore has been male-oriented, this would be a
movement toward an integration of male and female aesthetics and sensibilities and, consequently, an enrichment
of our culture, perhaps even its salvation. The same notion
can be seen at greater length in Annis Pratt's previously
cited article and at book length in Carolyn G. Heilbrun,
Toward a Recognition of Androgyny (New York: Knopf,
1973). Heilbrun's book is less concerned with the sociopolitical "prescriptivism" of some feminist criticism than with
tracing the historical ideal of androgyny and expressing a
hope and expectation "That great androgynous works will
soon be written" (p. 171).

III. GENRE CRITICISM

Genre criticism, criticism of "kinds" or "types," like several of the approaches described in this chapter (Aristotelian,
rhetorical, history of ideas, source study), is a traditional
way of approaching a piece of literature, having been used
in this case at least as far back as Aristotle's *Poetics.* But
like some of those approaches which are "traditional" (see
Chapter 1) yet which are treated in this chapter as well,
genre criticism has been given revitalized attention in this
century, modifying somewhat that which was accepted as
genre criticism for some 2,000 years.

For those many years (since the time of the classical
Greeks and especially during the neoclassical period) it
was assumed that if one knew into what genre a piece of
literature fell, he knew much about the work itself. Put
simply, an Athenian citizen going to see a play by Sophocles knew in advance that the story would be acted out by
a small group of actors, he knew that he would be seeing
and hearing a chorus as part of the production, and he
knew that a certain kind of music would accompany the
chorus. When Virgil set out to write an epic for Augustan
Rome, he chose to work within the genre that he knew

already from Homer. He conventionally announced his theme in his opening line, he set his hero out on journeys and placed him in combat situations, he saw to it that the gods were involved as they had been in the *Iliad* and the *Odyssey*, and in the two halves of his *Aeneid* he even provided actions that were roughly parallel to the actions of the *Odyssey* (journey) and the *Iliad* (warfare). Because Alexander Pope and his readers were schooled in the classics, and the genres of classic literature, it was easily recognizable when he parodied the epic, turned it inside out, and produced a mock-epic, *The Rape of the Lock*. Pope took the conventions of the epic genre and deliberately reversed them: The epic theme is "mighty contests" arising from "trivial things"; the hero is a flirtatious woman with her appropriate "arms"; the journey is to Hampton Court, a place of socializing and gossip; the battle is joined over a card table, with the cards as troops; the epic weapon is a pair of scissors; the epic boast is about cutting off a lock of hair. The same use of a genre with deliberate twisting of its conventions can be found in Thomas Gray's "Ode on the Death of a Favourite Cat, Drowned in a Tub of Gold Fishes," where again high style and low matter join. Here odes, death, cats, and goldfish come together in such fashion that one genre becomes its mirror image.

Such are the kinds of comments that traditional genre criticism could provide. It held sway through the eighteenth century, when it was even dominant. It was less vital as a form of criticism in the century that followed, though the conventional types, such as drama, lyric, and romance, were still recognized and useful for terminology, as they still are. In this century, however, new interest has been developed in genre criticism, especially in theoretical matters.

Of major significance is Northrop Frye's *Anatomy of Criticism: Four Essays* (Princeton, N.J.: Princeton University Press, 1957). In his introduction Frye points to our debt to the Greeks for our terminology for and our distinctions among some genres, and he also notes that we have not gone much beyond what the Greeks gave us (p. 13). This he proposes to correct in his "anatomy." Although much of his book is archetypal criticism, and hence has relevance for Chapter 4, much of it—especially the first essay, "Historical Criticism: Theory of Modes," and the fourth essay, "Rhetorical Criticism: Theory of Genres"—also bears upon genre criticism. Summarizing Frye is a challenge we shall gladly ignore, but two particular passages will illustrate his technique of illuminating a critical problem and at the same time will provide insight especially into genre criticism. Calling attention to the "origin of the words drama, epic, and lyric," Frye says that the "central principle of genre is simple enough. The basis of generic distinctions in literature appears to be the radical of presentation. Words may be acted in front of a spectator; they may be spoken in front of a listener; they may be sung or chanted; or they may be written for the reader" (pp. 246–247). Later he says, "The purpose of criticism by genres is not so much to classify as to clarify such traditions and affinities, thereby bringing out a large number of literary relationships that would not be noticed as long as there were no context established for them" (pp. 247–248). On the face of it these passages, though helpful, are not much different from what Aristotle offered in the *Poetics,* but on such bases Frye ranges far and wide (much more than we can here suggest) in his study of "modes" and "genres," classifying, describing, dividing, subdividing.

Monumental as the work is, it has provoked mixed responses, and we may cite two works that differ from Frye's, sometimes explicitly, as they offer other insights into genre criticism.

E. D. Hirsch's *Validity in Interpretation* (New Haven: Yale University Press, 1967) makes only small reference to Frye, and presents (among other things) a quite different approach to genre criticism (Chap. 3, "The Concept of Genre"). Less concerned with the extensive anatomizing of literature and of literary criticism (he implies that Frye's classification is "illegitimate" [pp. 110–111]), Hirsch insists on the individuality of any given work. More important, he shows again and again how the reader's understanding of meaning is dependent on the reader's accurate perception of the genre that the author intended as he wrote the work. (Hirsch is not, however, thinking simplistically of "short story," for example, in contrast to "masque," "epic," or the like.) If the reader assumes that a work is in one genre but it is really in another, only misreading can result: "An interpreter's notion of the type of meaning he confronts will powerfully influence his understanding of details. This phenomenon will recur at every level of sophistication and is the primary reason for disagreements among qualified interpreters" (p. 75). And again: "Understanding can occur only if the interpreter proceeds under the same system of expectations [as the speaker, or writer]" (p. 80). Such a statement reminds us that if a person reads *The Rape of the Lock* without any previous knowledge of the epic, we must wonder whether he has truly read Pope's poem. For if a reader does not recognize conventions, he is reading at best at a superficial level. As Hirsch says, "every shared type of meaning [every genre] can be defined as a system of conventions" (p. 92). Elsewhere, Hirsch is helpful in showing that when we read a work with which we are not previously familiar, or read a work that is creating a new genre, we operate ("triangulate") by moving back and forth from what we know to what we do not know yet as well.

Still another work that qualifies Frye's treatment of genres while offering its own insights (though basically on fiction) is Robert Scholes's *Structuralism in Literature: An Introduction* (New Haven: Yale University Press, 1974). Scholes's discussion (pp. 117–141) is closer to Frye's than is Hirsch's, but brings to the treatment not only qualifications of Frye's classifications but also the influences of recent work in structuralism (see below), whereas Frye's emphasis is archetypal and rhetorical.

All three of these works—those of Frye, Hirsch, and Scholes—although they are challenging and stimulating, are sometimes difficult. Part of the difficulty when they are dealing with genres derives from the fact that pieces of literature do not simply and neatly fall into categories, or genres (even the folk ballad, seemingly obvious as a narrative form, partakes of the lyric and of the drama, the latter through its dialogue). This difficulty arises from the nature of literature itself: It is original, imaginative, creative, and hence individualistic. But regardless of this protean quality, it does help if we can recognize a genre, if we can therefore be provided with a set of "expectations" and conventions, and if we can then recognize when the expectations are fulfilled and when they are imaginatively adapted. Perhaps one of the most beneficial aspects of engaging in genre criticism is that in our efforts to decide into what genre a challenging piece falls, we come to experience the literature more fully: "how we finally categorize the poem becomes irrelevant, for the fact of trying to categorize—even through the crudest approach—has brought us near enough to its individual qualities for genre-criticism to give way to something more subtle" (Allan Rodway, "Generic Criticism: The Approach Through Type, Mode, and Kind," in Contemporary Criticism, Stratford-upon-Avon Studies, 12, ed. Malcolm Bradbury and David Palmer [London: Arnold, 1970], p. 91).

IV. THE HISTORY OF IDEAS

Studying a piece of literature in the light of the history of ideas is somewhat similar to the historical approach presented in Chapter 1. For example, the concept of revenge as found in certain Renaissance English plays can be tied directly to the study of Seneca in the universities of the sixteenth century, and thus to the rise of interest in classical Greece and Rome during the Renaissance. Such a consideration must deal simultaneously with an idea, with historical developments, and with the contents of literature. Similarly, any consideration of the biography of an author may well deal with the history of his period and with the influence of the spirit of the times on a given work, an influence that may in turn be the result of antecedent developments. In this century the relationship between existentialism and the theater of the absurd provides an example.

However, when one speaks of the "history of ideas" he may be thinking more precisely of an area of philosophy than of history, and of a form of study more recent than the traditional "historical-biographical" approach of Chapter 1. This subdivision of philosophy has been best described by the scholar Arthur O. Lovejoy, in his now classic *The Great Chain of Being: A Study of the History of an Idea* (first published in 1936). Of the history of ideas, Stanley Edgar Hyman has said what most other readers would acknowledge: The history of ideas is a "philosophic field largely invented and pre-empted by Professor Arthur O. Lovejoy of Johns Hopkins. The history of ideas is the tracing of the unit ideas of philosophies through intellectual history, and just as it finds its chief clues in literary expression, literary criticism can draw on it for the philosophic background of literature" (*The Armed Vision*, rev. ed. [New York: Random House (Vintage Books), 1955], pp. 187–188). The "unit ideas" mentioned by Hyman are of central importance in this field of study, as we can see from Lovejoy's introductory chapter in *The Great Chain of Being*.

There Lovejoy says, "By the history of ideas I mean something at once more specific and less restricted than the history of philosophy. It is differentiated primarily by the character of the units with which it concerns itself" ([New York: Harper & Row (Torchbook edition), 1960], p. 3). Lovejoy differentiates a "unit idea" from the "compounds" whose names usually end with -*ism*: idealism, romanticism, rationalism, transcendentalism, pragmatism, and the like. Among the principal types of ideas, that which most concerns him he describes in part as follows:

> any unit-idea which the historian thus isolates he next seeks
> to trace through more than one—ultimately, indeed, through
> all—of the provinces of history in which it figures in any
> important degree, whether those provinces are called philos-

ophy, science, literature, art, religion, or politics.... [The history of ideas] is concerned only with a certain group of factors in history, and with these only in so far as they can be seen at work in what are commonly considered separate divisions of the intellectual world; and it is especially interested in the processes by which influences pass over from one province to another. [pp. 15–16]

Lovejoy singles out the need for seeing the relationships between philosophy and modern literature:

Most teachers of literature would perhaps readily enough admit that it is to be *studied*—I by no means say, can solely be enjoyed—chiefly for its thought-content, and that the interest of the history of literature is largely as a record of the movement of ideas.... [It] is by first distinguishing and analyzing the major ideas which appear again and again [in literature], and by observing each of them as a recurrent unit in many contexts, that the philosophic background of literature can best be illuminated. [pp. 16–17]

After this introduction, Lovejoy puts into practice the concept of pursuing a "unit idea" by studying the notion of the great chain of being in its genesis and its later diffusion in various places, eras, philosophers, and literary figures.

At the risk of extending the concept of the unit idea to works that Lovejoy may not have accepted as examples of the history of ideas (some may be labeled simply as "comparative literature," and one even antedates *The Great Chain of Being*), we shall now only cite by title some books that at least partake of Lovejoy's approach and method. The titles themselves provide glosses on how the history of ideas impinges upon literary criticism:

H. R. Patch. *The Goddess Fortuna in Medieval Literature*. 1927; New York: Octagon Books, 1967.

C. S. Lewis. *The Allegory of Love: A Study in Medieval Tradition*. 1936; New York: Oxford University Press (Galaxy Books), 1958.

Walter Jackson Bate. *From Classic to Romantic:*

Premises of Taste in Eighteenth-Century England. 1946; New York: Harper & Row (Torchbook), 1961.

Leo Marx. *Machine in the Garden: Technology and the Pastoral Ideal in America.* New York: Oxford University Press, 1964.

Stanley Stewart. *The Enclosed Garden: The Tradition and the Image in Seventeenth-Century Poetry.* Madison: University of Wisconsin Press, 1966.

Elizabeth Armstrong. *Ronsard and the Age of Gold.* London: Cambridge University Press, 1968.

Harry Levin. *The Myth of the Golden Age in the Renaissance.* Bloomington: Indiana University Press, 1969.

Nicolas James Perella. *The Kiss Sacred and Profane: An Interpretative History of Kiss Symbolism and Related Religio-Erotic Themes.* Berkeley: University of California Press, 1969.

M. H. Abrams. *Natural Supernaturalism: Tradition and Revolution in Romantic Literature.* New York: Norton, 1971.

George D. Economou. *The Goddess Natura in Medieval Literature.* Cambridge, Mass.: Harvard University Press, 1972.

George S. Rousseau, ed. *Organic Form: The Life of an Idea.* London: Routledge and Kegan Paul, 1972.

Ricardo J. Quinones. *The Renaissance Discovery of Time.* Cambridge, Mass.: Harvard University Press, 1972.

S. K. Heninger, Jr. *Touches of Sweet Harmony: Pythagorean Cosmology and Renaissance Poetics.* San Marino, Calif.: Huntington Library, 1974.

Leonard Barkan. *Nature's Work of Art: The Human Body as Image of the World.* New Haven: Yale University Press, 1975.

The list could go on, but these titles suggest the richness of the possibilities when one pursues an idea, discovered first perhaps in a piece of literature, and then traced to its philosophic roots and its manifestations in other disciplines, such as religion and science. Finally, we may mention the *Journal of the History of Ideas*, founded by Lovejoy; *The History of Ideas: An Introduction* (New York: Scribner, 1969), by George Boas, with whom Lovejoy sometimes collaborated; and Lovejoy's *Essays in the History of Ideas* (Baltimore: Johns Hopkins University Press, 1948). This last is a collection of some of Lovejoy's articles, the first of which, "The Historiography of Ideas," is helpful for showing in brief compass the interdisciplinary nature of this kind of study.

V. THE LINGUISTICS APPROACH

In the twentieth century, linguistics, the study of language, has become a discipline in itself (even, many would claim, a science), and in a university it is not unusual for the department of linguistics to be separate from the department of literature (or "English"). As the new discipline transcended traditional philological studies, a number of new questions arose: Is literature merely a part of language? Is the object of literary criticism totally different from the object of linguistic analysis? Is the language of literature susceptible to the same kind of study that can be brought to bear, for example, on language in its spoken form? If it is susceptible, then in what manner and in what areas can a work of art be studied by a scientific or quasiscientific discipline? Surely this kind of study, whether it derives from structural linguistics, transformational-generative grammar, or some other modulation of modern linguistics, goes beyond the historical study of language that was important to the nineteenth and early-twentieth-century "philologists," who concerned themselves, for example, with the rediscovery of Chaucer's pronunciation and the meanings of words in *Beowulf*.

Consequently, there is debate about linguistics as an approach to literature, and not the least of the difficulties in pursuing it is the overlapping quality of what in this handbook we are separating, for the sake of convenience and clarificaton, into several different approaches to literature—the linguistic, the stylistic, the structuralist, and in some instances the rhetorical approaches.

Both the debate and the overlap can be seen as we now turn to some items illustrative of the work being done either within the approach or because of it. Two articles intended for the general reader show the cautionary view. Mark Lester begins "The Relation of Linguistics to Literature" (*College English,* 30 [February 1969], 366-375) by asking, ". . . what can a student of literature learn from the discipline of linguistics?" He suggests "two main claims" that are made by those who wish to see linguistics as an approach to literature: the proposition that since "language is the medium of literature . . . the more we know about the medium, the more we will know about literature"; and the proposition that the "critic may gain insight into the writer or the work or both by discovering patterns in the linguistic choices that the writer, consciously or unconsciously, has made." He concludes that one area of modern language study, structural linguistics, has provided attempts at literary analysis that were mostly "out-and-out failures"; and another, transformational grammar, overlaps the interests of the literary critic only slightly, so that even in the area where it might help, the area of metrics and stylistics, the "insight into literature [is] correspondingly small" (p.375). Similarly, at the conclusion of "Notes on Linguistics and Literature" (*College English,* 32 [November 1970], 184-190), Elias Schwartz says flatly, "There is no such thing as a distinctive literary language. And if this is true, it means that, though linguists may tell us a great deal about language, they can tell us nothing about literature" (p. 190).

But although one might accept, at least partially, this cautionary view about the limitations of linguistics for literary analysis, there are areas that one might investigate profitably from a linguistic perspective. Such a middle view might be represented by Eugene V. Mohr, who cites these difficulties (and Lester's article) at the same time that he can demonstrate briefly but cogently some areas of successful overlap ("Linguistics and the Literature Major," *CEA Forum*, 3 [April 1973], 4-6). It is easy to agree with Mohr's first point—that a knowledge of historical information about language changes and about "devices which were operative at earlier stages in the development of English" is helpful in literary interpretation. Mohr cites the distinction between *thou* and *you* in an earlier day, and how Shakespeare, among others, could use the distinction. Second, he suggests that close analysis of the language of criticism itself (for example, Wordsworth's statements about language in the preface to the second edition of *Lyrical Ballads*) can help us to be more perceptive students of criticism, and this leads him to comment on how the objective data provided by modern linguistics can be helpful in appreciating stylistics (see the discussion of stylistics below). Finally, he cites dialect study as a potential field for the legitimate overlap of linguistics and literary criticism, because dialects (clearly open to linguistics study) have been used for literary effects in English at least since the time of Chaucer and appear in novelists and playwrights since then.

Another article that illustrates the qualified view of the literary critic who is willing to use linguistic techniques (while pointing out the difficulties) is by Stanley B. Greenfield ("Grammar and Meaning in Poetry," PMLA, 82 [October 1967], 377-387). Less helpful to the beginning student because of its range and depth, it is useful for all at least for its bibliographical citations and annotations. In addition, it shows how linguistics and stylistics overlap (Greenfield uses the term "linguistic stylistics" [p. 378] and implicitly suggests how linguistics analysis shades into stylistics criticism). Using 1960 as a convenient date for citing the appearance of several linguistics-oriented studies, Greenfield almost casually helps locate this approach to literature in terms of others: "[Here] is a testimony to the 'new linguistics' that gave rise to both linguistic and critical interest in elements of language other than diction, imagery, and symbolism, those staples of the New Criticism" (p. 377).

From Mohr's and Greenfield's qualified view of the usefulness of linguistics as an approach to literature, one might move to more concerted efforts to bring the one kind of study to bear upon the other. Very extensive, for example, is the increasingly recognized importance of structural linguistics (Lester's view notwithstanding) in the development of structuralism as an approach to literature (see the section on structuralism below). Somewhat more intensive is the study of prosody, alluded to by Lester. We may illustrate this by beginning with some less-than-qualified comments from a review of a study of contemporary English. In 1956 Harold Whitehall reiterated (originally expressed in 1951) that *An Outline of English Structure*, by George L. Trager and Henry Lee Smith, was a "work that literary criticism cannot afford to ignore...." "No criticism," he said, "can go beyond its linguistics. And the kind of linguistics needed by recent criticism for the solution of the pressing problems of metrics and stylistics, in fact, for all problems of the linguistic surface of letters, is not semantics, either epistemological or communicative, but down-to-the-surface linguistics, microlinguistics not metalinguistics" ("From Linguistics to Criticism," *Kenyon Review*, 18 [Summer 1956], 415; reprint of a review in the autumn 1951 issue). When Whitehall reprinted this review in 1956, he did so as a prologue to some detailed applications to verse ("Prosodic Implications," pp. 416-421). Whitehall's article, we should note, is part of a group of studies in that issue. The studies, entitled "English Verse and What It Sounds Like," provide further evidence of what linguistics critics try to do in the specialized area of prosody. The group of studies is "moderated" by poet-critic John Crowe Ransom, who sees himself as a "prosodist," not as a linguist. Ransom concludes that both the prosodists and the linguists have something to tell each other.

Both the intensiveness and the extensiveness of the

linguistics approach to literature can be suggested by calling attention to the collection that appeared in 1967 as *Essays on the Language of Literature* (ed. Seymour Chatman and Samuel R. Levin [Boston: Houghton Mifflin]). In the preface the editors admonish their readers that the causes of the "rift" between the linguists and the literary critics "are less important than its repair." "Reconciliation" between the two disciplines is in the air, a reconciliation that in some ways would take us back to the nineteenth and early twentieth centuries, when scholars would have seen, as a matter of course, that "linguistics and literary history were simply two peas in the philological pod." This return, however, would be made in the light of more recent investigations, and the editors cite the evidence of "some classics of criticism in the past three decades [that is, up to 1967]—*Seven Types of Ambiguity, The Structure of Complex Words, Articulate Energy: An Enquiry into the Syntax of English Poetry, The Verbal Icon, English Poetry and the English Language, Words and Poetry, The Language of Poetry....* " Their anthology of essays includes works from as early as 1900, but most are from the 1950s and 1960s. Among the essayists are some whose names can be found in bibliographies for structuralism, and among their five sections is one entitled "Style and Stylistics," so that on both counts we must be aware of the interrelationships of structuralism, stylistics, and linguistics as approaches to literature. (Their four other sections are "Sound Texture," "Metrics," "Grammar," and "Literary Form and Meaning.")

The interrelationships between linguistics and stylistics as approaches to literature can be further illustrated by an older work, Leo Spitzer's *Linguistics and Literary History,* the subtitle of which is *Essays in Stylistics* (Princeton, N. J.: Princeton University Press, 1948; New York: Russell and Russell, 1962). Spitzer's opening essay, which gives the book its name, describes and illustrates his "philological circle," in which he uses, among other things, etymologies, recurrence of words, and word patterns to get at the spirit not only of the work but also of the times in which it was written, and even at the " 'psychogram' of the individual artist" (p. 15).

Spitzer, whose early work dates back to 1910, serves to remind us that the linguistic approach in itself is not new. As we said earlier, however, linguistics as a discipline is rather new, and with the increasing use of the computer in linguistic and stylistic analysis, we must be alert to the possibilities that might be developed by critics who have both the gifts of literary perceptiveness and the skills of the new discipline and new technology.

VI THE PHENOMENOLOGICAL APPROACH (THE CRITICISM OF CONSCIOUSNESS)

Through much of Henry James's famous novel *The Ambassadors*, the reader shares with the central intelligence, Lambert Strether, a particular set of notions and beliefs, only to find at a later time along with Strether that a considerable reorientation and reinterpretation of apparent facts is necessary. In T. S. Eliot's *The Waste Land*, the reader is deliberately deprived of transitions and explanations, forcing him to perceive juxtapositions, to grasp allusions and echoes, and to develop patterns of relationships. In F. Scott Fitzgerald's *The Great Gatsby* the reader must see the world of Gatsby through the eyes of Nick Carraway, but must simultaneously evaluate and then accept or reject Nick's judgments about Gatsby and the people around him. In *The Sound and the Fury* the reader must first experience the world as perceived by Benjy, the idiot from whose point of view is told the first of four sections of Faulkner's novel; then the reader moves through the other three sections, each with its own point of view, so that he must successively reorient his consciousness to live in the world (or worlds) created. For that matter, the reader might take all of Faulkner, or any other writer whose works form a totality, and live not only in an individual work but in the full consciousness of the author, what has been called the "living unity" of his work. The mind of the artist, a consciousness, has created an art object, or a number of them, with which the mind of the reader, a different consciousness, must interact in a dynamic process of perception, so dynamic that objects may cease to exist as objects, becoming subsumed in the subjective reality of the reader's consciousness.

In other words, when a reader places himself in the hands of an author, surrendering his time and attention to that author's creation, he begins to live within the world that the author has created. Conversely, the text, which has been waiting for a reader, begins to come alive, for the text can live only when read. The space and time dimensions of the reader's everyday life and the facts of that life do not cease to exist, of course, but they are augmented by the space-time relationships and the facts of the fictive world that the reader now inhabits. In addition, the manner in which the reader now lives, discovers, and experiences in that world is akin to the manner in which he lives, learns, and experiences in "real" life; his subjective consciousness is involved in that world, and seemingly objective data are important to him insofar as they merge into his subjective consciousness. In the first half of the twentieth century the perceptions of the phenomena of "reality" became the concern of phenomenological philosophy and psychology. In the second half of the twentieth century the phenomena of the fictive world, the perceptions within that world, the very process of reading, and the understanding of consciousness (the author's and the critic's) have become the subject matter of literary criticism as well.

The development of this approach to literature is understandable because the made object (novel, play, epic), the various occurrences and "realities" of the fictive world, and the reader himself are all coexistent phenomena. David Halliburton, using a concept credited to Hans-Georg Gadamer, has suggested that art "is not a means of securing pleasure, but a revelation of being. The work is a phenomenon through which we come to know the world"

(*Edgar Allan Poe: A Phenomenological View* [Princeton, N. J.: Princeton University Press, 1973], p. 32). Halliburton says:

> my chief concern is with the existential situation of the work—the way it stands against the horizon of interrelated phenomena that we call life. I am not speaking of some mystic spirit or *Geist*, but of everyday things: of consciousness, identity, process, body, love, fear, struggle, the material world. Phenomenology, as a philosophical discipline, has investigated these things, and, within its powers, has described and analyzed their operations and structures. "Literary phenomenology," in its own way, must, I believe, try to do the same. [p. 34]

The philosophical discipline alluded to by Halliburton dates especially from the works of Edmund Husserl, early in the twentieth century, and includes, at least to some extent, the work of Martin Heidegger, Jean-Paul Sartre, Maurice Merleau-Ponty, and Pierre Thévenaz. Merleau-Ponty's *Phenomenology of Perception* is frequently cited. Thévenaz is not as well known as some of these others, but a useful work by him is available in English in paperback: *What Is Phenomenology? And Other Essays* (ed. James M. Edie [New York: Quadrangle, 1962]. Besides "What Is Phenomenology?" the book contains other essays by Thévenaz, bibliographies, and an introduction by the editor. Near the end of the title essay, Thévenaz repeats the question, and answers: "[Phenomenology] is above all method—a method for changing our relation to the world, for becoming more acutely aware of it. But at the same time and by that very fact, it is already a certain attitude vis-à-vis the world, or more exactly a certain attitude vis-à-vis our relation to the world" (p. 90). As a method and an attitude, the philosophical discipline known as phenomenology reaches out to touch a number of man's concerns—psychology, psychiatry, social studies, and literary criticism. In this far-reaching effect, phenomenology compares with structuralism (see below) as a movement that has had European roots but that is now felt in America, including American literary criticism.

One of the more influential European phenomenological critics whose works are becoming available in English is the Belgian Georges Poulet, whose *Proustian Space* has been translated by Elliott Coleman (Baltimore: Johns Hopkins University Press, 1977). The emphasis on the interrelationship of space and time in Proust (time transformed into space) is consonant with the concerns with time and space in other phenomenological critics. (Other works by Poulet that Coleman has translated are *The Metamorphoses of the Circle, The Interior Distance,* and *Studies in Human Time.*)

This spreading from Europe to America can be further illustrated by Wolfgang Iser's *The Implied Reader: Patterns of Communication in Prose Fiction from Bunyan to Beckett.* First published in Germany (Munich, 1972), it was then published in English in this country (Baltimore: Johns Hopkins University Press, 1974). Iser's treatment of the novel is especially important in our seeing the world within which the reader can live—for the reader is "involved" in the "world of the novel" in such manner that he better understands that world—"and ultimately his own world—more clearly" (p. xi). Iser's final essay, which had appeared earlier in *New Literary History,* 3 (1972), 279-299—"The Reading Process: A Phenomenological Approach"—gives a helpful overview of the process of reading as seen phenomenologically, laying stress on "not only the actual text but also, and in equal measure, the actions involved in responding to that text" (p. 274). Among other things, Iser deals with time and its importance in the reading process. For example, reading a work of fiction involves us in a process that has duration, and necessarily involves a changing self as the reader reads. Similarly, subsequent rereadings of a text create an interaction between text and reader that is necessarily different, because the reader is different, because he now knows what is to come, and reads in a different way from his initial reading, thus experiencing the phenomena in a different way.

If something of *time* can be seen in Iser's work, Cary

Nelson uses *space* as his central fact and metaphor in *The Incarnate Word: Literature as Verbal Space* (Urbana: University of Illinois Press, 1973). Nelson would see "literature as a unique process in which the self of the reader is transformed by an external verbal structure" (p. 4). Individual works—or even chapters of his book—set beside one another, "are a series of alternative spaces which can be entered and energized by the imagination" (p. 5). When we read, the "word becomes flesh," for "we evacuate a space in our bodies which we ... encircle and fill.... To read is to fold the world into the body's house" (p. 6). Nelson, unlike Iser, who concentrates on fiction, offers chapters on a range of genres—a medieval poem, Shakespeare's *The Tempest*, Milton's *Paradise Regained*, and other prose and poetry from the eighteenth, nineteenth, and twentieth centuries.

Sometimes the term "criticism of consciousness" is used to describe the kind of literary criticism represented by Poulet, Iser, and Nelson, but the term often extends beyond the study of particular works. In "criticism of consciousness," some critics would pursue not only the text, but the whole range of texts of an author—his corpus—so that the critic's consciousness tries to identify with the author's consciousness, a "union of subject with another subject," an approach not particularly favored by W. K. Wimsatt ("Battering the Object: The Ontological Approach," in *Contemporary Criticism*, Stratford-upon-Avon Studies, 12 [London: Arnold, 1970], p. 66).

Associated with this approach is the so-called Geneva School, including, for example, Georges Poulet (mentioned earlier) and, in this country, J. Hillis Miller and Geoffrey H. Hartman (for example, *The Unmediated Vision* [New Haven: Yale University Press, 1954]). Poulet has written that "When reading a literary work, there is a moment when it seems to me that the subject *present* in this work disengages itself from all that surrounds it, and stands alone"; at such a time, he senses that he has "reached the common essence present in all the works of a great master," an essence that now stands out and beyond the particular manifestations in individual works ("Phenomenology of Reading," *New Literary History*, 1 [1969], 68). Two of Miller's works—*The Disappearance of God: Five Nineteenth-Century Writers* (Cambridge, Mass.: Harvard University Press, 1963) and *Poets of Reality: Six Twentieth-Century Writers* (Cambridge, Mass.: Harvard University Press, 1965)—have been cited (by Halliburton [p. 17]) as important in preparing the way for such developments in American literary thought. The following passage from Miller will help to show how criticism of consciousness drives from, or is synonymous with, the phenomenological movement:

> Literature is a form of consciousness, and literary criticism is the analysis of this form in all its varieties. Though literature is made of words, these words embody states of mind and make them available to others. The comprehension of literature is a process of what Gabriel Marcel calls "intersubjectivity." Criticism demands above all that gift of participation, that power to put oneself within the life of another person, which Keats called negative capability. If literature is a form of consciousness the task of a critic is to identify himself with the subjectivity expressed in the words, to relive that life from the inside, and to constitute it anew in his criticism. [*The Disappearance of God*, p. ix]

Such a view compares with what Halliburton says early in his study of Poe. Calling into question the emphasis of earlier twentieth-century criticism on seeing the literary work as a "discrete object, a kind of inert and neutral 'thing,'" in studying which the critic need not concern himself with the author's intentions, Halliburton points out that such a view totally disconnects the text "from the consciousness that creates it and from the consciousness that interprets it." "The phenomenologist holds a different view. Without denying that the work has, in some sense, a life of its own, the phenomenologist believes that the work cannot be cut off from the intentionality that made it or from the intentionality that experiences it after it is made" (p. 21). In stressing intention, the phenomenologist would therefore call us back to the consciousness of the author and the critic, a call that would set him apart from the formalistic or New Critical approach. But, like the New Critics, he would emphasize the text, for "The intentionality he seeks out is not in the author but in the text" (p. 22). In pursuing a comprehension of the work, the phenomenologist must seek out in each work "its own way of going." The interpreter must "find this way and go along with it, experiencing the process of the work *as* a process" (p. 36).

Among the other works in the growing bibliography of phenomenological criticism, we might mention these: John Vernon, *The Garden and the Map: Schizophrenia in Twentieth-Century Literature and Culture* (Urbana: University of Illinois Press, 1973); Paul Brodtkorb, Jr., *Ishmael's White World: A Phenomenological Reading of "Moby Dick"* (New Haven: Yale University Press, 1965); and Sarah N. Lawall, *Critics of Consciousness: The Existential Structures of Literature* (Cambridge, Mass.: Harvard University Press, 1968).

VII. THE RHETORICAL APPROACH

Rhetorical criticism in the second half of this century, like several of the other approaches treated in this chapter, has been seen as a corrective to the New Critic's tendency to set up what John C. Gerber has called a *"cordon sanitaire* between the reader and the work that distances the work almost as successfully as the historical approach" ("Literature—Our Untamable Discipline," *College English,* 28 [February 1967], 354). Gerber ascribes the rise of this "new" rhetoric (for rhetoric is among our most ancient disciplines) to the interest in the late 1940s in communication skills, out of which came the renewed awareness that in communication, a "something" must be "communicated" to a "someone." Gradually, what was after World War ll a pragmatic, elementary need in composition classes became (or became again) a method of literary criticism that preserved the New Critic's interest in the work but also directed attention to author and audience.

Looking back at that development in his very helpful introduction to a collection of rhetorical analyses, Edward P. J. Corbett has written:

> rhetorical criticism is that mode of internal criticism which considers the interactions between the work, the author, and the audience. As such, it is interested in the *product*, the *process*, and the *effect* of linguistic activity, whether of the imaginative kind or the utilitarian kind. When rhetorical criticism is applied to imaginative literature, it regards the work not so much as an object of aesthetic contemplation but as an artistically structured instrument for communication. It is more interested in a literary work for what it does than for what it *is*. [*Rhetorical Analyses of Literary Works* (New York: Oxford University Press, 1969), p. xxii]

While dealing with the work itself (hence, "internal"), rhetorical criticism considers "external factors" insofar as it "uses the text for its 'readings' about the author and the audience" (p. xviii). Particularly important is the effect of the work on its audience ("what it *does*"). This is not surprising, in that the original emphasis of rhetoric was on persuasion, and for that we go back to the classical Greeks.

As a matter of fact, literary criticism itself really had some of its beginnings in rhetorical analysis, for our first critics—Plato, Aristotle, Longinus, Horace—were devoted students, indeed formulators, of rhetoric. (Corbett, by the way, would stress the influence of Horace more than of Aristotle in the later development of rhetorical criticism.) As late as the eighteenth century, rhetorical considerations played an important role in criticism, for learned men and women still knew and practiced formal rhetoric. Today much of the criticism of medieval, Renaissance, and neoclassical English and Continental literature can still profitably explore rhetorical strategies if only because we have and can work from the evidence of textbooks and manuals of rhetoric that were earnestly studied by the writers of those ages. Recently, however, the conscious and often impressive efforts to realize once again the advantages of rhetorical analyses of literature have not been limited to such earlier works. Even further, one area of rhetorical criticism—style—has developed so much that it now deserves its own emphasis (see our later discussion of stylistics). Today's "new rhetoric" may be expressed either in terms of classical rhetoric or through the insights gained in "practical" rhetoric without the use of Greek and Latin terms. Corbett, for example, points out that many a piece of practical criticism may be good rhetorical criticism even though the critic seems to be unaware of the long history of the mode within which he is operating, and may not at all use the terminology of the rhetorical critic. Similarly, a creative author may address himself to his *audience*, while *arranging* his *argument* and working within a *style*, without realizing that these are four of the "traditional concerns of rhetoricians." If the reader should desire a convenient compilation of traditional terms of classical rhetoric, however, he will find useful Richard A. Lanham, *A Handlist of Rhetorical Terms: A Guide for Students of English Literature* (Berkeley: University of California Press, 1968).

As already indicated, a rhetorical approach helps us to stay inside the work, although we may go outside for terms and strategies, being always aware that in those strategies the original author was a person choosing between options available to him. In this methodology, then, rhetorical analysis, on the one hand, is similar to and supportive of the formalistic approach, but, on the other, may go beyond it. Among the questions raised by the rhetorical approach are these: What can we know of the speaker or narrator? To whom is he allegedly speaking? What is the nature of that addressee, that audience? What setting is established or implied? How are we asked to respond to the situation created? Are we being asked to make a distinction between the *ethos* (the ethical stance) of the author and the statements of the central character (for example, a distinction between the comprehensive view of Mark Twain and the limited view of Huckleberry Finn)?

As "persuasive discourse," the rhetoric of a literary work requires or invites the reader to participate in an imagined experience. If we recognize such rhetorical devices as metaphor, irony, syllogism, or induction, so much the better. But even without such terminology and accompanying sophistication, by close reading and from the experience of even a good course in freshman composition, we can recognize that Marvell (or his *persona*) is skillfully using "persuasive discourse." Consequently, "To His Coy Mistress" takes on the structure of argument. We could see just as easily that lyric poems can be structured on the basis of a definition, a process, an analysis, a causal relation; that they may provide examples; or that they may be arranged in a spatial or temporal pattern—rhetorical matters all. In every case, we can see that literature must be related to established forms of saying things; even syntax and diction, "punch lines" and sober conclusions, arrangement and emphasis are forms familiar to the writer before he begins his work, just as they are forms familiar to us before we read the work. The awareness of such special features and structures of words tells us a great deal about the author and the created "voice." Our response to manipulated language tells us even more about the *meaning* of the work and quite a bit about ourselves as registers of meaning. Although lyric poetry seems to be the favorite genre for displays of rhetorical analysis, it can be used effectively with fiction, as has been demonstrated by Ian Watt ("The First Paragraph of *The Ambassadors:* An Explication," *Essays in Criticism,* 10 [July 1960], 250-274; reprinted in Corbett, pp. 184-203). There Watt examines diction and syntax in six sentences for the implications of their functions within the paragraph, the effects upon the reader, the revelations of the character of Lambert Strether, James's own attitudes toward experience, and our understanding of the "meaning" of the style.

Though his collection includes studies of modern and traditional authors, Corbett noted that he could not find a study of the short story from a rhetorical perspective. To fill that gap, the reader might find helpful the essay by Michael Squires, "Teaching a Story Rhetorically: An Approach to a Short Story by D. H. Lawrence" (*College Composition and Communication*, 24 [May 1973], 150-156). Except perhaps for the short story, Corbett provides an extensive bibliography of works of rhetorical criticism, including both "general background" and specific works and authors. Not the least of the works in the first list is Wayne Booth's *The Rhetoric of Fiction* (Chicago, 1961), a work regularly cited by practitioners of rhetorical criticism.

Among more recent contributions that show what is being done in this approach are Walter J. Ong, S. J., "The Writer's Audience Is Always a Fiction" *PMLA*, *90* [January 1975], 9-21); S. M. Halloran, "On the End of Rhetoric, Classical and Modern (*College English*, 36 [February 1975], 621-631); and E. D. Hirsch, Jr., " 'Intrinsic' Criticism" (*College English*, 36 [December 1974], 446-457), which is especially helpful for the comments on reader-writer relationships and the ethical-social role of literature.

VIII. THE SOCIOLOGICAL APPROACH (INCLUDING MARXIST CRITICISM)

The sociological approach to literature, from one point of view, is a traditional approach, in that whenever a work has been studied in its social milieu, we have had sociological criticism. It certainly has been "traditional" to see Chaucer's *Canterbury Tales* and William Langland's *Piers Plowman* as both reflections of and commentaries on fourteenth-century English society. Such an interaction between social milieu and literary work is evident in the exponential view of *Adventures of Huckleberry Finn* offered in Chapter 5 of this book. A similar view might be taken of Twain's *Connecticut Yankee in King Arthur's Court*. Even more explicit in social commentary, and therefore clearly open to sociological criticism, is William Dean Howells's *A Traveler from Altruria* or any other utopian work that deals with the social fabric of a real or imagined time (for example William Morris's *News from Nowhere*). In one way or another, social themes are important in dealing with literature as diverse as Frank Norris's *The Octopus*, Upton Sinclair's *The Jungle*, John Steinbeck's *The Grapes of Wrath*, William Faulkner's *Intruder in the Dust*, John Updike's *Couples*, and Kurt Vonnegut's *God Bless You, Mr. Rosewater*. American naturalists like Stephen Crane (*Maggie, A Girl of the Streets*) and Theodore Dreiser (*An American Tragedy*) can especially be studied from a sociological point of view, for they themselves were conscious of the effect of society on individuals. Arthur Miller's *Death of a Salesman*, though much more than a sociological tract, is nevertheless a commentary on the economic system within which Willy Loman tries to find his place in the sun. All of these works can be studied from a traditionalist sociological point of view, without recourse to an avowedly Marxist worldview.

During the 1930s, however, a number of our writers expressed special interest in social reform, and there was considerable stress on the uses of literature in the proletarian revolt and on seeing literature as a projection of the movement of social history. Some believed that dialectical materialism could provide a sufficiently large frame of reference, a worldview, within which literature would have a practical, even a polemical role. Among American writers of some prominence who have written such criticism are Granville Hicks (*The Great Tradition* [New York: Macmillan, 1933; New York: Quadrangle, 1969] and *Figures of Transition* [New York: Macmillan, 1939]), Lionel Trilling (*The Liberal Imagination: Essays on Literature and Psychology* [1950; Garden City, N. Y.: Doubleday (Anchor Books), 1957]), and Edmund Wilson (*The Triple Thinkers* [New York: Harcourt Brace Jovanovich, 1948]). But there came a decline in interest in this kind of criticism, what with the effects of World War II, the "cold war" with the Communist bloc, and the awakening to the crisis that faced the democracies. Stanley Edgar Hyman was able to write in *The Armed Vision,* rev. ed. (New York: Random House [Vintage Books], 1955), "Marxism in practice has hardly made good its claim as an all-embracing integrative system" (p. 389), and in his revised edition Hyman omitted two chapters on sociologically oriented critics, Christopher Caudwell and Edmund Wilson, that he had included earlier.

But once again the pendulum has swung. Partly because of the pressures brought on by the Vietnam War of the 1960s and early 1970s and partly because of a developing wave of critical effort, Marxist—or "neo-Marxist"—criticism has received renewed consideration. We can find, for example, Frederic Jameson admitting that the Marxist critics of the 1930s have been "relegated to the status of an intellectual and historical curiosity"; but then Jameson stresses that, "In recent years . . . a different kind of Marxist criticism has begun to make its presence felt upon the English-language horizon. This is what may be called—as opposed to the Soviet tradition—a relatively Hegelian kind of Marxism . . . " (*Marxism and Form: Twentieth-Century Dialectical Theories of Literature* [Princeton N. J.: Princeton University Press, 1971], p. ix).

From a different perspective this renewed interest in Marxist criticism is the result of the opinion of many that the formalist approach, especially as practiced by the New Critics, has been inadequate in treating the literary work. The formalistic approach, a Marxist might say, is even elitist and deals too restrictedly with the made object, with the art work's internal or aesthetic form, and not enough with the social milieu in which it found its being or the social circumstances to which it ought to speak. Consequently, among the schools of criticism that have found formalistic criticism inadequate, none have been more direct in their attack than the new Marxists.

Though acknowledging, for example, that Marxist criticism, in its stress on content, has some difficulty in dealing

with form, a Marxist-oriented writer can and will challenge the formalists: they need to explain how their own
methodologies can come to grips with class, race, sex, with
oppressions and liberation." That comment was made by
Richard Wasson, in "New Marxist Criticism," written as
an introduction to an edition of *College English* (34 [No-
vember 1972]) especially devoted to Marxist criticism.
Similarly Ira Shor, who, along with Wasson, was coeditor
of the issue, noted in "Questions Marxists Ask About
Literature" that "These questions are primarily theme-and-
content oriented, though they can illuminate subtleties of
consciousness and literature's paradigmatic relation to society" (p. 179). The special issue, he said, should show that
"marxist criticism is a tense dialectic between society and
literature, between an attitude toward history and an
appreciation of art" (p. 178). This is not to say that form is
neglected by the Marxist critics—only that they themselves
admit that content tends be emphasized. For example, in
the same special issue, James G. Kennedy offers "The
Content and Form of *Native Son*" (pp. 269-283), and in
analyzing Richard Wright's novel he consciously wants to
preserve the "dialectic of content and form." His first two
sections, consequently, are "Content: Class Character" and
"Content: World View," but his latter two are "Form: Plot"
and "Form: Sub-Plot." Frederic Jameson's *Marxism and
Form,* already mentioned, is not as helpful to the beginning student in matters of form as its title might suggest.
The book is quite theoretical, offering the reader an introduction to several major European figures. Jameson then
provides an essay entitled "Towards Dialectical Criticism,"
a synthesis "that would account for the relationship of the
achieved work to larger structures within which it draws
its significance, as well as explain the uniqueness of the
work, its intrinsic configurations of theme and technique."

The latter comment comes from the helpful, if brief,
annotated bibliography of M. L. Raina, "Marxism and
Literature—A Select Bibliography," in the same issue of

College English already mentioned (pp. 308-314). Raina's bibliography, highly adequate for the beginning student, ranges from "Marxist Aesthetics," through "Marxism and Literary Criticism," to "Applications." The bibliography guides the user not only to major literary and philosophical figures (Georg Lukács, Herbert Marcuse, Christopher Caudwell), but also to major Marxist theoreticians (Marx himself, Lenin, Trotsky, Mao) and even to other figures who, though not Marxists, have written about realism or other socially oriented matters. For a comprehensive bibliography, Raina recommends Lee Baxandall's *Marxism and Aesthetics—An Annotated Bibliography* (New York: Humanities Press, 1968).

In any bibliography of new Marxist criticism, the preeminent figure, commanding respect regardless of one's political or philosophical leanings, is the Hungarian Georg Lukács (1885-1971), whose scholarly publishing spanned half a century. Besides his considerable work in aesthetics, other studies by him that are often cited are *The Theory of the Novel*, which first appeared in book form in 1920 (Cambridge, Mass.: M.I.T. Press, 1971); *Studies in European Realism* (New York: Grosset & Dunlap [Universal Library], 1971); *The Historical Novel* (London: Merlin Press, 1962; Boston: Beacon Press: 1962), and *The Meaning of Contemporary Realism* (London: Merlin Press, 1963), which is available in paperback as *Realism in Our Time: Literature and the Class Struggle* (New York: Harper & Row, 1964). His criticism ranges wide, and he has praise for figures as diverse as Walter Scott and Alexander Solzhenitsyn (in *Solzhenitsyn* [Cambridge, Mass.: M.I.T. Press, 1971]). Lukács's works were first published in Hungarian and German and are now becoming increasingly available in English translations.

One theoretician who wrote in English and has been given some renewed attention because of the rise of the New Marxists is Christopher Caudwell (a pseudonym for Christopher St. John Sprigg). Though Caudwell is scarcely mentioned in Jameson's book, he is stressed in a useful overview of both his ideas and the 1930s done by Andrew Hawley, "Art for Man's Sake: Christopher Caudwell as Communist Aesthetician" (*College English*, 30 [October 1968], 1-19). Perhaps this interest is partly the result of Caudwell's almost Romantic death, a symbolic act. Like others who were drawn to the Spanish Civil War for ideological reasons, the Englishman Caudwell went to Spain in 1937, at the age of 29—and died on his first day of battle. Ultimately more significant, of course, is his work, some of which has been recently published or republished. Samuel Hynes, editor of Caudwell's *Romance and Realism: A Study in English Bourgeois Literature* (Princeton, N.J.: Princeton University Press, 1970), goes so far as to say that Caudwell's "essays on literature and literary figures, together with *Illusion and Reality*, are certainly the most important Marxist criticism in English" (p. 14). Hynes, whose comment might need revision in light of work done since 1970, was alluding to *Studies in a Dying Culture* (New York: Dodd, Mead, 1938), *Further Studies in a Dying Culture* (London: Monthly Review Press, 1971), and *Illusion and Reality* (1937: New York: Russell and Russell, 1955). Noting that Caudwell's work is only partly oriented to literature as such, Hynes points out that Caudwell was interested in relationships, in offering a world view that he found lacking in others (Freud, for example): "Caudwell did not choose analytic criticism because the task he had set himself was to synthesize. Caudwell acknowledged this point by making his only essay on literature a part of his synthetic study of bourgeois culture; *Romance and Realism* is far more concerned with literature than any other of Caudwell's writings, but like the other studies it sets its subject in relation to the general movement of society" (pp. 24-25). Thus we note once again that the tendency of the Marxist critic is to deal with content, for in content is to be found literature's importance in the movement of history.

With that notion in mind we can understand better the words of George Levine when he expressed his concern about the breach between the practice of criticism and any concern for society: He hoped for a "step toward healing the terrible breach between the study of literature and the life that surrounds that study, between this hall, where we think about politics and literature, and those streets, which our thinking about politics and literature has so far helped keep as they are" ("Politics and the Form of Disenchantment," *College English,* 36 [December 1974], 435).

IX. SOURCE STUDY AND RELATED APPROACHES (GENETIC)

The kind of approach we want to survey here, or the set of related approaches, does not have a generally accepted name. It would be pleasant but not altogether helpful if we could settle upon what Kenneth Burke called it—a "high-class kind of gossip"—for Burke was describing part of what we are interested in—the "inspection of successive drafts, notebooks, the author's literary habits in general" *(Poems in the Making,* ed. Walker Gibson [Boston: Houghton Mifflin, 1963], p. 171).

We might call the approach *genetic,* because that is the word sometimes used when a work is considered in terms of its "origins." We would find the term appropriate in studying the growth and development of the work, its genesis, as from its sources. However, the term seems effectively to have been preempted by critics for the method of criticism, as David Daiches says, that accounts for the "characteristics of the writer's work" by looking at the sociological and psychological phenomena out of which the work grew ("Criticism and Sociology," in *Critical Approaches to Literature* [Englewood Cliffs, N.J.: Prentice-Hall, 1956], pp. 358-375). Similarly, the *Princeton Encyclopedia of Poetry and Poetics,* enlarged ed. (ed. Alex Preminger [Princeton, N.J.: Princeton University Press, 1974]) uses the term "genetic" in surveying the methods of criticism that treat how the work "came into being, and what influences were at work to give it exactly the qualities that it has. Characteristically, [genetic critics] try to suggest what is in the poem by showing what lies behind it" (p. 167). These phrases would come near to what we care calling "source study and related approaches," except for the fact that these statements tend to be in a sociological context, where the work is seen as a piece of "documentary evidence" for the milieu that gave rise to it.

More precisely, then, by "source study and related approaches" we mean the growth and development of a work as seen through a study of the author's manuscripts during the stages of composition of the work, of his notebooks, of sources and analogues, and of various other influence (not necessarily sociological or psychological) that lie in the background of the work. In such study, our assumption is that we can derive therefrom clues to a richer, more accurate appreciation of the work. It may be that such an assumption is something of a will-o'-the wisp, for we can never be precisely sure of how the creative process works, of the accuracy of our guesses, of the "intention" of the author (a vexed question in modern criticism). Well suited as an introduction to this kind of criticism and a pleasant indication of both the advantages and the disadvantages of this approach to literature is the collection of pieces from which we took the Kenneth Burke quotation: Walter Gibson's *Poems in the Making*. Introducing the pieces he has gathered, Gibson calls attention to the problem of the "relevance of any or all of these accounts" in our gaining a "richer appreciation of poetry," but at the same time he clearly believes that this high-class kind of gossip offers possibilities. Accordingly, he provides a variety of specific approaches—different kinds of manuscript study, essays by the original authors (for example, Edgar Allan Poe and Stephen Spender on their own works), the classic study (in part) of "Kubla Khan" by John Livingston Lowes, and T. S. Eliot's "devastating" attack on that kind of scholarship. Not in Gibson's compendium but of interest because of the popularity of the poem is a similar study of Robert Frost's "Stopping by Woods on a Snowy Evening." An analysis of the manuscript of the poem shows how Frost worked out his words and his rhyme scheme, crossing out words not conducive to the experience of the poem. At the same time, Frost's own (separate) comments on the writing of the poem help us to interpret what the marks in the manuscript suggest (for this study see Charles W. Cooper and John Holmes, *Preface to Poetry* [New York: Harcourt Brace Jovanovich, 1946]. An excellent example of this kind of work is Robert Gittings's *The Odes of Keats and Their Earliest Known Manuscripts* (Kent, Ohio: Kent State University Press, 1970), a handsome volume that provides an essay on how five of Keats's greatest poems were written and numerous, clear facsimile pages of the manuscripts.

These examples tend to come from poems of the nineteenth and twentieth centuries, but source and analogue study has long been a staple of traditional scholarship on literature of an earlier day, such as various works on Shakespeare's plays and *Sources and Analogues of Chaucer's Canterbury Tales* (ed. W. F. Bryan and Germaine Dempster, 1941; New York: Humanities Press, 1958). A work like this last, it should be noted, provides materials for the scholar or student to work with, whereas other works are applications of such materials. An example of application can be found in the study of Sir Thomas Malory's *Le Morte Darthur*. Study of Malory's French and English sources helps us greatly in evaluating the art of his romance and the establishment of his purposes and have contributed to the debate as to whether he intended to write one book (see *Malory's Originality: A Critical Study of Le Morte Darthur*, ed. R. M. Lumiansky [Baltimore: Johns Hopkins, University Press, 1964] or a compendium of eight stories (see *The Works of Sir Thomas Malory*, 2d ed., ed. Eugène Vinaver [Oxford: Oxford University Press, 1967]). Milton's notes and manuscripts over a long period of time show us how he gradually came to write *Paradise Lost* and something of his conception of what he was working toward. This and more can be seen, aided again by facsimile pages, in Allan H. Gilbert, *On the Composi-*

tion of Paradise Lost: A Study of the Ordering and Insertion of Material (1947; New York: Octagon Books, 1966). More helpful to the beginning student is the somewhat broader view of a briefer work by Milton offered by Scott Elledge in *Milton's "Lycidas," Edited to Serve as an Introduction to Criticism* (New York: Harper & Row, 1966). There Elledge provides not only manuscript facsimiles of the poem, but materials on the pastoral tradition, examples of the genre, passages on the theory of monody, and information both from Milton's life and from his times.

For an example of the application of this approach to fiction, the reader might look at Matthew J. Bruccoli, *The Composition of Tender Is the Night: A Study of the Manuscripts* (Pittsburgh: University of Pittsburgh Press, 1963). Bruccoli worked from 3,500 pages of holograph manuscript and typescript, plus proof sheets, which represented seventeen drafts and three versions of the novel (p. xv). Perhaps this is more than the beginning student cares to have in this critical approach to literature. It may be well to mention, therefore, that, like Gibson's and Elledge's works on poetry cited earlier, there are some books on pieces of fiction that are intended for the student and offer opportunity to approach a piece of fiction by means of source and influence study. Such are, for example, some of the novels (*The Scarlet Letter, Adventures of Huckleberry Finn, The Red Badge of Courage*) in the Norton Critical Editions, where the text of the novel is accompanied by source and influence materials. Similar to these is *Bear, Man, and God: Eight Approaches to William Faulkner's "The Bear,"* 2d ed. (ed. Francis Lee Utley, Lynn Z. Bloom, and Arthur F. Kinney [New York: Random House, 1971]). In introducing the section on "Other Versions of 'The Bear,'" the editors point to some of the advantages of this kind of study:

> Criticism based on a close comparison of texts has recently come under attack; often such collation is seen as pedantic and fruitless. But a short time ago an examination of Mark

Twain papers demonstrated that Twain had never composed "The Mysterious Stranger"; rather, an editor had combined selected fragments of his writing after his death to "make" the book. Perhaps in the same spirit of inquiry, critics have examined the various texts of "The Bear" in order to determine through textual changes something of Faulkner's evolving art: such an examination is the closest we can come to seeing Faulkner in his workshop. [p. 121]

Perhaps that is a good place to engage in a "high-class kind of gossip."

X. THE STRUCTURALIST APPROACH

Like several of the approaches described in this chapter, particularly the linguistic and the stylistic approaches, the structuralist approach to literary criticism has an interdisciplinary quality, it has European sources or influences (here, Russian and French), and it has close relationships to structural linguistics, particularly the work of Ferdinand de Saussure. To reduce a definition of structuralism to a few words is an act of courage, but some have tried. Dorothy B. Selz, for instance, says that structuralism is a "study of the laws of composition both of nature and of man's creations" ("Structuralism for the Non-Specialist: A Glossary and a Bibliography," *College English*, 37 [1975], 164). We might say that structuralism at one level is the study of how the three quatrains of a Shakespearean sonnet compare with each other and generate the concluding couplet. (Sonnet 73, "That time of year thou mayst in me behold," is an excellent example.) At quite a different level, structuralism might be the study of how recurrent patterns may be detected, not just within a particular work, but throughout literature, perhaps revealing something about the way the human mind works. Reducing the highly complex idea to a phrase, we would say that structuralism is the study of relationships.

The simplicity of that definition contrasts with the range and detail of the structuralist approach. Something of that range can be suggested by a mere glance at any one of a number of books on the subject, which will usually show that structuralism is nothing if it is not interdisciplinary. An instance is Jean Piaget's little book *Structuralism* (tr. and ed. Chaninah Maschler [New York: Basic Books, 1970]. Although it does not deal with literature as such, the book is important for its definition of structuralism and because of its range, as the chapter titles show: "Mathematical and Logical Structures," "Physical and Biological Structures," "Psychological Structures," "Linguistic Structuralism," "Structural Analysis in the Social Sciences," and "Structuralism and Philosophy." Piaget's opening sentence alludes to the difficulty of defining structuralism, but having said that a "structure is a system of transformations," he goes on to state that the "notion of structure is comprised of three key ideas: the idea of wholeness, the idea of transformation, and the idea of self-regulation" (p. 5). Structuralism is not new, he points out, despite its only recent formulations and intensive study (p. 136); and, as many others say, it is "essentially a method" (p. 136).

However old structuralism as a method may be, it is true that the recent wave of interest makes it seem like a new way of seeing the world. For example, in 1966 an international symposium was held at Johns Hopkins University out of which came, among other things, *The Language of Criticism and the Sciences of Man: The Structuralist Controversy* (ed. Richard Macksey and Eugenio Donato [Baltimore: Johns Hopkins University Press, 1970]). (When this book was later reissued in paperback, with the main title and the subtitle reversed, "controversy," appropriately enough, seemed to be given some emphasis.) Because of the volume of work in the field and a measure of controversy, there clearly was a developing need among critics, teachers, and students of literature for an overview of literary aspects of structuralism. In 1974 Robert Scholes published his response to that need, *Structuralism in Literature: An Introduction* (New Haven: Yale University Press). This "introduction" is a full-length book, and its bibliographical appendix alone is sixteen pages long, including a large number of items that have been published in languages other than English. Consequently, a reading of Scholes's book and a study of the bibliography make clear the international nature of discussions of structuralism. A similar book, Jonathan Culler's *Structuralist Poetics: Structuralism, Linguistics and the Study of Literature* (Ithaca, N.Y.: Cornell University Press, 1975), gives something of the same effect with its twenty-page bibliography.

But perhaps more easily accessible and more immediately helpful for the general reader are the several articles in the October 1975 issue of *College English*. The titles of two suggest their helpfulness: one, cited earlier, is Selz's "Structuralism for the Non-Specialist"; the other is Isaiah Smithson's "Structuralism as a Method of Literary Criticism." Smithson provides a definition dependent on Piaget and Claude Lévi-Strauss (the latter an anthropologist who has had a large influence on the movement), identifies four "basic principles of structuralism" ([1] the emphasis upon relations among elements; [2] the structuralist concern with the "synchronic" rather than the "diachronic"; [3] the contention that "structures exist below the surface"; and [4] the universal presence of structures and the necessary relations among them), notes some inadequacies of structuralism as a method of literary study, and provides a structuralist reading of D. H. Lawrence's *The Rainbow*. That Selz has provided a glossary of structuralist terms is in itself a reminder that here we have a new effort to articulate an approach to literature (not forgetting what Piaget has already said about "new" and "old"), an approach with its own methodology and terminology. (One is reminded of the need experienced by teachers and critics of literature, to say nothing of students, when the New Criticism was sweeping American universities. That need was responded to in similar fashion by William Elton, with *A Guide to the New Criticism* [Chicago: Modern Poetry Association, 1953].) Another of the articles in *College English* begins on a cautionary note that we would do well to remember, a note that can be heard in Scholes's book and elsewhere. Quentin G. Kraft, in "Science and Poetics, Old and New," warns against "imposing scientific method on the study of literature and art and other human things." Kraft is concerned "to show that its scientism is only the most recent and perhaps strongest manifestation of a tendency which has long influenced our collective sense of what art is." There is, he believes, a "strong link between the new poetics and the old, between structuralism and the criticism once known as 'new' " (p. 167).

A few comments on Scholes's book will now give some dimension to these notes on the movement. In his preface Scholes calls attention to his deliberate limitation of his book to literature, acknowledging that he has "necessarily deemphasized other aspects," neglecting "any discusssion of structuralism in philosophy, in psychology, in history, in the physical sciences or mathematics" (p. ix). For Scholes, structuralism is a "response to the need . . . for a 'coherent system' that would unite the modern sciences and make the world habitable for man again" (p. 2); it is "in its broadest sense . . . a way of looking for reality not in individual things but in the relationships among them" (p. 4). Nor has the movement been merely scientific: It "has affected the arts as well, for it is a general movement of mind—one of those currents of thought that from time to time sweep through a culture and move its most disparate elements in the same direction" (p. 7). Structuralism is not only a "movement of mind," says Scholes: as Piaget had observed, it is a method:

> [It] may claim a privileged place in literary study because it seeks to establish a model of the system of literature itself as the external reference for the individual works it considers. By moving from the study of language to the study of literature, and seeking to define the principles of structuration that operate not only through individual works but through the relationships among works over the whole field of literature, structuralism has tried—and is trying—to establish for literary studies a basis that is as scientific as possible. [p. 10]

Central to the "idea of structuralism is the idea of system: a system: a complete, self-regulating entity that adapts to new conditions by transforming its features while retaining its systematic structure." In such a system, "Every literary unit from the individual sentence to the whole order of words can be seen in relation to the concept of system," and the study of works, genres, and the whole of literature can be made in this structural or relational way (p. 10).

Having set forth these general principles, Scholes then devotes much of his book to tracing the development of structuralism—for example, the linguistic theories of Ferdinand de Saussure and Roman Jakobson; various other structuralist approaches, such as "forms" and "dramatic situations"; the Russian formalists (of great importance in the development of the movement); and such "mythographers" as Claude Lévi-Strauss. Scholes not only surveys but also makes interesting applications of his own, showing for example, Romantic theories of poetic language in a structuralist manner and offering a "structural perspective" on Joyce's *Ulysses*. He concludes with an almost religious hope for the future, when the structuralist imagination may produce an ideology as much as a method, an ideology that "we need most desperately today," one that would show the relationship between structuralism and love (p. 197). In such a hope Scholes consciously differs from other critics who would restrict structuralism to method.

XI. THE STYLISTICS APPROACH

Style has traditionally been a concern of rhetoric (see "The Rhetorical Approach"), but recently style has had such a development in its own right that we will treat it here not only as a division of the "new rhetoric" but also as an approach in its own right, as "stylistics."

Stylistics, defined in a most rudimentary way, is not the study of the words and grammar an author uses, but the study of the *way* the author uses his words and grammar— as well as other elements—both within the sentence (where some would see it) and within the text as a whole.

Although the distinction between linguistics and stylistics as approaches to literature is difficult (and sometimes impossible) to make (see "The Linguistics Approach"), we offer these parallel statements: (1) in linguistics we have a study of the materials available to users of language—the syntactic forms, the grammar—materials, in other words, available to all users by virtue of their ability to recognize and to duplicate sentence patterns (that is, a grammar can be formulated in advance of its implementation in a given sentence or literary work); (2) in stylistics we have a study of the particular choices an author makes from the "available materials," choices that are largely culture oriented and situation bound. This distinction seems to be something of the meaning of Roger Fowler when he says, "A text is structured in a certain way because it is a distinct use of certain distinctive materials given in advance. We need to make a fundamental division between the . . . linguistic materials available (grammatical facts) and the use made of them (stylistic facts)" ("The Structure of Criticism and the Languages of Poetry: An Approach Through Language," in *Contemporary Criticism*, ed. Malcolm Bradbury and David Palmer, Stratford-upon-Avon Studies, 12 [London: Edward Arnold, 1970], p. 182). Fowler recognizes the assistance offered the literary critic by the linguist, but calls for a "sufficiently rich theory of linguistic *performance*" (p. 185; emphasis ours). Language, he asserts, has a cultural dimension so that not merely "grammatical competence" but "sociolinguistic competence" (p. 187) is important to the "mature member of the English-speaking community"—and of course to the author and reader therein. The performance, consequently, becomes the crucial element in a stylistic approach to a literary work. Fowler gives brief examples from *The Essay on Man, Washington Square,* and *Mansfield Park* to show the principles at work and then says:

> A language is a structured repository of concepts, and every use of language is a particular ordering in a (partly language-dependent) circumscribed cultural situation. This ought to be

a tacit principle for criticism, because it is an inevitable fact
of all writing. The reader, whose linguistic conceptualization
of experience answers closely to that of a poet who uses the
same language, has his perceptions guided by the poet's
performance in language. [p. 193]

Because of the emphasis on choices and performance
(rather than on "availability" of grammar), stylistics concerns the full text rather than the sentence. Although it
may move toward evaluation of texts, this last point is
debated. On the one hand, for example, David Lodge says
that a certain kind of stylistics "can never become a fully
comprehensive method of literary criticism" (*Language of
Fiction* [New York: Columbia University Press, 1966], p.
56). According to Lodge, the stylistician looks at a linguistic
element in the context of the language as a whole, whereas
the critic takes as his context the text as a whole; more
importantly, the stylistician is less concerned with questions of value than is the critic, who "undertakes to combine analysis with evaluation": "It is the essential characteristic of literature that it concerns values. And values are
not amenable to scientific method" (p. 57). On the other
hand, Stanley B. Greenfield, in "Grammar and Meaning in
Poetry" (*PMLA*, 82 [1967], 377-387), takes issue with that
statement, and tries to demonstrate not only how linguistics
moves into the domain of stylistics, but also how stylistics
can be judgmental. Greenfield, whose annotations will be
of great help to anyone seeking to go further in these
related approaches, expresses his concern as being

particularly with the voyages of *linguists* among poetic texts,
and with the values of their new methodologies, for our
understanding of "how a poem means." They have staked
large claims for the objectivity and scientific nature of their
investigations as opposed to the intuitive and impressionistic
vagaries of the critical mind. And it is perhaps time that their
newfoundland became as widely known and explored by
readers of critical journals as it has been by those of linguistic ones. [p. 378]

Just about the time that Greenfield was calling for a wider acceptance in the critical journals of the techniques being presented in the linguistic publications, the journal *Style* was being founded (1967). The periodical has as its expressed aims the publication of "meritorious analyses of style, particularly those which deal with literature in the English language and which provide systematic methods of description and evaluation of style," the reviewing of books "which contribute significantly to our understanding of style," and the provision of an "annual bibliography of stylistic criticism" as well as of occasional bibliographies that focus on aspects of style. The journal also aims to survey international developments in stylistics and to provide information on the teaching of style. We may note here that the reference to international matters of stylistics in an American journal that emphasizes literature in English reminds us of the European roots of stylistics. It was only a year earlier that David Lodge was saying: "The first thing that must be said about modern stylistics is that it is largely a Continental phenomenon. Stylistics as such scarcely exists as an influential force in Anglo-American criticism of literature in English. We have no Spitzer, no Auerbach, no Ullmann" (*Language of Fiction*, p. 52).

A further appreciation of the interest in stylistics can be gained from two major collections of papers and commentaries on those papers: *Style in Language* (ed. Thomas A. Sebeok [Cambridge, Mass.: M. I. T. Press, 1960]); and *Literary Style: A Symposium* (ed. Seymour Chatman [New York: Oxford University Press, 1971]). Each book is the result of a major conference on style. The first, held at Indiana University in the spring of 1958, was attended by Americans and was heavily interdisciplinary; the second, held at the Villa Serbelloni in August 1969, was less interdisciplinary in its intent, but was very much international, with ten European nations being represented. Each book has short biographical sketches of the participants and extensive annotations; Sebeok's additionally has a list of 462 references. Taking the two volumes together, one can realize the difficulty of deciding what style is, the variety of approaches to the nature of style, the European—especially Continental—sources of this critical approach, and the variety of stylistic aspects of literary works that can be investigated.

There are almost thirty papers and "statements" in the Sebeok volume, but one essay that might be cited for its accessibility to the beginning student is John B. Carroll's "Vectors of Prose Style" (pp. 283-292). Crediting psychologist L. L. Thurstone's *The Vectors of Mind* (1935) with introducing the technique called *factor analysis,* Carroll employs a "statistical procedure for identifying and measuring the fundamental dimensions ('vectors') that account for the variation to be observed in any set of phenomena" (p. 283). Carroll describes six "factors": good-bad, personal-impersonal, ornamental-plain, abstract-concrete, serious-humorous, and characterizing-narrating. His procedure is to have a team of "raters" evaluate selected passages of literature in terms of these factors. The result of such a close evaluation can be produced in graph form, so that, for example, the different profiles of two authors might be superimposed and compared.

Another essay in the Sebeok volume, Sol Saporta's "The Application of Linguistics to the Study of Poetic Language," raises points we have already alluded to: Is poetry language? Can poetry, as language, be studied scientifically? Can linguistics be the scientific study of poetry? Saporta suggests that

> there seems to be an essential difference in the aims and consequently the results of linguistics and what can be called stylistics. A linguistic description is adequate to the extent that it predicts grammatical sentences beyond those in the corpus on which the description is based. Now, stylistic analysis is apparently primarily classificatory rather than predictive in this sense. . . . the result of a linguistic analysis is a grammar which generates unobserved (as well as observed) utterances. The aim of stylistic analysis would seem

to be a typology which would indicate the features by which they may be further separated into subclasses. [p. 86]

Saporta adds: "Such a view suggests that whereas linguistics is concerned with the description of a code, stylistics is concerned with the differences among the messages generated in accordance with the rules of that code" (p. 87). This sounds like the nonevaluative methodology that Greenfield was seeking to transcend; nevertheless, the passages do supply another differentiation between linguistics and stylistics, and like other commentators, Saporta points out that linguistics tends to take the sentence as its limit of concern, whereas stylistics must concern itself with a "larger unit, the text, . . . as the basis for stylistic analysis" (p. 88).

The volume edited by Seymour Chatman, with another score of papers and contributors, is also rich and wide-ranging. The papers are arranged under six headings: "Theory of Style," "Stylistics and Related Disciplines," "Style Features," "Period Style," "Genre Style," and "Styles of Individual Authors and Texts." In his introduction Chatman says, "It would be presumptuous to attempt to summarize in a brief introduction the richness and complexity of this Symposium. But perhaps I can give the reader some sense of its unity and focus by noting certain persistent themes in the discussion. They are perhaps best formulated by [three] questions" (p. xi): (1) "What is style?" (2) "How do style features emerge?" and (3) "Is linguistics sufficient to describe literary style? That is, Is stylistics merely a branch of linguistics?" To this last, Chatman says, "The general opinion of the Symposium is 'No.'" He then cites from the essays a number of passages that "should relieve the fears of those (mostly Anglo-Saxon) scholars who worry about the 'encroachment' of linguistics into literary studies" (p. xiv). The consensus is that there are important "things in literature *beyond* language" that deserve study.

One critic cited by Chatman is René Wellek, who had

also contributed to the Sebeok volume. Because Wellek, very much the literary critic, voiced a healthy corrective to the Indiana conference, it is appropriate to quote here his words at the very end of the "closing statement" of that volume:

> Interpretation, understanding, explication, analysis are not, at least in the study of literature and art, separate from evaluation and criticism. There is no collection of neutral, value-proof traits that can be analyzed by a science of stylistics. A work of literature is, by its very nature, a totality of values which do not merely adhere to the structure but constitute its very nature. Thus criticism, a study of values, cannot be expelled from a meaningful concept of literary scholarship. This is not of course a recommendation of pure subjectivity, of "appreciation," of arbitrary opinion. It is a plea for literary scholarship as a systematic inquiry into structures, norms, and functions which contain and *are* values. Stylistics will form an important part of this inquiry, but only a part. [*Style in Language,* p. 419]

But it is just as appropriate to close this section on stylistics by citing an article with a different bent, one that would complement—even implement—Wellek's words, particularly his last sentence. Erwin R. Steinberg, in "Stylistics as a Humanistic Discipline" (*Style,* 10 [1976], 67–68), argues that it is a humane activity to seek and analyze "verbal patterns" in works of literature, for the very discovery and reporting of such patterns says, ". . . here is an ordering, an organizing principle, that has not been pointed out before. What might have been thought to have been random is in fact patterned. Here is the evidence: the tools, the procedure, and the results" (p. 68). Steinberg would see no inconsistency between humanistic endeavor and the use of statistics or even of the computer. He suggests five ways of commenting on a discovered pattern: merely reporting the pattern for the sake of recording it; reporting the way a certain effect, already perceived, is achieved; citing evidence of how a pattern supports the meaning of a text;

noting a pattern counter to the surface meaning that in turn sets up a "tension which adds an additional dimension to the meaning of the work"; and citing evidence of a pattern that weakens a work of art "by running counter to all the other patterns available in the text" (pp. 68–69). Steinberg then asks, "Is such pattern-seeking an appropriate occupation for followers of humanistic disciplines? Inasmuch as pattern-seeking itself seems to be a basic intellectual interest and inasmuch as the finding and describing of language patterns can help us to understand texts that assert 'the dignity and worth of man and his capacity for self-realization through reason,' I would assume that it is" (p. 69).

EPILOGUE

"How do you learn to *read* this way? *Where* do you learn this? Do you take a course in *symbols* or something?"

With a rising, plaintive pitch to her voice, with puzzled eyes and shaking head, a college student once asked those questions after her class had participated in a lively discussion of the multiple levels in Henry James's *The Turn of the Screw*. As with most students when they are first introduced to a serious study of literature, members of this group were delighted, amazed—and dismayed—as they themselves helped to unfold the rich layers of the work, to see it from perspectives of form and of psychology, to correlate it with the author's biography and its cultural and historical context.

But that particular student, who was both fascinated and dismayed by the "symbols," had not yet taken a crucial step in the learning process: She had not perceived that the practice of close reading, the bringing to bear of all kinds of knowledge, and the use of several approaches are in themselves the "course in symbols or something." What we have traced in this volume is not a course in the occult; it is not something only for those who have access to the inner sanctum. For, after all, as Wordsworth wrote in 1800 in his Preface to the *Lyrical Ballads*, the poet "is a man speaking to men." A poet or a dramatist embodies an experience in a poem or a play, embodies it—usually—for us, his readers; and we respond simply by reliving that experience as fully as possible.

To be sure, not all of us may want to respond to that extent. There was, for example, the secondary school teacher who listened to a fairly long and detailed explication of "The Death of the Ball-Turret Gunner," a five-line poem by Randall Jarrell. Later she took the lecturer aside and said, with something more than asperity, "I'd *never* make my class try to see all of *that* in a poem." Perhaps not. But is the class better or worse because of that attitude?

Clearly, the authors of this book believe that we readers are the losers when we fail to see in a work of literature all that may be legitimately seen there. We have presented a number of critical approaches to literature, aware that many have been only briefly treated and that much has been generalized. But we have suggested here some of the tools and some of the approaches that enable a reader to "criticize" —that is, to judge and to discern so that he may see better the truth of a literary work, to relate it to the range of human experience, to appreciate its form and style.

Having offered these tools and approaches, we would also urge caution against undue or misdirected enthusiasm in their use, for judgment and discernment imply reason and caution. Too often even seasoned critics, forgetting the etymology of the word "critic," become personal and subjective or preoccupied with tangential concerns. Not-so-seasoned students, their minds suddenly open to psychoanalytic criticism, run gaily through a pastoral poem and joyously find Freudian symbols in every rounded hill and stately conifer. Some read a simple poem like William Carlos Williams's "The Red Wheelbarrow" and, unwilling to see simplicity and compression as virtues enough (and as much more than mere "simpleness"), stray from the poem into their individual mazes. They forget that any interpretation must be supported logically and fully from the evidence within the literary work and that the ultimate test of the validity of an interpretation must be its selfconsistency. Conversely, sometimes they do establish a fairly legitimate pattern of interpretation for a work, only to find something that seems to be at odds with it; then, fascinated with or startled by what they assume to be a new element, they forget that this new possibility is not valid unless it permits a unified picture of both the original pattern and the new insight. In short, an object of literary art has its unique aesthetic experience; the reader is no more at liberty to mar it with careless extensions than the author would have been free to damage its organic unity with infelicitous inclusions.

We must also remember to be flexible and eclectic in our choices of critical approaches to a given literary work. Our choices are determined by the same discretion that controls what we exclude, by our concern for the unique experience and nature of a piece of literature. Not all approaches are useful in all cases. Perhaps we would not be too far wrong to suggest that there are as many approaches to literary works as there are literary works. All we can do is to draw from the many approaches the combination that best fits a particular literary creation. As David Daiches said at the end of his book *Critical Approaches to Literature* (Englewood Cliffs, N.J.: Prentice-Hall, 1956), "Every effective literary critic sees some facet of literary art and develops an awareness with respect to it; but the total vision, or something approximating it, comes only to those who learn how to blend the insights yielded by many critical approaches" (p. 393).

That is why we have chosen to present a variety of approaches and why some of the chapters have even blended several methods. This blending is as it should be. It is not easy—and it would be unwise to try—to keep the work always separate from the life of the author and a view of his times; to divide the study of form from the study of basic imageries; to segregate basic imageries from archetypes or from other exponents of the experience of the work. And it would be unwise to ignore how, for example, a work long known and interpreted by conventional methods might yield fresh insights if examined from the perspectives of neo-Marxist criticism, feminist criticism, or phenomenological criticism.

Our final word, then, is this: We admit that literary criticism can be difficult and sometimes esoteric, but it is first of all an attempt of a reader to understand fully what he is reading. To understand in that manner, he does well to bring to bear whatever is in the human province that justifiably helps him to achieve that understanding. For literature is a part of the richness of human experience: It at once thrives on it, feeds it, and constitutes a significant part of it. When we realize this, we never again can be satisfied with the simple notions that a story is something only for the idler or the impractical dreamer, that a poem is merely a "pretty" combination of sounds and sights, that a significant drama is equivalent to an escapist motion picture or a television melodrama. Browning's Fra Lippo Lippi says:

> This world's no blot us us,
> Nor blank; it means intensely, and means good:
> To find its meaning is my meat and drink.

So too must be our attitude toward any worthy piece of literature in that world.

APPENDIXES

ANDREW MARVELL
TO HIS COY MISTRESS

Had we but world-enough, and time,
This coyness, Lady, were no crime.
We would sit down and think which way
To walk and pass our long love's day.   5
Thou by the Indian Ganges' side
Shouldst rubies find; I by the tide
Of Humber would complain. I would
Love you ten years before the Flood,
And you should, if you please, refuse
Till the conversion of the Jews.   10
My vegetable love should grow
Vaster than empires, and more slow;
An hundred years should go to praise
Thine eyes and on thy forehead gaze;
Two hundred to adore each breast,   15
But thirty thousand to the rest;
An age at least to every part,

And the last age should show your heart.
For, Lady, you deserve this state,
Nor would I love at lower rate.   20

But at my back I always hear
Time's wingèd chariot hurrying near;
And yonder all before us lie
Deserts of vast eternity.
Thy beauty shall no more be found,   25
Nor, in thy marble vault, shall sound
My echoing song; then worms shall try
That long preserved virginity,
And your quaint honor turn to dust,
And into ashes all my lust: 30
The grave's a fine and private place,
But none, I think, do there embrace.

Now therefore, while the youthful hue
Sits on thy skin like morning dew,
And while thy willing soul transpires   35
At every pore with instant fires,
Now let us sport us while we may,
And now, like amorous birds of prey,
Rather at once our time devour
Than languish in his slow-chapped power.   40
Let us roll all our strength and all
Our sweetness up into one ball,
And tear our pleasures with rough strife
Thorough* the iron gates of life:
Thus, though we cannot make our sun   45
Stand still, yet we will make him run.

*thorough: through

NATHANIEL HAWTHORNE
YOUNG GOODMAN BROWN

Young Goodman Brown came forth at sunset into the street at Salem village; but put his head back, after crossing the threshold, to exchange a parting kiss with his young wife. And Faith, as the wife was aptly named, thrust her own pretty head into the street, letting the wind play with the pink ribbons of her cap while she called to Goodman Brown.

"Dearest heart," whispered she, softly and rather sadly, when her lips were close to his ear, "prithee put off your journey until sunrise and sleep in your own bed to-night. A lone woman is troubled with such dreams and such thoughts that she's afeard of herself sometimes. Pray tarry with me this night, dear husband, of all nights in the year."

"My love and my Faith," replied young Goodman Brown, "of all nights in the year, this one night must I tarry away from thee. My journey, as thou callest it, forth and back again, must needs be done 'twixt now and sunrise.

What, my sweet, pretty wife, dost thou doubt me already, and we but three months married?"

"Then God bless you!" said Faith, with the pink ribbons; "and may you find all well when you come back."

"Amen!" cried Goodman Brown. "Say thy prayers, dear Faith, and go to bed at dusk, and no harm will come to thee."

So they parted; and the young man pursued his way until, being about to turn the corner by the meeting-house, he looked back and saw the head of Faith still peeping after him with a melancholy air, in spite of her pink ribbons.

"Poor little Faith!" thought he, for his heart smote him. "What a wretch am I to leave her on such an errand! She talks of dreams, too. Methought as she spoke there was trouble in her face, as if a dream had warned her what work is to be done to-night. But no, no; 'twould kill her to think it. Well, she's a blessed angel on earth; and after this one night I'll cling to her skirts and follow her to heaven."

With this excellent resolve for the future, Goodman Brown felt himself justified in making more haste on his present evil purpose. He had taken a dreary road, darkened by all the gloomiest trees of the forest, which barely stood aside to let the narrow path creep through, and closed immediately behind. It was all as lonely as could be; and there is this peculiarity in such a solitude, that the traveller knows not who may be concealed by the innumerable trunks and the thick boughs overhead; so that with lonely footsteps he may yet be passing through an unseen multitude.

"There may be a devilish Indian behind every tree," said Goodman Brown to himself; and he glanced fearfully behind him as he added, "What if the devil himself should be at my very elbow!"

His head being turned back, he passed a crook of the road, and, looking forward again, beheld the figure of a man, in grave and decent attire, seated at the foot of an old tree. He arose at Goodman Brown's approach and walked onward side by side with him.

"You are late, Goodman Brown," said he. "The clock of the Old South was striking as I came through Boston, and that is full fifteen minutes agone."

"Faith kept me back a while," replied the young man, with a tremor in his voice, caused by the sudden appearance of his companion, though not wholly unexpected.

It was now deep dusk in the forest, and deepest in that part of it where these two were journeying. As nearly as could be discerned, the second traveller was about fifty years old, apparently in the same rank of life as Goodman Brown, and bearing a considerable resemblance to him, though perhaps more in expression than features. Still they might have been taken for father and son. And yet, though the elder person was as simply clad as the younger, and as simple in manner too, he had an indescribable air of one who knew the world, and who would not have felt abashed at the governor's dinner table or in King William's court, were it possible that his affairs should call him thither. But the only thing about him that could be fixed upon as remarkable was his staff, which bore the likeness of a great black snake, so curiously wrought that it might almost be seen to twist and wriggle itself like a living serpent. This, of course, must have been an ocular deception, assisted by the uncertain light.

"Come, Goodman Brown," cried his fellow-traveller, "this is a dull pace for the beginning of a journey. Take my staff, if you are so soon weary."

"Friend," said the other, exchanging his slow pace for a full stop, "having kept covenant by meeting thee here, it is my purpose now to return whence I came. I have scruples touching the matter thou wot'st of."

"Sayest thou so?" replied he of the serpent, smiling apart. "Let us walk on, nevertheless, reasoning as we go; and if I convince thee not thou shalt turn back. We are but a little way in the forest yet."

"Too far! too far!" exclaimed the goodman, unconsciously resuming his walk. "My father never went into the woods on such an errand, nor his father before him. We have been a race of honest men and good Christians since the days of the martyrs: and shall I be the first of the name of Brown that ever took this path and kept—"

"Such company, thou wouldst say," observed the elder person, interpreting his pause. "Well said, Goodman Brown! I have been as well acquainted with your family as with ever a one among the Puritans; and that's no trifle to say. I helped your grandfather, the constable, when he lashed the Quaker woman so smartly through the streets of Salem; and it was I that brought your father a pitch-pine knot, kindled at my own hearth, to set fire to an Indian village, in King Philip's war. They were my good friends, both; and many a pleasant walk have we had along this path, and returned merrily after midnight. I would fain be friends with you for their sake."

"If it be as thou sayest," replied Goodman Brown, "I marvel they never spoke of these matters; or, verily, I marvel not, seeing that the least rumor of the sort would have driven them from New England. We are a people of prayer, and good works to boot, and abide no such wickedness."

"Wickedness or not," said the traveller with the twisted staff, "I have a very general acquaintance here in New England. The deacons of many a church have drunk the communion wine with me; the selectmen of divers towns make me their chairman; and a majority of the Great and General Court are firm supporters of my interest. The governor and I, too— But these are state secrets."

"Can this be so?" cried Goodman Brown, with a stare of amazement at his undisturbed companion. "Howbeit, I have nothing to do with the governor and council; they have their own ways, and are no rule for a simple husbandman like me. But, were I to go on with thee, how should I meet the eye of that good old man, our minister, at Salem village? Oh, his voice would make me tremble both Sabbath day and lecture day."

Thus far the elder traveller had listened with due gravity; but now burst into a fit of irrepressible mirth, shaking himself so violently that his snake-like staff actually seemed to wriggle in sympathy.

"Ha! ha! ha!" shouted he again and again; then composing himself, "Well, go on, Goodman Brown, go on; but, prithee, don't kill me with laughing."

"Well, then, to end the matter at once," said Goodman Brown, considerably nettled, "there is my wife, Faith. It would break her dear little heart; and I'd rather break my own."

"Nay, if that be the case," answered the other, "e'en go thy ways, Goodman Brown. I would not for twenty old women like the one hobbling before us that Faith should come to any harm."

As he spoke he pointed his staff at a female figure on the path, in whom Goodman Brown recognized a very pious and exemplary dame, who had taught him his catechism in youth, and was still his moral and spiritual adviser, jointly with the minister and Deacon Gookin.

"A marvel, truly, that Goody Cloyse should be so far in the wilderness at nightfall," said he. "But with your leave, friend, I shall take a cut through the woods until we have left this Christian woman behind. Being a stranger to you, she might ask whom I was consorting with and whither I was going."

"Be it so," said his fellow-traveller. "Betake you to the woods, and let me keep the path."

Accordingly the young man turned aside, but took care to watch his companion, who advanced softly along the road until he had come within a staff's length of the old dame. She, meanwhile, was making the best of her way, with singular speed for so aged a woman, and mumbling some indistinct words—a prayer, doubtless—as she went. The traveller put forth his staff and touched her withered neck with what seemed the serpent's tail.

"The devil!" screamed the pious old lady.

"Then Goody Cloyse knows her old friend?" observed the traveller, confronting her and leaning on his writhing stick.

"Ah, forsooth, and is it your worship indeed?" cried the good dame. "Yea, truly it is, and in the very image of my old gossip, Goodman Brown, the grandfather of the silly

fellow that now is. But—would your worship believe it?—
my broomstick hath strangely disappeared, stolen, as I
suspect, by that unhanged witch, Goody Cory, and that,
too, when I was all anointed with the juice of smallage,
and cinquefoil, and wolf's bane—"

"Mingled with fine wheat and the fat of a new-born
babe," said the shape of old Goodman Brown.

"Ah, your worship knows the recipe," cried the old lady,
cackling aloud. "So, as I was saying, being all ready for the
meeting, and no horse to ride on, I made up my mind to
foot it; for they tell me there is a nice young man to be
taken into communion to-night. But now your good worship will lend me your arm, and we shall be there in a
twinkling."

"That can hardly be," answered her friend. "I may not
spare you my arm, Goody Cloyse; but here is my staff, if
you will."

So saying, he threw it down at her feet, where, perhaps,
it assumed life, being one of the rods which its owner had
formerly lent to the Egyptian magi. Of this fact, however,
Goodman Brown could not take cognizance. He had cast
up his eyes in astonishment, and, looking down again,
beheld neither Goody Cloyse nor the serpentine staff, but
his fellow-traveller alone, who waited for him as calmly as
if nothing had happened.

"That old woman taught me my catechism," said the
young man; and there was a world of meaning in this
simple comment.

They continued to walk onward, while the elder traveller exhorted his companion to make good speed and
persevere in the path, discoursing so aptly that his arguments seemed rather to spring up in the bosom of his
auditor than to be suggested by himself. As they went, he
plucked a branch of maple to serve for a walking stick, and
began to strip it of the twigs and little boughs, which were
wet with evening dew. The moment his fingers touched
them they became strangely withered and dried up as with
a week's sunshine. Thus the pair proceeded, at a good free
pace, until suddenly, in a gloomy hollow of the road,

Goodman Brown sat himself down on the stump of a tree and refused to go any farther.

"Friend," said he, stubbornly, "my mind is made up. Not another step will I budge on this errand. What if a wretched old woman do choose to go to the devil when I thought she was going to heaven: is that any reason why I should quit my dear Faith and go after her?"

"You will think better of this by and by," said his acquaintance, composedly. "Sit here and rest yourself a while; and when you feel like moving again, there is my staff to help you along."

Without more words, he threw his companion the maple stick, and was as speedily out of sight as if he had vanished into the deepening gloom. The young man sat a few moments by the roadside, applauding himself greatly, and thinking with how clear a conscience he should meet the minister in his morning walk, nor shrink from the eye of good old Deacon Gookin. And what calm sleep would be his that very night, which was to have been spent so wickedly, but so purely and sweetly now, in the arms of Faith! Amidst these pleasant and praiseworthy meditations, Goodman Brown heard the tramp of horses along the road, and deemed it advisable to conceal himself within the verge of the forest, conscious of the guilty purpose that had brought him thither, though now so happily turned from it.

On came the hoof tramps and the voices of the riders, two grave old voices, conversing soberly as they drew near. These mingled sounds appeared to pass along the road, within a few yards of the young man's hiding-place; but, owing doubtless to the depth of the gloom at that particular spot, neither the travellers nor their steeds were visible. Though their figures brushed the small boughs by the wayside, it could not be seen that they intercepted, even for a moment, the faint gleam from the strip of bright sky athwart which they must have passed. Goodman Brown alternately crouched and stood on tiptoe, pulling aside the branches and thrusting forth his head as far as he durst without discerning so much as a shadow. It vexed him the more, because he could have sworn, were such a thing possible, that he recognized the voices of the minister and Deacon Gookin, jogging along quietly, as they were wont to do, when bound to some ordination or ecclesiastical council. While yet within hearing, one of the riders stopped to pluck a switch.

"Of the two, reverend sir," said the voice like the deacon's, "I had rather miss an ordination dinner than tonight's meeting. They tell me that some of our community are to be here from Falmouth and beyond, and others from Connecticut and Rhode Island, besides several of the Indian powwows, who, after their fashion, know almost as much deviltry as the best of us. Moreover, there is a goodly young woman to be taken into communion."

"Mighty well, Deacon Gookin!" replied the solemn old tones of the minister. "Spur up, or we shall be late. Nothing can be done, you know, until I get on the ground."

The hoofs clattered again; and the voices, talking so strangely in the empty air, passed on through the forest, where no church had ever been gathered or solitary Christian prayed. Whither, then, could these holy men be journeying so deep into the heathen wilderness? Young Goodman Brown caught hold of a tree for support, being ready to sink down on the ground, faint and overburdened with the heavy sickness of his heart. He looked up to the sky, doubting whether there really was a heaven above him. Yet there was the blue arch, and the stars brightening in it.

"With heaven above and Faith below, I will yet stand firm against the devil!" cried Goodman Brown.

While he still gazed upward into the deep arch of the firmament and had lifted his hands to pray, a cloud, though no wind was stirring, hurried across the zenith and hid the brightening stars. The blue sky was still visible, except directly overhead, where this black mass of cloud was sweeping swiftly northward. Aloft in the air, as if from the depths of the cloud, came a confused and doubtful sound of voices. Once the listener fancied that he could distinguish the accents of townspeople of his own, men and women, both pious and ungodly, many of whom he had met at the communion table, and had seen others rioting at the tavern. The next moment, so indistinct were the sounds, he doubted whether he had heard aught but the murmur of the old forest, whispering without a wind. Then came a stronger swell of those familiar tones, heard daily in the sunshine at Salem village, but never until now from a cloud of night. There was one voice, of a young woman, uttering lamentations, yet with an uncertain sorrow, and entreating for some favor, which, perhaps, it would grieve her to obtain; and all the unseen multitude, both saints and sinners, seemed to encourage her onward.

"Faith!" shouted Goodman Brown, in a voice of agony and desperation; and the echoes of the forest mocked him, crying, "Faith! Faith!" as if bewildered wretches were seeking her all through the wilderness.

The cry of grief, rage, and terror was yet piercing the night, when the unhappy husband held his breath for a response. There was a scream, drowned immediately in a louder murmur of voices, fading into far-off laughter, as the dark cloud swept away, leaving the clear and silent sky above Goodman Brown. But something fluttered lightly down through the air and caught on the branch of a tree. The young man seized it, and beheld a pink ribbon.

"My Faith is gone!" cried he, after one stupefied moment. "There is no good on earth; and sin is but a name. Come, devil; for to thee is this world given."

And, maddened with despair, so that he laughed loud and long, did Goodman Brown grasp his staff and set forth again, at such a rate that he seemed to fly along the forest path rather than to walk or run. The road grew wilder and drearier and more faintly traced, and vanished at length, leaving him in the heart of the dark wilderness, still rushing onward with the instinct that guides mortal man to evil. The whole forest was peopled with frightful sounds— the creaking of the trees, the howling of wild beasts, and the yell of Indians; while sometimes the wind tolled like a distant church bell, and sometimes gave a broad roar around the traveller, as if all Nature were laughing him to scorn. But he was himself the chief horror of the scene, and shrank not from its other horrors.

"Ha! ha! ha!" roared Goodman Brown when the wind laughed at him. "Let us hear which will laugh loudest. Think not to frighten me with your deviltry. Come witch, come wizard, come Indian powwow, come devil himself, and here comes Goodman Brown. You may as well fear him as he fear you."

In truth, all through the haunted forest there could be nothing more frightful than the figure of Goodman Brown. On he flew among the black pines, brandishing his staff with frenzied gestures, now giving vent to an inspiration of horrid blasphemy, and now shouting forth such laughter as set all the echoes of the forest laughing like demons around him. The fiend in his own shape is less hideous than when he rages in the breast of man. Thus sped the demoniac on his course, until, quivering among the trees, he saw a red light before him, as when the felled trunks and branches of a clearing have been set on fire, and throw up their lurid blaze against the sky, at the hour of midnight. He paused, in a lull of the tempest that had driven him onward, and heard the swell of what seemed a hymn, rolling solemnly from a distance with the weight of many voices. He knew the tune; it was a familiar one in the choir of the village meeting-house. The verse died heavily away, and was lengthened by a chorus, not of human voices, but of all the sounds of the benighted wilderness pealing in awful harmony together. Goodman Brown cried out, and his cry was lost to his own ear by its unison with the cry of the desert.

In the interval of silence he stole forward until the light glared full upon his eyes. At one extremity of an open space, hemmed in by the dark wall of the forest, arose a rock, bearing some rude, natural resemblance either to a an altar or a pulpit, and surrounded by four blazing pines, their tops aflame, their stems untouched, like candles at an evening meeting. The mass of foliage that had overgrown the summit of the rock was all on fire, blazing high into the night and fitfully illuminating the whole field. Each pendent twig and leafy festoon was in a blaze. As the red light arose and fell, a numerous congregation alternately shone forth, then disappeared in shadow, and again grew, as it were, out of the darkness, peopling the heart of the solitary woods at once.

"A grave and dark-clad company," quoth Goodman Brown.

In truth they were such. Among them, quivering to and fro between gloom and splendor, appeared faces that would be seen next day at the council board of the province, and others which, Sabbath after Sabbath, looked devoutly heavenward, and benignantly over the crowded pews, from the holiest pulpits in the land. Some affirm that the lady of the governor was there. At least there were high dames well known to her, and wives of honored husbands, and widows, a great multitude, and ancient maidens, all of excellent repute, and fair young girls, who trembled lest their mothers should espy them. Either the sudden gleams of light flashing over the obscure field bedazzled Goodman Brown, or he recognized a score of the church members of Salem village famous for their special sanctity. Good old Deacon Gookin had arrived, and waited at the skirts of that venerable saint, his revered pastor. But, irreverently consorting with these grave, reputable, and pious people, these elders of the church, these chaste dames and dewy virgins, there were men of dissolute lives and women of spotted fame, wretches given over to all mean and filthy vice, and suspected even of horrid crimes. It was strange to see that the good shrank not from the wicked, nor were the sinners abashed by the saints. Scattered also among their pale-faced enemies were the Indian priests, or powwows, who had often scared their native forest with more hideous incantations than any known to English witchcraft.

"But where is Faith?" thought Goodman Brown; and, as

hope came into his heart, he trembled.

Another verse of the hymn arose, a slow and mournful strain, such as the pious love, but joined to the words which expressed all that our nature can conceive of sin, and darkly hinted at far more. Unfathomable to mere mortals is the lore of fiends. Verse after verse was sung; and still the chorus of the desert swelled between like the deepest tone of a mighty organ; and with the final peal of that dreadful anthem there came a sound, as if the roaring wind, the rushing streams, the howling beasts, and every other voice of the unconverted wilderness were mingling and according with the voice of guilty man in homage to the prince of all. The four blazing pines threw up a loftier flame, and obscurely discovered shapes and visages of horror on the smoke wreaths above the impious assembly. At the same moment the fire on the rock shot redly forth and formed a glowing arch above its base, where now appeared a figure. With reverence be it spoken, the apparition bore no slight similitude, both in garb and manner, to some grave divine of the New England churches.

"Bring forth the converts!" cried a voice that echoed through the field and rolled into the forest.

At the word, Goodman Brown stepped forth from the shadow of the trees and approached the congregation, with whom he felt a loathful brotherhood by the sympathy of all that was wicked in his heart. He could have well-nigh sworn that the shape of his own dead father beckoned him to advance, looking downward from a smoke wreath, while a woman, with dim features of despair, threw out her hand to warn him back. Was it his mother? But he had no power to retreat one step, nor to resist, even in thought, when the minister and good old Deacon Gookin seized his arms and led him to the blazing rock. Thither came also the slender form of a veiled female, led between Goody Cloyse, that pious teacher of the catechism, and Martha Carrier, who had received the devil's promise to be queen of hell. A rampant hag was she. And there stood the proselytes beneath the canopy of fire.

"Welcome, my children," said the dark figure, "to the communion of your race. Ye have found thus young your nature and your destiny. My children, look behind you!"

They turned; and flashing forth, as it were, in a sheet of flame, the fiend worshippers were seen; the smile of welcome gleamed darkly on every visage.

"There," resumed the sable form, "are all whom ye have reverenced from youth. Ye deemed them holier than yourselves, and shrank from your own sin, contrasting it with their lives of righteousness and prayerful aspirations heavenward. Yet here are they in all my worshipping assembly. This night it shall be granted you to know their secret deeds: how hoary-bearded elders of the church have whispered wanton words to the young maids of their households; how many a woman, eager for widows' weeds, has given her husband a drink at bedtime and let him sleep his last sleep in her bosom; how beardless youths have made haste to inherit their fathers' wealth; and how fair damsels—blush not, sweet ones—have dug little graves in the garden, and bidden me, the sole guest, to an infant's funeral. By the sympathy of your human hearts for sin ye shall scent out all the places—whether in church, bedchamber, street, field, or forest where crime has been committed, and shall exult to behold the whole earth one stain of guilt, one mighty blood spot. Far more than this. It shall be yours to penetrate, in every bosom, the deep mystery of sin, the fountain of all wicked arts, and which inexhaustibly supplies more evil impulses than human power—than my power at its utmost—can make manifest in deeds. And now, my children, look upon each other."

They did so; and, by the blaze of the hell-kindled torches, the wretched man beheld his Faith, and the wife her husband, trembling before that unhallowed altar.

"Lo, there ye stand, my children," said the figure, in a deep and solemn tone, almost sad with its despairing awfulness, as if his once angelic nature could yet mourn for our miserable race. "Depending upon one another's hearts, ye had still hoped that virtue were not all a dream.

Now are ye undeceived. Evil is the nature of mankind. Evil must be your only happiness. Welcome again, my children, to the communion of your race."

"Welcome," repeated the fiend worshippers in one cry of despair and triumph.

And there they stood, the only pair, as it seemed, who were yet hesitating on the verge of wickedness in this dark world. A basin was hollowed, naturally, in the rock. Did it contain water, reddened by the lurid light? or was it blood? or, perchance, a liquid flame? Herein did the shape of evil dip his hand and prepare to lay the mark of baptism upon their foreheads, that they might be partakers of the mystery of sin, more conscious of the secret guilt of others, both in deed and thought, than they could now be of their own. The husband cast one look at his pale wife, and Faith at him. What polluted wretches would the next glance show them to each other, shuddering alike at what they disclosed and what they saw!

"Faith! Faith!" cried the husband, "look up to heaven, and resist the wicked one."

Whether Faith obeyed he knew not. Hardly had he spoken when he found himself amid calm night and solitude, listening to a roar of the wind which died heavily away through the forest. He staggered against the rock, and felt it chill and damp; while a hanging twig, that had been all on fire, besprinkled his cheek with the coldest dew.

The next morning young Goodman Brown came slowly in to the street of Salem village, staring around him like a bewildered man. The good old minister was taking a walk along the graveyard to get an appetite for breakfast and meditate his sermon, and bestowed a blessing, as he passed, on Goodman Brown. He shrank from the venerable saint as if to avoid an anathema. Old Deacon Gookin was at domestic worship, and the holy words of his prayer were heard through the open window. "What God doth the wizard pray to?" quoth Goodman Brown. Goody Cloyse, that excellent old Christian, stood in the early sunshine at her own lattice, catechizing a little girl who had brought her a pint of morning's milk. Goodman Brown snatched away the child as from the grasp of the fiend himself. Turning the corner by the meeting-house, he spied the head of Faith, with the pink ribbons, gazing anxiously forth, and bursting into such joy at sight of him that she skipped along the street and almost kissed her husband before the whole village. But Goodman Brown looked sternly and sadly into her face, and passed on without a greeting.

Had Goodman Brown fallen asleep in the forest and only dreamed a wild dream of a witch-meeting?

Be it so if you will; but, alas! it was a dream of evil omen for young Goodman Brown. A stern, a sad, a darkly meditative, a distrustful, if not a desperate man did he become from the night of that fearful dream. On the Sabbath day, when the congregation were singing a holy psalm, he could not listen because an anthem of sin rushed loudly upon his ear and drowned all the blessed strain. When the minister spoke from the pulpit with power and fervid eloquence, and, with his hand on the open Bible, of the sacred truths of our religion, and of saint-like lives and triumphant deaths, and of future bliss or misery unutterable, then did Goodman Brown turn pale, dreading lest the roof should thunder down upon the gray blasphemer and his hearers. Often, awaking suddenly at midnight, he shrank from the bosom of Faith; and at morning or eventide, when the family knelt down at prayer, he scowled and muttered to himself, and gazed sternly at his wife, and turned away. And when he had lived long, and was borne to his grave a hoary corpse, followed by Faith, an aged woman, and children and grandchildren, a goodly procession, besides neighbors not a few, they carved no hopeful verse upon his tombstone, for his dying hour was gloom.

GLOSSARY

This is not intended to be a complete glossary of literary terms. Such a list would be, rightfully, a book in itself, and adequate reference and source books of that sort are available. The terms given here do, however, appear in the present book—sometimes italicized to call attention to their being glossed here—and have special relevance for the types of literary interpretation that are here discussed.

Aesthetics. The study of beauty (actually, a branch of philosophy). As the term is used in this book, it refers principally to the combination of feeling and thought stimulated by literary art. It does not concern what is merely "pretty" or picturesque, but what is effective. See ART and ARTIFACT.

Allegory. A narrative that has two meanings, one a literal or surface meaning (the story itself) and one a metaphorical meaning (the characters or actions or even the objects of which have a one-to-one equivalence with those of the literal narrative). Frequently the allegory has distinct moral, political, or philosophical implications embedded in its body of SYMBOLS. (Examples are John Bunyan's *Pilgrim's Progress* and the medieval play *Everyman*.)

Alliteration. The repetition of initial sounds (for example, "right as rain," "Kit-Cat Club," "the fickle finger of Fate").

Allusion. Any reference, direct or indirect, to a person, place, event, or character in history, literature, mythology, or sacred books like the Koran and the Bible.

Ambiguity. A vagueness, often intentonal, that may enrich an author's MEANING by evoking any or all of a number of possibilities, which, when played off one against the other, heighten the dramatic or aesthetic effect. Sometimes, a deliberate ambiguity may be contained in puns or plays on words (for example, "son" and "sun").

Apostrophe. A figure of speech in which a person who is absent is directly addressed as if he were present (for example, "Milton! thou shouldst be living at this hour"); also a form of personification in which a nonhuman or inanimate thing is directly addressed as if it were human or animate (for example, "O Rose, thou art sick!").

Archetype. An image, MOTIF, or thematic pattern that has recurred so regularly in history, literature, religion, or folkways as to have acquired transcendent symbolic force. According to Jungian psychology, archetypes or "primordial images" are MYTH-forming structural elements that are always present in the unconscious psyche; they are not inherited ideas but "belong to the realm of activities of the instincts and in that sense . . . represent inherited forms of psychic behaviour" (*Psyche and Symbol* [New York: Doubleday, 1958], p. xvi).

Art. Generally, any concrete creation of the imagination that so blends FORM and content as to appeal to the emotions and the intellect of the perceiver in an aesthetically satisfying way.

Artifact (literary). The literary work of ART itself: poem, drama, short story, novel; that is, a structure of words that is produced or created, just as a vase, a symphony, or a sculpture is produced.

Catastrophe. The concluding action of a tragedy, wherein the principal character or characters meet death or other significant defeat. By extension the term may also designate an unhappy event in other forms of literature.

Catharsis. Aristotle's term for the purgation or purification of the emotions of pity and fear, a purgation that results from the viewing of a tragic drama. The term, itself a metaphor, has had varied interpretations. Perhaps the effect of tragedy would have been better described in terms of the beneficial stimulation of the viewer's total being—moral, emotional, and intellectual.

Classicism.   That aesthetic temper characterized by an emphasis on rational order, discipline, balance and symmetry, clarity and simplicity, and decorum. Generally, Classicism is conservative, looking to the tradition transmitted from the past, especially from classical Greece and Rome, as a means of knowing man's limitations and the universality of human nature. Unlike ROMANTICISM, Classicism downplays emotion, hyperindividualism, and subjectivism. *See also* REALISM.

Comedy.   Any literary work, but especially a play, that aims primarily to amuse and that ends happily. Note that the term is derived from the Greek *komoidos,* meaning a "singer in the [Dionysian] revels." See TRAGEDY.

Connotation.   An overtone of "evocative" meaning, the suggested or emotional meaning of a word as compared with its "dictionary" or "conceptual" meaning. For example, the connotative values of "home" may in some instances be more important than the denotative values. *See* DENOTATION.

Context.   The setting or frame of reference in which an event takes place, a speech is made, an idea is conceived, or a word is used.

Denotation.   The literal ("conceptual" or "dictionary") meaning of a word, more objective than its connotation. *See* CONNOTATION.

Denouement.   The conclusion of a plot, the unraveling of the mystery, the resolution of various strands of action in a DRAMA or a story. The denouement of a tragedy is often called the CATASTROPHE.

Dialectic.   In formalistic criticism, a pattern of opposition betwen two attitudes, or character traits, or systems of ideas. Like PARADOX and TENSION, dialectic suggests a pull of opposed forces that, nevertheless, move toward synthesis or resolution. (In *Hamlet,* for example, dialectic manifests itself on several levels, as in the disparity between appearance, and reality, between things as they are and things as they should be, between the godlike in man and the complex of traits that Hamlet calls the "quintessence of dust.")

Drama.   That genre of imaginative literature in which characters act out their roles, conventionally on a stage, although some dramas (called "closet dramas") are meant primarily to be read.

Explication (*explication de texte*). A critical analysis, commentary, and interpretation based on a close reading of a literary work.

Exponent. A sign or symbol in a literary work that points toward a pattern of MEANING, a recurrent idea, or an emotion or attitude. It may serve as a clue for a steadily deepening appreciation of a work. (The several allusions to traps, nets, and springes point to the animal IMAGERY in *Hamlet*; in turn, the animal imagery helps suggest and develop the thematic question, "What is a man?")

Figurative language. A type of expression that achieves aesthetic effect by transcending or by departing from the literal and conventional phrasing. *See, for example,* METAPHOR, HYPERBOLE, and PARADOX.

Foil. A character used to compare and contrast with another character, so that the more important character is better delineated. For example, Hamlet is better understood by our seeing him in relation to Horatio and Laertes. Customarily, the term is used for certain characters in drama, though it may be used in fiction as well. Thus, Tom Sawyer may be viewed as a "foil" for Huck Finn.

Form. *See* ORGANIC FORM and FORMALISTIC; not to be confused with GENRE.

Formalistic. A term used to describe that type of literary criticism having as its major concern the form of a work of art, ranging from its typography to the STRUCTURE its ideas build. The interplay of these variations of form results in a totality of effect that INFORMS or shapes inwardly the work and gives its parts a relevance to the whole and vice versa. (Related terms are *analytical, ontological,* and *New Critical.*)

Genre. A literary type: poetry, drama, fiction. To these basic ones may be added others like biography and the personal essay. Sometimes subdivisions of these basic types are also called genres, as with the novel and the short story as the main divisions of fiction, or tragedy and comedy in drama, or epic and lyric in poetry. A genre like ROMANCE may exist in both prose fiction and poetry.

Gothic. A term originally used to describe a particularly melodramatic and sensational kind of novel in the eighteenth century. Now used to refer to anything that is ghostly, eerie, mysterious, or horrifying (such as much of Poe's fiction and much of present day fiction by Southern writers).

Gustatory imagery. *See* IMAGERY.

Humor character. A character, not necessarily "humorous" in the sense of being funny, who is distinguished by some particular trait or dominated by some aspect of his personality. The term derives from medieval physiology, which held that the body consisted of four humors—phlegm, blood, yellow bile, and black bile—and that a preponderance of any one gave rise to certain personality traits.

Hyperbole. A type of figurative language characterized by exaggeration or overstatement for some special effect (for example, John Donne's "Go and catch a falling star, / Get with child a mandrake root . . . ").

Imagery. Any verbal appeal to any of the senses; a stimulation of the IMAGINATION through sense experience (note that "image" and "imagination" are cognates). *Visual* imagery, the type most familiar to readers at large, appeals to the sense of sight; thus any object that can be seen can be a visual image. Similarly, *aural* imagery is that which can be heard ("thunderous"). *Kinesthetic* imagery and *kinetic* imagery—perhaps more strange for the beginning student of literature, because the senses stimulated are not among the classical five—are closely related. We may make a distinction, however, if by "kinetic" we mean an appeal to a sense of motion and by "kinesthetic" we mean an appeal to a sense of muscular tensions and activity. Not only words, but prose and verse rhythms can create these effects (for instance, both kinetic and kinesthetic senses are stimulated in Browning's "I sprang to the saddle, and Joris, and he . . . "). Other types of imagery that may be perceived are *gustatory*, *tactile*, *olfactory*, and *thermal*, which make their appeals, respectively, to taste ("salty"), touch ("velvety smoothness"), smell ("stench"), and sensitivity to temperature ("scorch," "frigid"). Some of these tend to overlap, because what stimulates the taste often stimulates the sense of smell as well, and what can be heard can also suggest motion, and so on. In some writers (notably John Keats) the various sense experiences may be associated or mingled in such a way as to produce the effect of *synesthesia*.

Imagination. That human mental faculty, distinguished from intellect, will, and memory, that, as Coleridge observed, shapes and fuses the perceptions brought to the mind; or, more generally, that level of the mind's activity at which things are created or conceived, or from which they begin to rise to consciousness in the mind of the writer, musician, painter, or thinker.

Inform. To shape inwardly, to present the primary characteristic of an object or idea (not to be confused with the idea of simply presenting information). The term denotes an inner process that gives life to a particular entity. (For example, when we say that Poe's single effect of "the redness and the horror of blood" informs "The Masque of the Red Death," we mean that this quality both pervades the story and gives it its essential MEANING.)

Irony. A literary device, a manner of expression, a tone characterized by a duality wherein what is said or seen or otherwise perceived at one level is at another level either incongruous or misconstrued or diametrically opposed to what is expected. Note that there are several kinds of irony. *Socratic irony* is a dialectic technique using the pretense of ignorance to enable others to perceive their own logic and illogic (the word "irony" is derived from the Greek *eironeia*, meaning "dissembling, feigned ignorance"). *Verbal irony* means the opposite of what one says (for example, Mark Antony's famous oration following the death of Julius Caesar: "Brutus is an honorable man ..."). *Dramatic irony* is a device by which a reader or member of an audience is made aware of something the protagonist or characters do not know (for example, the audience is aware, before the protagonist knows, that the murderer of Laius whom Oedipus is so intent upon discovering is Oedipus himself). This device is also called *tragic irony*. *Cosmic irony* (the *irony of fate*) is the manipulation of events by the gods or by destiny so that the protagonist is frustrated and mocked (for example, the actual outcome of events is the opposite of that expected by the protagonist; see *situational irony*). *Situational irony* (the *irony of events*) involves an unexpected turn of events, sometimes with cosmic overtones but often merely humorous or absurd.

Lyric. A major class of poetry, the subject matter of which is usually emotion, often subjectively perceived and presented, and the STYLE of which is highly charged with IMAGERY. Love and nature are two of the subjects with which lyric poets are frequently concerned.

Meaning. The content, the moral or intellectual or emotional signification, perhaps even the "message," of a given work, which is, however, integral to and inseparable from the work itself. Frequently the "meaning" of a work is stated by the critic in terms of the work's THEME.

Melodrama. A species of DRAMA that lays particular stress on emotion and pays little attention to the probability of action, accurate characterization, or genuine feeling. The typical "western" story and the "mystery" tale offer familiar examples of melodrama. Now, more often than not, melodrama is a term of disparagement in literary criticism.

Metaphor. Broadly, FIGURATIVE LANGUAGE used to draw comparisons imaginatively, as opposed to literal STATE-MENT. Specifically, a comparison of things essentially unlike, drawn without the use of words such as "like" and "as." (Metaphor occurs when one thing is directly called something else, as when Hamlet declares, "Denmark's a prison.")

Metaphysical. In literary criticism and history, a type of poetry that flourished in the seventeenth century, the style of which has recurred since then, especially in the twentieth century. It is characterized by bizarre, grotesque, unconventional, even shocking figures of speech, and by wit and IRONY and a kind of detached intellectualism. (The term—actually borrowed from philosophy—received its classic literary definition in Samuel Johnson's *Life of Cowley*.)

Meter. The pattern of stressed (accented) and unstressed (unaccented) syllables by means of which the rhythm of verse is conveyed (from the Greek *metron*, meaning "measure"). The basic unit of measurement within a line of verse is the *foot*; the standard feet in English verse are the *iambic* (an unstressed followed by a stressed syllable: *today*); *trochaic* (a stressed followed by an unstressed syllable: *colder*); *anapestic* (two unstressed syllables followed by a stressed syllable: *in the book*); *dactyllic* (a stressed syllable followed by two unstressed syllables: *syllable*); and *spondaic* (two stressed syllables: *daybreak*). Lines of verse are designated by the number of feet within each line (one foot = *monometer*, two feet = *dimeter*, three feet = *trimeter*, four feet = *tetrameter*, five feet = *pentameter*, six feet = *hexameter*, seven feet =

heptameter). Samuel Taylor Coleridge's "Lesson for a Boy" is often quoted as a device for helping students to identify the kinds of feet:

> Trochee trips from long to short;
> From long to long in solemn sort
> Slow Spondee stalks, strong foot, yet ill able
> Ever to come up with Dactyl trisyllable.
> Iambics march from short to long;
> With a leap and a bound the swift Anapests throng.

Mood. The atmosphere or emotional effect generated by the words, images, situations in a literary work (the emotional ambience of the work), for example, melancholy, joyous, tense, oppressive, and so on.

Motif. A THEME, an IMAGE, a type of action, or an ARCHE-TYPE that by its recurrent appearance traces itself through a work and heightens its aesthetic appeal. In literature, it may become a sign or index (*see* EXPONENT) for the meaning or experience of a work.

Motive. The reason for a character's action (that is, his psychological motivation); the word is sometimes used also for what in this book is called MOTIF.

Myth. In the traditional sense, an anonymous story reflecting primitive beliefs or explaining the mysteries of the natural universe. In more recent theory, myth is the symbolic projection of a people's collective values—a communal, almost instinctive, articulation of reality. Sometimes defined as the verbal aspect of ritual.

New Criticism. A critical position that emphasizes the literary ARTIFACT itself and tends to minimize such matters as the biographical and historical facts about an author and his work. It stresses close analysis of the literary work itself as an entity worthy of attention in its own right.

Novel. An extended, fictional, prose narrative that portrays characters in a PLOT. The novel may stress adventure for its own sake or character development or a partisan position on some issue or a blend of these and other emphases. The plot of the novel is more extended than that of the SHORT STORY, having usually many more episodes. In modern fiction it is possible to find novels that treat at length one or a few episodes in psychological depth and with a modified concept of time that plays down sequence and stresses relationship. Especially in our day, the distinction between a novel and a novella becomes difficult.

Oedipus complex. A term used in Freudian psychology to denote the strong attachment, sometimes romantic, of a son to his mother. It may in some cases be sublimated and take conventionally acceptable channels; in others, it may give rise to feelings of jealousy of the father as a rival for the mother's love; in its extreme form it may result in incest. (The term derives from the classical MYTH of Oedipus, who unwittingly killed his father and married his mother.)

Omniscient narrator (or author). *See* POINT OF VIEW.

Organic form. The structural, necessary interrelationship of the parts of a literary work, which gives it, as it were, a life of its own that grows from within. The literary work becomes an organism.

Paradox. A figure of speech containing a contradiction that is, nevertheless, somehow true. It is frequently used to express the complexities of life that do not easily lend themselves to simple statement. (Paradoxes abound, for example, in the Scriptures: "For whosoever will save his life shall lose it: but whosoever will lose his life for my sake, the same shall save it.")

Plot. The action, that which happens—narratively speaking—in a literary work. Technically, it involves not only a sequence of episodes but their interaction and interrelation in a dynamic STRUCTURE.

Poem. A literary composition characterized by a high degree of verbal compression and FIGURATIVE LANGUAGE, in which pleasure, its primary end, is derived from an appreciation of the parts simultaneously with a perception of the whole. The poem should not be confused with mere verse; although, like verse, it may have a regular rhythm and rhyme, the poem achieves its identity through its heightened and compressed language rather than through mere jingle effects.

Point of view. A device used in narration that indicates the position from which an action is observed and narrated. For example, a FIRST-PERSON POINT OF VIEW is that in which the narrator is a participant in the action; he may be a major character, perhaps even the central character; or he may be more of an observer, one who is on the fringes of the action. The OMNISCIENT NARRATOR is a kind of third-person narrator; he speaks with the authority of the creating author who knows all; he is not confined to what he sees or hears; he may even comment on or interpret action or character. Still another point of view, variously called THIRD-PERSON LIMITED or LIMITED OMNISCIENT, presents only that which can be seen or heard; it does not tell what the characters are thinking or feeling, although we may see the action more from the vantage point of one character than another. The SCENIC or DRAMATIC POINT OF VIEW resorts to dialogue even more than the others, resulting in the objective reporting of what is said. In all of these there is a possibility of overlap, and sometimes an author will shift from one to another within a story.

Psychoanalysis.   The diagnosis and treatment of mental disorder premised on the Freudian theory that such disorders are caused by repression of desires, desires that the afflicted person may have consciously rejected but that nevertheless persist strongly in his subconscious. In this book, Chapter 3 is predicated in large measure on the psychoanalytic theories of psychology pioneered by Sigmund Freud.

Realism.   A manner of presentation in literature that stresses an accurate, perhaps even factual, treatment of subject matter. The emphasis is on the rational and probable, as opposed, for example, to the romantic.

Romance.   A type of narrative fiction characterized by the fanciful, often idealistic, treatment of subject matter; love and adventure are often its principal themes. (The genre is an old one, including, for example, prose and verse from the Middle Ages, such as the Arthurian stories, as well as such later work as Tennyson's *Idylls of the King*.) The romance may be contrasted with the NOVEL. (See, for example, Nathaniel Hawthorne's Preface to *The House of the Seven Gables*.)

Romanticism.   The aesthetic temper or philosophy characterized by an emphasis on freedom from restraint; interest in the exotic, the far, the ideal, the past, the picturesque; subjectivism; and individualism. Often opposed to the tenets of CLASSICISM, Romanticism in the critical sense does not concern "romance" in courtship and sentimental love.

Sentimentality. An excess of sentiment or emotion beyond what the circumstances seem to call for; often a stereotyped response.

Setting. A combination of locale; historical period, season, or hour; and spiritual, ethnic, and cultural background.

Short story. A short, fictional, prose narrative (which, according to Edgar Allan Poe, should work toward a single preconceived effect). As opposed to the tale, the short story in its most finished form fuses its few characters, its few episodes, and its details into a tightly knit STRUCTURE.

Sonnet. A fourteen-line LYRIC POEM usually in iambic pentameter. The essential characteristic of most sonnets is the dynamic interrelationship of their parts: in the *Petrarchan* or *Italian* sonnet, the octave (the first eight lines) with the sestet (the last six); or in the *Shakespearean* or *English* sonnet, the three quatrains (four-line stanzas) with each other and the concluding couplet.

Stanza. A grouping of lines in poetry that results in formalized units held together by recurrent patterns of rhyme or sometimes only by thought or by the poet's decision to use units of a given number of lines. *See also* VERSE PARAGRAPH.

Statement. In literary criticism, a first or surface level of communication; a paraphrase of the message or THEME or content of a literary work. The term is often opposed to "suggestion" or subsurface levels of MEANING and to the AESTHETIC quality of the art object.

Stereotype. An oversimplified conception; something that duplicates something else without variation or individualizing characteristics. Contrast the stereotype, which is static and superficial, with the ARCHETYPE, which is dynamic and profound.

Stress. In metrics, an accented beat in a verse line.

Structure. A formal pattern of words, images, actions, or ideas. *See* ORGANIC FORM, FORMALISTIC, INFORM, and TEXTURE.

Style. The particular way in which an author uses words; it is a manifestation not only of his vocabulary and his rhetorical tendencies, but also of his personality. It might be influenced in given instances by POINT OF VIEW, SETTING, and other considerations that develop verisimilitude or other desired effects. In the hands of a skillful writer, style becomes an important key to MEANING (as in much of Hemingway's fiction).

Symbol. An image or object or action that is charged with meaning beyond its denotative value. Although the term presents difficulty and perhaps should be used with caution and for relatively concrete objects, it is not altogether inaccurate to speak of a character's being a symbol. In its most sophisticated forms, the symbol tends to become more and more indefinite in its meanings in contrast to the fixed meaning of ALLEGORY.

Tension. Generally, a pull of opposing forces; in criticism, a quality of opposition that gives inner life to a poem or play or work of fiction by unifying its disparate elements. Thus we may point out the "tension" between THEME and FORM in a given work. See PARADOX, IRONY, and FORMALISTIC.

Texture. The tone, connotations of individual words, or "felt life" of the literary work which combines with STRUCTURE to produce the total meaning of the work.

Theme. The underlying idea, relatively abstract, that is given concrete expression by the literary work.

Tone. A term used, sometimes broadly, to denote an attitude or feeling of the speaker or author as conveyed by the language in its artful arrangement (for example, ironic, pensive, sly, acerbic, humorous). Tone describes the attitude of the narrator or *persona* of the work whereas MOOD refers to the emotional impact felt by the reader of the work. Although often similar, these feelings are not necessarily the same.

Tragedy. A literary work (traditionally a drama) in which the protagonist is engaged in a morally significant struggle that ends in calamity or great disappointment. In his *Poetics* Aristotle defined Greek tragedy as "an artistic imitation of an action that is serious, complete in itself, and of adequate magnitude" involving a hero neither superlatively good nor wholly bad who, because of some human flaw such as pride (*hubris*), was destined to be "brought low through some error of judgment or shortcoming" (*hamartia*). The proper tragedy, suggested Aristotle, would arouse emotions of *pity* and *terror* in the audience, leading to *catharsis* (a wholesome emotional purgation). Though later dramatists—particularly the modern playwrights—departed from many of the criteria set forth by

Aristotle (concerning the *unities* of plot and action, for instance), tragedy has continued to be viewed as a special genre informed by a serious mood and featuring a strong protagonist who challenges the gods or the forces of his environment with great courage and accepts his unfortunate fate with dignity.

Vers de Société. A type of light verse characterized by a frivolous subject and an elegant, sophisticated treatment. It is usually witty and urbane and often satiric, written for upper-class and aristocratic audiences and customarily demonstrating the author's technical proficiency. Any implied seriousness of theme is masked by the brilliant and refined treatment. Herrick's "Gather Ye Rosebuds" and Pope's *The Rape of the Lock* are two excellent examples of the genre.

Verse paragraph. A grouping of lines in verse based primarily on thought content rather than on rhyme pattern. (*See* STANZA.) Conventionally, the verse paragraph is either indented or separated by some spacing device from preceding and following passages.

BIBLIOGRAPHY

We four authors have found the following books to be particularly useful in our own study and teaching of the various critical approaches discussed in the foregoing pages. As with this book, our list is intended to be suggestive rather than definitive or exhaustive. (Books discussed in Chapter 6 are not included in this bibliography.)

Works of General Interest and Surveys of Critical History

Daiches, David. *Critical Approaches to Literature.* Englewood Cliffs, N.J.: Prentice-Hall, 1956.

Holman, C. Hugh, ed. *A Handbook to Literature.* 3d ed. New York: Odyssey, 1972.

Hyman, Stanley Edgar. *The Armed Vision: A Study of the Methods of Literary Criticism.* Rev. ed. New York: Random House, 1955.

Lipking, Lawrence I., and A. Walton Litz, eds. *Modern Literary Criticism, 1900-1970.* New York: Atheneum, 1972.

Polletta, Gregory T., ed. *Issues in Contemporary Literary Criticism.* Boston: Little, Brown, 1973.

Scott, Wilbur, ed. *Five Approaches of Literary Criticism.* New York: Macmillan, 1962.

Thorpe, James, ed. *Relations of Literary Study: Essays on Interdisciplinary Study.* New York: Modern Language Association, 1967.

Wimsatt, William K., Jr., and Cleanth Brooks. *Literary Criticism: A Short History.* New York: Knopf, 1957.

Works Helpful for the Particular Approaches (Numbers indicate the chapters for which the books have special relevance.)

Altick, Richard D. *The Art of Literary Research.* Rev. ed. New York: Norton, 1975. 1

Aristotle. *Poetics* (available in several paperback editions, for example, Hill & Wang, University of North Carolina Press, University of Michigan Press, Dutton [Everyman]). 1, 6

Auden, W. H. *The Enchaféd Flood, or The Romantic Iconography of the Sea.* London: Faber & Faber, 1951. 4

Baird, James. *Ishmael: A Study of the Symbolic Mode in Primitivism.* Baltimore: The Johns Hopkins University Press, 1956. 4

Basler, Roy P. *Sex, Symbolism, and Psychology in Literature.* 1948: New York: Octagon Books, 1967. 3

Bodkin, Maud. *Archetypal Patterns in Poetry: Psychological Studies of Imagination.* 1934; New York: Random House, 1958. 4

Bonaparte, Marie. *The Life and Works of Edgar Allan Poe: A Psychoanalytic Interpretation.* Trans. John Rodker. London: Imago Publishing Company, 1949. 3

Bradbury, John M. *The Fugitives: A Critical Account.* Chapel Hill: University of North Carolina Press, 1958. 2

Bradley, A. C. *Shakespearean Tragedy.* London: Macmillan, 1941. 1

Brooks, Cleanth. *The Well Wrought Urn: Studies in the Structure of Poetry.* Rev. ed. London: D. Dobson, 1968. 2

Brooks, Cleanth, and Robert B. Heilman, eds. *Understanding Drama: Twelve Plays.* New York: Holt, Rinehart and Winston, 1948. 2

Brooks, Cleanth, and Robert Penn Warren, eds. *Understanding Fiction.* 2d ed. Englewood Cliffs, N.J.: Prentice-Hall, 1959. 2

———. *Understanding Poetry.* 3d ed. New York: Holt, Rinehart and Winston, 1960. 2

Bibliography

Brooks, Van Wyck. *The Ordeal of Mark Twain*. New York: Dutton, 1920. 1, 2

Burke, Kenneth. *Counter-Statement*. Rev. ed. Los Altos, Calif.: Hermes, 1953. 2, 5

Campbell, Joseph. *The Flight of the Wild Gander: Explorations in the Mythological Dimension*. New York: Viking Press, 1969. 4

———. *The Hero with a Thousand Faces*. Rev. ed. Princeton, N.J.: Princeton University Press, 1968. 4

Carpenter, Frederic I. *American Literature and the Dream*. New York: Philosophical Library, 1955. 4

Cirlot, J. E. *A Dictionary of Symbols*. Trans. Jack Sage. New York: Philosophical Library, 1962. 4

Coleridge, Samuel Taylor. *Biographia Literaria, 1817* (available in collections of Coleridge's work and in anthologies of English literature, especially English Romanticism). 5

Cowan, Louise. *The Fugitive Group: A Literary History*. Baton Rouge: Louisiana State University Press, 1950. 2

Crews, Frederick C. *The Sins of the Fathers: Hawthorne's Psychological Themes*. New York: Oxford University Press, 1966. 3

———, ed. *Psychoanalysis and Literary Process*. Cambridge, Mass.: Winthrop, 1970. 3

Drew, Elizabeth. *Discovering Poetry*. New York: Norton, 1933. 2

Eliot, T. S. *The Sacred Wood: Essays on Poetry and Criticism*. London: Methuen, 1920. 2

Fiedler, Leslie. *An End to Innocence: Essays on Culture and Politics*. Boston: Beacon Press, 1955. 3, 4

Fogle, Richard Harter. *Hawthorne's Fiction: The Light and the Dark*. Rev. ed. Norman: University of Oklahoma Press, 1964. 2

Frazer, Sir James George. *The Golden Bough: A Study in Magic and Religion*. One vol. abridged ed. New York: Macmillan, 1958. 4

Freud, Sigmund. *New Introductory Lectures on Psychoanalysis*. Trans. and ed. James Strachey. New York: Norton, 1933. 3

———. *On Dreams*. Trans. and ed. James Strachey. New York: Norton, 1949. 3

———. *An Outline of Psycho-Analysis*. New York: Norton, 1949. 3

Friedman, Albert B. *Myth, Symbolic Modes and Ideology: A Discursive Bibliography*. Claremont, Calif.: Claremont Graduate School, 1976.   4

Fromm, Erich. *The Forgotten Language: An Introduction to the Understanding of Dreams, Fairy Tales and Myths*. New York: Grove Press, 1957.   3, 4

Frye, Northrop. *Anatomy of Criticism: Four Essays*. Princeton, N.J.: Princeton University Press, 1957.   4, 5

Gottesman, Ronald, and Scott Bennett, eds. *Art and Error: Modern Textual Editing*. Bloomington: Indiana University Press, 1970.   1

Handy, William J. *Kant and the Southern New Critics*. Austin: University of Texas Press, 1963.   2

Hoffman, Daniel. *Form and Fable in American Fiction*. New York: Oxford University Press, 1965.   4

Hoffman, Frederick J. *Freudianism and the Literary Mind*. 2d ed. Baton Rouge: Louisiana State University Press, 1957.   3

Holland, Norman N. *The Dynamics of Literary Response*. New York: Oxford University Press, 1968.   3

Jacobi, Jolande. *The Psychology of C. G. Jung*. Trans. Ralph Manheim. Rev. ed. New Haven, Conn.: Yale University Press, 1962.   4

James, Henry. *Theory of Fiction*. Ed. James E. Miller, Jr. Lincoln: University of Nebraska Press, 1972.   2

Johnson, Samuel. *Lives of the Poets*. New York: Dutton, 1925, 2 vols.   1

Jung, C. G. *The Archetypes and the Collective Unconscious*. Vol. 9, part 1 of the *Collected Works*. Trans. R. F. C. Hull. 2d ed. Princeton, N.J.: Princeton University Press, 1968.   4, 5

———. *Modern Man in Search of a Soul*. Trans. W. S. Dell and Cary F. Baynes. 1933; New York: Harcourt Brace Jovanovich, n.d.   4

———, ed. *Man and His Symbols*. Garden City, N.Y.: Doubleday, 1964.   4

Jung, C. G., and C. Kerenyi. *Essays on a Science of Mythology: The Myths of the Divine Child and the Divine Maiden*. New York: Pantheon Books, 1949.   4

Karanikas, Alexander. *Tillers of a Myth: Southern Agrarians as Social and Literary Critics*. Madison: University of Wisconsin Press, 1966.   2

Kenner, Hugh. *The Art of Poetry*. New York: Holt, Rinehart and Winston, 1959.   2

Kirk, G. S. *Myth: Its Meaning and Functions in Ancient and Other Cultures.* Berkeley: University of California Press, 1970. 4

———. *The Nature of Greek Myths.* Woodstock, N.Y.: Overlook Press, 1975. 4

Kris, Ernst. *Psychoanalytic Explorations in Art.* New York: Schocken Books, 1967. 3

Lesser, Simon O. *Fiction and the Unconscious.* Boston: Beacon Press, 1957. 3

Lewis, R. W. B. *The American Adam: Innocence, Tragedy, and Tradition in the Nineteenth Century.* Chicago: University of Chicago Press, 1955. 4

Lowes, John Livingston. *The Road to Xanadu: A Study in the Ways of the Imagination.* Boston: Houghton Mifflin, 1927. 5

Morris, Wesley. *Toward a New Historicism.* Princeton, N.J.: Princeton University Press, 1972. 1

Morrison, Claudia C. *Freud and the Critic: The Early Use of Depth Psychology in Literary Criticism.* Chapel Hill: University of North Carolina Press, 1968. 3

Nethercot, Arthur H. *The Road to Tryermaine: A Study of the History, Background, and Purposes of Coleridge's "Christabel."* 1939; New York: Russell and Russell, 1962. 5

Neumann, Erich. *The Great Mother: An Analysis of the Archetype.* Trans. Ralph Manheim. Princeton, N.J.: Princeton University Press, 1963. 4

———. *The Origins and History of Consciousness.* Trans. R. F. C. Hull. Princeton, N.J.: Princeton University Press, 1970. 4

Ohmann, Richard M., ed. *The Making of Myth.* New York: Putnam, 1962. 4

Paris, Bernard J. *A Psychological Approach to Fiction: Studies in Thackeray, Stendhal, George Eliot, Dostoevsky, and Conrad.* Bloomington: Indiana University Press, 1974. 3

Pearce, Roy Harvey. *Historicism Once More: Problems and Occasions for the American Scholar.* Princeton, N.J.: Princeton University Press, 1969. 1

Perrine, Laurence. *Sound and Sense: An Introduction to Poetry.* 4th ed. New York: Harcourt Brace Jovanovich, 1973. 2

Raine, Kathleen. *On the Mythological.* Fullerton, Calif.: The College English Association, 1969. 4

Ransom, John Crowe. *The New Criticism.* New York: New Directions, 1941. 2

Richards, I. A. *Practical Criticism: A Study of Literary Judgment.* New York: Harcourt Brace Jovanovich, 1929.   2

Richter, David H. *Fable's End: Completeness and Closure in Rhetorical Fiction.* Chicago: University of Chicago Press, 1974.   2

Ruitenbeek, Hendrik M., ed. *Psychoanalysis and Literature.* New York: Dutton, 1964.   3

Sebeok, Thomas A., ed. *Myth: A Symposium.* Bloomington: Indiana University Press, 1965.   4

Shumaker, Wayne. *Literature and the Irrational: A Study in Anthropological Backgrounds.* Englewood Cliffs, N.J.: Prentice-Hall, 1960.   3, 4

Sidney, Sir Philip. *The Defense of Poesy,* 1580 (available in collections of Sidney's work and in anthologies).   1

Slochower, Harry. *Mythopoesis: Mythic Patterns in the Literary Classics.* Detroit: Wayne State University Press, 1970.   4

Smith, Henry Nash. *Virgin Land: The American West as Symbol and Myth.* 1950; New York: Random House, 1957; reissued with new preface, Cambridge, Mass.: Harvard University Press, 1970.   4

Spitzer, Leo. *Linguistics and Literary History: Essays in Stylistics.* 1948; New York: Russell and Russell, 1962.   5

Spurgeon, Caroline. *Shakespeare's Imagery and What It Tells Us.* 1935; Boston: Beacon Press, 1958.   5

Stallman, Robert Wooster, ed. *Critiques and Essays in Criticism, 1920–1948, Representing the Achievement of Modern British and American Critics.* New York: Ronald Press, 1949.   2

Stevick, Philip. *The Chapter in Fiction: Theories of Narrative Division.* Syracuse, N.Y.: Syracuse University Press, 1970.   2

Taine, H. A. *Histoire de la Littérature Anglaise.* 1863.   1

Thorpe, James. *Principles of Textual Criticism.* San Marino, Calif.: The Huntington Library, 1972.   1

Ulanov, Ann Belford. *The Feminine in Jungian Psychology and in Christian Theology.* Evanston, Ill.: Northwestern University Press, 1971.   4

Van Ghent, Dorothy. *The English Novel: Form and Function.* New York: Harper & Row, 1961.   2

Vickery, John B. *The Literary Impact of The Golden Bough.* Princeton, N.J.: Princeton University Press, 1973.   4

———, ed. *Myth and Literature: Contemporary Theory and Practice.* Lincoln: University of Nebraska Press (Bison Books), 1969.   4

Walcutt, Charles Child, and J. Edwin Whitesell, eds. *The Explicator Cyclopedia*. 3 vols. New York: Quadrangle, 1968.　　2

Wetherill, P. M. *The Literary Text: An Examination of Critical Methods*. Berkeley: University of California Press, 1974.　　1

Wilson, J. Dover. *What Happens in Hamlet*. London: Cambridge University Press, 1935.　　1

Wimsatt, W. K., Jr. *The Verbal Icon: Studies in the Meaning of Poetry*. Lexington: University of Kentucky Press, 1954.　　2

Wimsatt, W. K., Jr., ed. *Explication as Criticism: Selected Papers from the English Institute, 1941–1952*. New York: Columbia University Press, 1963.　　2

Young, Philip. *Ernest Hemingway: A Reconsideration*. University Park: Pennsylvania State University Press, 1966. First published as *Ernest Hemingway*. New York: Holt, Rinehart and Winston, 1952.　　1, 3, 4, 5

INDEX

88 89 90   20 19 18 17